Psychoanalytic Group Dynamics

Basic Readings

PSYCHOANALYTIC GROUP DYNAMICS

Basic Readings

edited by

SAUL SCHEIDLINGER, PH.D.

INTERNATIONAL UNIVERSITIES PRESS, INC.

New York

Library of Congress Cataloging in Publication Data

Main entry under title:

Psychoanalytic group dynamics.

    Bibliography: p.
    Includes index.
    1.   Group psychoanalysis—Addresses, essays, lectures.
2.   Small groups—Addresses, essays, lectures.
I.   Scheidlinger, Saul, 1918-
RC510.P79   616.8′915   79-20604
ISBN 0-8236-4445-6

Chapters 1 and 7 are reprinted by special permission of W. W. Norton Co., New York; chapters 2 and 6 by special permission of the William Alanson White Psychiatric Foundation, Inc.; chapter 3 with permission from the *International Journal of Psycho-Analysis;* chapter 4 with permission of Cambridge University Press, New York; and chapters 5, 8, 9, and 10 through the courtesy of International Universities Press, New York.

Manufactured in the United States of America

It is not thy duty to finish the work,
but thou art not at liberty to neglect it

Pirke Avot (Hebrew)
Ethics of the Fathers

CONTENTS

PREFACE

The idea for this book of readings on psychoanalytic group psychology evolved gradually in the course of my teaching numerous courses and workshops on group psychotherapy and group processes. Many students, including seasoned practitioners, were all too frequently unfamiliar with some of the seminal writings in this field.

Given the difficulty of locating so many separate contributions, some students had resorted to condensed versions of the literature, which I found often to be unreliable and, on occasion, even biased. An example of the latter is Irvin Yalom's (1975) otherwise excellent book on group psychotherapy wherein he minimized the import of what he termed "mass group process." He furthermore totally ignored the relevant contributions of Freud and of Redl, among others, and paid only slight attention to unconscious group-level manifestations in general.

I hope this volume will serve as a supplementary text in programs designed to train human services professionals in the use of groups to promote change in people, whether this be in the context of education or of psychotherapy.

My intent is to offer the student of group processes selected samples of the most significant contributions to the rich literature on this subject. The chosen emphasis in this selection is on theory rather than practice. The concern here is with the hypotheses and concepts utilized to explain the overt and covert aspects of small-group behavior. In other words, we are interested in the broader question of what makes groups tick rather than in the techniques and skills involved in group treatment practice. I nevertheless believe that the writings included here have relevance for theoretician and practitioner alike, for it is our theoretical understanding that makes it possible to effectively use groups to promote behavioral change or amelioration of personality problems in people.

I am aware that to read a single article by any given theoretician is a far cry from getting to know all about his work. The articles I have selected, however, will allow the reader to capture the flavor of each contributor and, together with my commentaries, to understand the essentials of each approach. The reader can then decide whether to follow up by reading the additional writings listed in the references.

The contributions have been grouped in three separate sections. Section I deals with the earliest psychoanalytic conceptualizations on group psychology, beginning with Freud's "Group Psychology and the Analysis of the Ego" and developed further by Redl. Section II contains three articles by prominent British group analysts who were in varying degrees influenced by Melanie Klein and other "object relations" theorists. Section III presents contributions by American writers which reflect the impact of ego psychology on group analytic theory.

Each section opens with editorial comments and concludes with editorial discussions which aim to place the material in historical and theoretical context.

A final chapter provides an overview of current theoretical developments in psychoanalytic group psychology and points to possible directions these might take in the future.

ACKNOWLEDGMENTS

I am indebted to my many colleagues, as well as to three generations of students, for having helped me develop my ideas about group behavior.

I also gratefully acknowledge the permission of the authors to reprint their work. Martin Azarian, President of the International Universities Press, offered me his warm support from the beginning of this undertaking, while Natalie Altman served as an invaluable guide and critic in her role as editor. Carol Corsa was most helpful in deciphering my handwritten materials and turning them into typewritten copy.

Last, but not least, without the patience and support of my wife Rosalyn Tauber Scheidlinger, this work could not have been completed.

Contributors

WILFRED R. BION, M.D.: *Psychoanalyst; formerly Consultant Psychiatrist, Tavistock Clinic, London, England.*

ERIK H. ERIKSON: *Professor Emeritus of Human Development, Harvard University, Cambridge, Massachusetts. Noted psychoanalyst, psychobiographer and psychohistorian.*

HENRY EZRIEL, M.D.: *Consultant Psychiatrist, Tavistock Clinic, London, England.*

S. H. FOULKES, M.D., F.R.C. PSYCH. (DECEASED 1976): *Founder of London Group Analytic Society and Institute, London, England.*

FRITZ REDL, PH.D.: *Distinguished Professor Emeritus of Behavioral Sciences, Wayne State University, Detroit, Michigan.*

STEPHEN M. SARAVAY, M.D.: *Coordinator, Psychiatric Services, L.I.J. Division, Long Island Jewish-Hillside Medical Center, New Hyde Park, New York.*

SAUL SCHEIDLINGER, PH.D.: *Professor of Psychiatry (Psychology), Albert Einstein College of Medicine, Bronx, New York.*

DOROTHY STOCK (WHITAKER), PH.D.: *Professor of Social Work, Department of Social Administration and Social Work, University of York, England.*

ROY M. WHITMAN, M.D.: *Professor of Psychiatry, University of Cincinnati College of Medicine, Cincinnati, Ohio.*

Section I

Early Freudian Concepts

INTRODUCTION

Freud's "Group Psychology and the Analysis of the Ego" originally appeared in 1921. Its length precludes reprinting it in full, so that an abstract is offered here (chap. 1).

As is true of all Freud's writings, one must place this publication's timing in relation to earlier as well as subsequent developments in psychoanalytic theory. Thus, this treatise on group psychology predates Freud's (1923) formulation of the structural theory (i.e., ego-id-superego) and that of his view of anxiety as the ego's danger signal against stimuli from within or from without (1926). The fuller consideration of aggression as one of the two basic drives as well as the evolution of ego psychology, were also later developments. In fact, to judge by its title, this "armchair" essay about groups was probably kindled less by the author's intrinsic interest in group psychology than by his efforts to develop his concept of the ego ideal (later termed superego) in relation to the ego, as well as to elaborate on the variety of identifications in interpersonal behavior and on their relationship to libidinal object ties. Possibly another purpose was to show that unconscious processes in crowds were demonstrable–a subject otherwise considerably removed from the primary area of psychoanalytic inquiry.

Freud's observations about group behavior, despite their vagueness and incompleteness, appear in some ways to be quite advanced and even astute when one considers the state of social psychological theory in 1921.

In contrast to most of his other works, this essay is not well organized. Not only does it fail to adhere to its main theme of group psychology in an orderly progression, but it is interspersed with theoretical and clinical observations appropriate for other topics.

The *Table of Contents* conveys the diverse steps Freud pursued in this inquiry on the dynamics of groups.

Though published over 20 years after Freud's contribution, Redl's article "Group Emotion and Leadership" (chap. 2) picks up where Freud left off. Redl's work aims to supplement, not substitute for Freud's ideas, especially his formula of group formation. Using his experiences with youth groups in schools and in summer camps as a base, Redl enlarges on ten varieties of leadership roles, on the durability of group psychological influences, on the concept of a group libido, and on group contagion.

1

FREUD'S GROUP PSYCHOLOGY

SAUL SCHEIDLINGER

At the very beginning of his "Group Psychology and the Analysis of the Ego," Freud asserted that there was no real dichotomy between individual and group psychology. Inasmuch as the earliest, most influential years of life are spent in the family setting, he viewed the family group and the patterns established therein as foundations for future individual and group relationships. To quote him, "In the individual's mental life someone else is invariably involved, as a model, as an object, as a helper, as an opponent; and so from the very first individual psychology, in this extended but entirely justifiable sense of the words, is at the same time social psychology as well" (p. 69). Although failing to elaborate on this, Freud seemed cognizant of the multiplicity of roles assumed by people in their course of living. He also acknowledged that individuals belonged to many groups, had identifications in many directions, and a variety of models upon which to build an ego ideal.

Freud disclaimed any intent to deal with the broad field of group psychology, but rather with those few aspects likely to throw light on questions of special concern to

Reprinted, abridged and revised, from the author's *Psychoanalysis and Group Behavior*. W. W. Norton, New York, 1952, with the permission of the publisher.

psychoanalysis. Questioning the usefulness of the notion of a special social instinct or a "group mind" to explain group behavior, he instead suggested two alternative paths for inquiry: that the social instinct may not be primary in origin and concept and that it may have its origins in the family. As he had noted in another context, given favorable circumstances, the child's personality evolves from a state of complete egocentrism, to an increasing capacity and desire to relate to the mother, to the parents as a couple, to siblings, and to other people. Furthermore, mature object relationships require a capacity to give as well as to take emotionally; the child has to learn to postpone, to renounce, and redirect many of his impulses if he is to become a socialized being. This learning to share and to cooperate flows from the reality of having to live together with a group of people—the members of the family. In general, family life necessarily involves some loss of privacy and individual identity, the giving up of personal desires, particularly if these interfere with the needs of others. The ability to adjust to the demands of family living depends on the individual's capacity to tolerate frustration as well as on the availability of substitute satisfactions. Being a member of the family group, although calling for certain sacrifices, also offers definite pleasures and advantages which are inherent in group living.

Freud acknowledged his debt to some contemporary sociological writings which dealt with the behavior of crowds. While quoting Le Bon (1920), Tarde (1890), Trotter (1916), and McDougall (1920), among others, he was particularly impressed by Le Bon's description of mob behavior, which touched directly on issues relevant for the psychology of unconscious mental life. Thus in elaborating on unconscious phenomena emerging in the behavior of crowds, Freud stated: "The mental superstructure, the development of which in individuals shows such dissimilarities, is removed, and the unconscious foundations which are similar in everyone, stand exposed to view. . . . the individual is brought under conditions which allow him to throw off the repressions of his unconscious instincts" (p. 74). While thus agreeing with Le Bon's assumption of primarily unconscious motivations in mob phenomena, Freud criticized Le Bon's theories for failing to give a satisfactory explanation of the role of the leader as well as of the nature and causes of group cohesion. Instead he offered the idea that the essence of groups might reside in the libidinal ties that held individuals together and that acted as a counter to narcissistic self-love with its intolerance and lack of consideration for others. He defined libido as ". . . the energy, regarded as a quantitative magnitude (though not at present actually measurable), of those instincts which have to do with all that may be comprised under the word 'love' " (p. 90). While Le Bon and McDougall attempted to depict group dynamics in terms of people's suggestibility, Freud believed that suggestion and other group processes could be explained in terms of underlying libidinal attachments between each group member and the leader, as well as among the members. These ties tended to counter individual egocentricity and self-love.

Freud was aware that there is a difference between temporary crowd phenomena as described by Le Bon and the stabler groupings that characterize society. In this connection, he reviewed McDougall's ideas on group behavior, stressing in particular the latter's distinction between crowds, as primary "unorganized" groups, and groups with a higher degree of organization. He accepted McDougall's following five characteristics for stable groups: (1) some elements of continuity in the group's existence; (2) awareness in the members regarding the essential nature and purposes of the group; (3) interaction of the group with other similar groups; (4) presence of a code determining the relations among the members; and (5) a structure, providing for the differentiation and division of functions. Freud noted that structured groups differed from crowds, especially insofar as they did not facilitate the lowering of individual intellectual functioning, distinctiveness, and sense of personal identity.

Freud voiced no basic disagreement with the content of McDougall's formulation of the characteristics of the more stable groups. He implied that the more "organized" the group, the greater the control over individual unconscious drives, the greater the resistance to forces of suggestion and regression, and the greater the preservation of the individual's identity.

While thus accepting the positions of Le Bon and McDougall to the effect that in crowds there occurred both an increased emotionality and a lowering of intellectual functioning, he showed that these often unwelcome consequences are at least to some extent prevented by a higher "organization" of the group. At another point, he spoke of crowd phenomena as showing, "an unmistakable picture of a regression of mental activity to an earlier stage" reminiscent of the behavior of primitive people and of children. A regression of this sort is a particularly essential characteristic of primary groups, whereas in organized and artificial groups it can to a large extent be checked. Freud acknowledged the power of emotional contagion, especially in group behavior where individuals are less prone to resist it. Freud referred to the complexity and variety of groupings in society, which differ in line with such elements as structure, duration, composition, and purpose. He distinguished between leaderless groups and those with leaders. He also differentiated natural spontaneous groups from artificial groups, such as church groups or an army, which are held together by external authority.

In fact, he used the illustrations of the Catholic Church

and of an army to spell out his hypotheses regarding the libidinal ties between group members and the leader as well as those prevailing among the members. He stressed the central role of the father-leaders in these two groups; in the Church, Christ, and in the army, its Commander-in-Chief. The illusionary belief of the followers that the father-leaders loved each of them in the same way represents the cementing force which holds these groups together and leads the members to perceive themselves as a community of believers–"brothers in Christ" or comrades in arms, respectively.

Freud used the example of military panic to support his view that the essence of a group's existence resides in the libidinal ties of each group member to the leader and to the other members. He stressed that such panic was rooted directly in the ". . . relaxation in the libidinal structure of the group" (p. 96) rather than in the external danger that might threaten the group. More specifically, the basis of panic was related to the actual or imagined loss of the leader or of his power.

In trying to examine the nature of the libidinal ties in group formation more deeply, Freud distinguished between libidinal object ties and identifications. In contrast to the ". . . straightforward sexual object cathexis," he depicted identification as an aim-inhibited, desexualized emotional tie. Identification precedes object ties in child development and is characterized by marked ambivalence, whereas in object love a person wants to *have* the object, in identification he wants to *be* like the object, to model himself after him. After distinguishing between a variety of identifications which could be at work in symptom formation, Freud referred to a nonsexual identification which arises in connection with people's perception of a shared common quality. This commonly shared quality may serve as the impetus for a new relationship. It is such an identification, based on the common tie with the leader, that operates in the mutual bond among group members. He subsequently used the example of the relation between the subject and his hypnotist to exemplify the desexualized attachment of the individual to the leader.

After distinguishing between identification where the object, by the mechanism of introjection, is put in the place of the ego or of the ego ideal (superego), Freud offered a formula for how groups that had a leader and were sufficiently unorganized not to have acquired individual characteristics were libidinally constituted: "*A primary group of this kind is a number of individuals who have put one and the same object in the place of their ego ideal and have consequently identified themselves with one another in their ego*" (p. 116).

In line with a later amendment, a common group ideal or strongly held interests in common could take the place of the leader and thus precipitate group formation. In considering the basis of *esprit de corps* in groups, Freud rejected Trotter's (1916) concept of an inborn "herd instinct," positing, instead, the notion that each person's envious wish for the exclusive tie to the leader gets replaced by an insistence on absolute equality. Lasting group formations thus entail an admired leader shared by a number of equals. In some groups, the Church being an example, the object tie to the leader can go hand in hand with identification with him. Furthermore, in addition to identifications, group members can also be bound to each other by object ties.

Although he failed to develop this in detail, Freud made mention of the existence of ambivalence and of direct aggression in group behavior. However, libidinal ties entailed in group formation tend to counteract intolerance and hatred in the sense that love for others serves as a civilizing force. At another point, he noted the possible role of hatred in sparking group cohesion, referring to the frequency with which group cohesion is sparked by a shared hatred against an individual or institution.

Having earlier rejected Trotter's view of a man as a herd animal, Freud asserted that man is rather "... a horde animal, an individual creature in a horde led by a chief " (p. 121). Reviving his hypothesis enunciated in "Totem and Taboo" (Freud, 1913) wherein the primal father-chief, who exclusively possessed the tribes' females, was killed by the younger men, who then became a community of brothers, Freud postulated a phylogenetic inheritance of the memory of this event in group formation. He listed the characteristics of crowd behavior that had been enumerated by Le Bon and McDougall and ascribed these to the primal horde. He concluded that "Just as primitive man survives potentially in every individual, so the primal horde may arise once more out of any random collection; in so far as men are habitually under the sway of group formation, we recognize in it the survival of the primal horde" (pp. 122-123).

While it would accordingly appear at first that the psychology of the group is the oldest human psychology, Freud juxtaposed this with the view that individual psychology was just as old as group psychology. For one also had to account for the psychologies of the individual members of the group and for that of the father-leader. He depicted the primal father-chief as uniquely self-centered and mean, prone to persecute his sons with equal intensity. In fact, he believed that the group members' feelings in artificial groups that they were loved equally by the leader was an illusion, a wishful restructuring of the opposite state of affairs which had prevailed in the primal horde.

Freud portrayed hypnosis as a group of two and as representing a revival of the individual's submissive relation to the primal chieftain, carried on in man's collective unconscious from prehistoric times.

While terming it a "hypothesis" at one point in the monograph, Freud labeled his theory of the archaic phylogenetic primal horde a "scientific myth" at another point. Following on Rank's ideas regarding mythology, he speculated further that, after the sons had killed the primal father, all of them had to renounce the idea of taking his place. The totem prohibitions served both to preserve as well as to expiate the memory of the father's murder. Gradually, the emergence of the family from the totemistic community of brothers opened the way for the father role, with each father, however, being limited by the rights of the others. The first epic poet was the man who invented the heroic myth regarding the hero who had slain the father, the latter appearing in the myth as a totemistic monster. "The myth, then, is the step by which the individual emerges from group psychology. . . . The poet who had taken this step and had in this way set himself free from the group in his imagination, is nevertheless able . . . to find his way back to it in reality" (p. 136).

Group ties between member and leader, as well as among members, are inhibited in their aims. In fact, direct sexual expression works against the group spirit. Freud made contradictory statements regarding heterosexual and homosexual libido in group ties, appearing to believe that the latter was more likely to lead to group cohesion.

Since neurotics can be characterized as having problems with the repression or inhibition of directly sexual tendencies, they are usually not part of group life. For, in a sense ". . . a neurosis has the same disintegrating effect upon a group as being in love. . . . [But] where a powerful impetus has been given to group formation neuroses may diminish and . . . temporarily disappear. Justifiable attempts have also been made to turn this antagonism between neuroses and group formation to therapeutic account" (p. 142). As an illustration, Freud pointed to the powerful impact of religious groupings both on the prevention and on "distorted cures" of all kinds of neuroses. It is noteworthy in this connection that he implied in one sense, at least, that regression in groups is not necessarily pathological. He pointed to such socially acceptable outlets for pent-up instinctual needs as group carnivals and orgies, which serve to lessen the inner conflict between ego and ego ideal, at least temporarily.

2

GROUP EMOTION AND LEADERSHIP

FRITZ REDL

Freud's (1921) article "Group Psychology and the Analysis of the Ego" has influenced psychoanalytic literature mainly in two directions. A series of valuable attempts have been made to expand psychoanalytic explorations through the application of sociological, anthropological, and socioeconomic theory. Then, in the field of education, some of the later publications in the *Zeitschrift für Psychoanalytische Pädagogik* clearly recognize the growing importance of group psychology especially for educational practice. Strictly speaking, however, Freud's article has not found supplementation. This is all the more surprising because during the last decade people have shown increasing interest in the problems he addressed. They clearly understand how futile it is to attempt to interpret events in the world at large without more thoroughly considering group psychology. In addition, there is no doubt that Freud's article is incomplete, and that it does invite more supplementation than many of his other writings. The methodological equipment he employed is markedly different from the one he would have used had he written the article

Reprinted from *Psychiatry*, 5:573-596 (1942), with the permission of the publisher and of the author.

15

after his concepts and fundamental theories had undergone their later changes. This would be especially true if it were applied to the following points:

His concept of the ego ideal–frequently called *ideal ego*–is not yet differentiated into the two components which he later distinguished as elements derived through an incorporation of parental threats–conscience–and the residues of a narcissistic cathexis of personality traits–ego ideal–in the later meaning of the term. He used the term ego ideal in a way which comprised both functions indiscriminately.

In his use of the term *identification*, Freud changed his meaning several times during the course of the article. In some places, he distinguished between the "establishment of an object in the ego ideal" on the one hand, and the "identification of the group members 'in their ego,' " on the other. Elsewhere, he used the term in its later meaning.

Freud's article appeared shortly before he developed his theory of the differentiation of love drives and aggressive drives. There is no doubt that the application of these concepts would have made a considerable difference. It seems especially promising to apply this differentiation to the chapter on explanations of group psychology in the army.

The material Freud used for his discussion is also responsible for some of the peculiarities of his publication. He applied the insight gained out of rich experience in handling individual patients and used these to draw analogies with situations in "the Church," "the army," and other group psychological phenomena. The generality of some of his formulations is clearly due to the fact that he did not compare concrete personality experience with equally direct group psychological experience. This is why his formula reads: "A primary group . . . is a number of individuals who have put one and the same object in the place of their ego ideal and have consequently identified themselves with one another in their ego" (1921, p. 116).

In general, there can be little doubt of the validity of this formula, but there is serious doubt of its adequacy for every group formation found in practice. Of course, Freud purposely excluded from his investigation those group formations which occur without the influence of a "leader." Even if one follows him in this limitation of the problem, it seems highly probable that this formula needs modification and supplementation. It must, perhaps, be partly replaced by other formulae if it is to cover the rich field of practical group formations around a *central* person of some kind.

The present investigation tries to supplement Freud's study in the points just mentioned. It attempts to utilize the methodological equipment developed after 1921; it applies this equipment to group psychological observations that could be gained from practical work with groups of children and adolescents in school and camp situations. Nevertheless, the fundamental object of investigation remains strictly the same: an attempt to examine the intrapsychic emotional and instinctual events in the members of groups, especially those which happen "around" some *central* person, and are constituent factors in group formative processes.

Psychoanalytic Exploration and Sociology

The final word about the relationship between the two fields has not been written–nor should this study be weighted with such an attempt. However, methodological considerations of this sort are sufficiently vital that a clear statement of the author's position might well help to avoid a number of possible misunderstandings. This can easily be done.

A psychoanalytic study of *group emotion* is not identical

with a psychoanalytic study of *the group* or *groups*. It is only
the first which is being attempted. To try the second seems
nonsensical. *Groups* are phenomena containing so many
different ingredients that the attempt to reduce them to
any one formula by the technique of psychoanalytic exploration must remain futile. Indeed, an attempt to do so
seems analogous to the idea that any one person could be
understood by psychoanalytic methods exclusively, elimi-
nating all the data about this person's organic structure,
for example. The importance of understanding the man-
ifold factors constituting group life–psychological, socioeconomic, and all others–is therefore fully recognized, but
this paper does not attempt to deal with all of them. It
purposely singles out only one of the aspects of group life,
the emotional and instinctual relationships between persons who constitute a group. This is therefore an attempt
to supplement, not to supplant, Freud's work with other
or wider aspects of the problem.

Neither is this an attempt to mix psychoanalytic with
"sociological" viewpoints. Such mixtures are frequently
offered as an advanced development. Attempts at keeping
the psychoanalytic technique in its *pure form* are threatened
with the stigma of narrow-mindedness and lack of "sociological sensitivity." Yet, this study obviously confines its
scope to the merely psychoanalytic sphere for the following
reasons.

It is hoped that some blend between psychoanalytic and
sociological insights may eventually be created. However,
it is definitely felt that the time is not yet ripe. One cannot
mix two things before one has them. Today, there is a
Sociology of the Group, on the one hand, and a *Psychoanalytic
Psychology of the Person*, on the other. The two do not blend.
The product of such mixing is either a sociology with a
certain number of friendly compliments to the contribution of psychoanalytic thought, or a psychoanalytic study

with more or less eager recognition of the importance of sociological research. The desirable blend would first require a *Psychoanalytic Psychology of the Group*. To develop this, following the steps made in that direction by Freud's article, seems to be the first task. Only after exhaustive studies will there be some meaningful integration between sociology and psychoanalysis.

Definitions and Basic Assumptions

Group Emotion

The term emotion is used here with the same wide meaning that is implied in phrases like "the emotional development of children." Emotion "proper" is not alone intended; drives are included as well. Since the word *drive* does not have an adequate adjective, a further complication has been introduced into these formulations. The term *instinctual* will be used as adjective for drive. The summarizing of emotions and drives under the same phrase is a deplorable shortcoming, but it corresponds to a widespread scientific habit based on terminological tradition and convenience.

When "group emotions" are discussed, it is realized that they do not occur in a vacuum, but are events that take place within and among the persons who constitute a group. In all probability they are composed of the same ingredients found in any "emotion," although they occasionally seem to obey their own special laws. The term *group* does not seem to designate some special quality, but rather, the "conditions for their arousal." Thus, by "group emotions," reference shall be made to *instinctual and emotional events taking place within persons under the pressure of group formative processes.*

From this definition it is obvious that further distinctions should be made. Not all of the emotion people have while they are in a group is really "group" emotion. Thus, for example, a pair of lovers holding hands in a political propaganda meeting might justly refuse to have the love emotion in which they participate considered under the category of group emotion. Where it seems necessary, this difference can be taken care of by calling emotions which are not the result or cause of the group formative processes going on concurrently "individual" emotions–although it is realized that this term is misleading insofar as any emotion is, basically, a process happening within a personal situation. Furthermore, not all group emotions are equally *basic* to the process of group formation. Some, for example, are the source of group formation. The adoration one hundred people have for one and the same person may make this person their leader. It is basic for the formation of the group. On the other hand, on the basis of this group formation, a number of other emotional relationships may develop between these persons which might not otherwise have been experienced. These emotions are the result of, rather than the cause for, group formative processes. Thus, for example, A may begin to distrust B, without any highly "personal" hate against him, merely on the basis of a general group aversion which has developed through the role B has played within his group. In that case, A's feeling toward B is the product of a special group emotional constellation. The following distinction will therefore be made: *constituent group emotions* are instinctual and emotional events in the potential members of a group which are basic to the group formative processes; *secondary group emotions* are such instinctual and emotional procedures within and among the members of a group which have developed on the basis of some group formative processes.

Of course, any emotion may be constituent in one situation and secondary in another. The diagnosis is not always easy, although vital for the judgment and influence of group formative processes.

The Central Person

Freud called the person around whom the group formative process crystallizes the "leader," following a well-rooted linguistic habit. Since 1921, however, quite a few things have happened which make everybody more sensitive to the tremendous differences of meaning which this word assumes under certain circumstances. The present investigation, especially, led to the discovery of a number of types of group formation which do occur "around a central person," but for the designation of which the word *leader* simply does not lend itself. It is therefore necessary to begin with a terminological correction, reserving the word leader for only one type of role of the person central for group formation and relationships with members, giving different names to the other forms.

By *central person* is meant person "around whom" group formative processes take place, the "crystallization point" of the whole affair. The word *central* is simply willful and should not be taken literally. "Focal" might be better for logical reasons, but for linguistic purposes it is unsatisfactory.

The term central person designates the one through emotional relationship to whom the group formative processes are evoked in the potential group members.

Ten types of "leadership"–ten different roles which this central person may play in group formation–can easily be distinguished.

The object of this investigation must be recognized as the study of drive-relationships and emotional procedures within each member of a group, on the basis of which group formative processes are evoked. Freud's limitation of the topic to those types of group formation which occur "around some person" is followed, excluding other mass psychological investigations from this study. The weight of the study is on the constituent group emotions; the secondary consequences of group formation on the emotional relationships between the members are only alluded to occasionally for the purpose of illustration. The interpersonal relations should provide the basis for another study, equally important for the purpose of education.

Basic Assumptions

In addition to the methodological equipment developed by Freud used in this study, two further assumptions are suggested, both of a metapsychological character. They are the assumption of the *guilt-and-fear-assuaging effect of the initiatory act*, and the assumption of the *infectiousness of the unconflicted on the conflicted personality constellation*, or of the *spatial repetition compulsion*. These two assumptions will be explained in detail and a partial attempt at their justification will be made.

TEN TYPES OF GROUP FORMATION

All the ten types presented deal with group formation "around" a central person. The difference between the ten types lies in the different role of the central person for the basic processes of group formation. The method that has been used to present these ten types is somewhat involved. Its peculiarity for the whole problem will become a topic of discussion later. Let it suffice at this point to say that an attempt has been made to present each type by describing one or more " illustrative examples." The explanation and formula which is thought to differentiate the type from others is then given. This summarizes the nature of the constituent group formative processes at work.

The examples are not necessarily identical with clinical material, nor are they to be used as "proof " for the formula that follows them. The examples are intended as illustrations for the purpose of introduction and explanation of each type. In condensing many observations into a composite picture, a host of practically irrelevant items were discarded in order to isolate one process. These illustrative examples will be best understood if they are taken as graphic slides. They all claim to be based on concrete reality experiences, but none of them pretends to be a photograph. Problems of frequency and actuality—for example—will be taken up in discussion of the ten types immediately following their presentation.

Type 1: The Patriarchal Sovereign

Illustrative Example: This group is composed of approximately ten-year-old children, most of whom are just at that point in their development when they most fully represent the end states of "childhood" immediately before the outbreak of preadolescent symptoms. In charge of them is a teacher who fits the following description: "He is an elderly gentleman of stern but not unfriendly exterior, decided but fundamentally mild in his manner. He stands for 'order and discipline,' but they are values so deeply ingrained in him that he hardly thinks of them explicitly, nor does it occur to anyone to doubt them in his presence. He believes in good and thorough work, knows very clearly what he expects, and leaves no doubt about it in the minds of his students." The atmosphere of the classroom may be easily described. The children accept his values without question. Their emotions about him are a mixture of love and adoration, with an element of anxiety in all those instances in which they are not quite sure of his approval. As long as they behave according to his code they feel happily secure–sheltered. Thoughts and imaginations which do not comply with his code are suppressed in his presence. The jokes he makes, or acknowledges, are funny. If one youngster is not quite so ready as the others to concentrate his filial adoration upon this type of a teacher, makes unfitting remarks, unruly gestures, or shows lack of submission, the others will experience a deep feeling of moral indignation–even though they may have enjoyed this youngster's jokes a few minutes earlier during the recreation period. They all love their teacher and trust him infinitely, but certain thoughts must never enter their minds in his presence. When questioned or doubted by this teacher, tears come more easily than words; behind the happy security felt in his presence there is a nagging fear of its loss, which streams into awareness every once in a while without apparent cause.

Explanation: These youngsters love their teacher, but that is not all that occurs. Their love is of a type which leads to "identification." It would be absurd to say that they want to be like their teacher, but they want to behave so that their teacher will approve of them.

Formula: These children become a group because they incorporate the superego–conscience–of the central person, into their own. On the basis of this similarity between them, they develop group emotions toward each other.

Type 2: The Leader

Illustrative Example: This group of boys are between fifteen and seventeen years of age. Most of them are far beyond their preadolescence–at the verge of transition from earlier adolescence into later adolescence. The teacher in charge of them is, or has the appearance of being, very young. He has an attractive exterior. He is somewhat juvenile but not too unpleasantly so in his views and behavior. He also stands for "work and discipline," and gets his youngsters to comply without much outward pressure. However, the basis on which he gets them to accept his authority is a little different. He differs from the patriarch mainly in that he strongly sympathizes with the drives of the children. They are clearly aware of this. He plays a dual role in his teaching. In his own superego, he is identified with the order and the demands of the school he represents; but he is keenly aware of the instinctual demands of the youngsters. In order to combine both, he has to display considerable technical skill. If he succeeds, he makes his class feel secure and happy; if he fails, they are frightened either of him or of their own drives. The children adore him, but they also accept what he stands for without much question. The boy who misbehaves is not the greatest danger to the emotional equilibrium of the group. He elicits moral pity rather than indignation from the others. The danger is the boy who tries to get a more intensive emotional counterresponse from the teacher than the others, while less ready to pay for it by conscientious output of work. The others hate and despise him. A single youngster in this group feeling negatively viewed by the teacher is unhappy rather than frightened. Undesirable thoughts and actions still remain confessable. To be "understood"–accepted–is the minimum requirement of group happiness in this class.

Explanation: A central person of this kind appeals to the love emotions as well as to the narcissistic tendencies in the children. However, it would be difficult to say that they put the teacher in the place of their "conscience." Rather, they place him in the other part of their superego, in what is usually called their ego ideal, which means that they start wishing to become the type of person he is.

Formula: The children become a group because they incorporate the teacher's personality into their ego ideal. On the basis of this similarity they develop group emotions toward each other. This formula coincides most closely with that of Freud (1921) in "Group Psychology and the Analysis of the Ego."

Type 3: The Tyrant

Illustrative Example: This is a class of children approximately ten years old, near the verge of preadolescence. In charge of them is an elderly, or middle-aged teacher, among whose motives for teaching were one or both of the following: He is compulsively bound to repeat a certain pattern of "discipline" against the children because this is the only way he can prove late obedience to some of the demands of his own parents; or his most intensive drive satisfactions lie in the direction of sadism, and he has to use the children as objects for that purpose. This teacher will not "stand for" anything, but has to "impose" some kind of capricious "order" or "discipline" all the time. Nor will he be satisfied to do so quietly. He will require a noisy machinery of special tricks, rules, and revenge techniques. His concept of discipline, too, will be of the most compulsive, unrealistic sort; the way he works it out is as "unchild-minded" as possible. In short, there is a "regular tyrant" in charge of this class. Everyday psychology might tempt one to expect children to hate the teacher and fight him as much as they dare. Indeed, this does happen in a few examples, which I will describe later. The entirely different reaction from the youngsters is surprising. They submit easily. They rebel against the silly pedantry of this tyrant less vehemently than other groups do against the reasonable demands of their beloved leader. Nor do they

submit only temporarily. What they show is genuine "identification." How strong is this identification? This is illustrated by the youngster who does dare to rebel in such a
class. He has a difficult time. He has everyone against him,
the teacher, the other youngsters, and himself. The others
show intensive signs of moral indignation, and eventually
become afraid of the child.

However, the emotional relations these youngsters develop among themselves seem less intensive than in the
other illustrations. Children of such classes develop little
"comradeship"–unlike those who just hate their teacher
without identifying with him–and they seem to be afraid
of each other, and distrustful. They seem to fear that too
much intimacy might endanger the successful repression
of their hostility and might force them to realize what
cowards they are.

Explanation: Doubtless, the identification of these children with their tyrant is genuine. He is the central person
for that group. Unlike the two previous illustrations, this
identification occurs from a different motive. It is not love
that causes them to identify, but fear. Of course, not all
fear leads into identification, but it does in the type just
described.

Formula: These children incorporate the superego of
the central person into their own by way of identification,
the outgrowth of fear of the aggressor, and on this basis
establish group emotions between each other.

Type 4: The Central Person as Love Object

Freud mentioned an example of group formation
which he exempted from the leadership type. It fits into
the pattern according to the broadened concept of the
Central Person I have introduced.

Imagine a number of women who are in love with a singer or pianist, and crowd around him after his performance. Certainly, each of them would prefer to be jealous of all the others. However, considering their large number and how impossible it is for them to reach the aim of their infatuation, they resign, and instead of pulling each other's hair they act like a uniform group. They bring ovations to their idol in common actions and would be glad to divide his locks among themselves.

Life in the school class furnishes two similar examples for illustration.

Illustrative Example, 1: There is a group of sixteen-year-old girls in a class of a girls' high school. In charge of them is a male teacher—young, attractive, but narcissistic enough so that they are not too greatly frightened sexually from the outset. It is known that in some such cases "the whole class falls in love with him." From that moment on, they will act like a group in many ways along the line of Freud's example. Despite their infatuation for him, it would not be surprising if the teacher complained that he had trouble with discipline—that these girls did not obey him or follow his wishes without pressure. It seems that this kind of "being in love" with the central person does not make for "identification" described in type 2.

Illustrative Example, 2: In a coeducational class of approximately sixteen-year-old children, there is one especially pretty girl, rather narcissistic. In similar situations one frequently finds a whole cluster of boys loving and adoring her in various ways, but equally unsuccessful insofar as their wish for exclusive possession goes. The girl is equipped with special skill for keeping them all equidistant and yet equally near. Symptoms of dense group formation may sometimes be observed among these boys. They seem very close to each other, and yet their relationship is not genuine friendship. It is on a group emotional basis. This becomes evident when the girl ultimately decides in favor of one of her suitors. The other boys then begin to hate him as their rival, with the exception, perhaps, of the one or two who may move even closer to the successful colleague and thus enjoy some of the satisfactions denied to them via the mechanism of *altruistic surrender* (A. Freud, 1936).

Explanation: There is no doubt that the group emotional symptoms are genuine and that the teacher in Example 1 and the girl in Example 2 are playing the role of the central person without whose presence this type of group formative process would not have been evoked. However, it is also evident that these central persons could not be called "leaders" by any interpretation of the term–that the other children do not "identify" with them. Nor do they incorporate their central person's standards. The central person remains "outside," but does call out a display of group emotional symptoms in these children.

Formula: The children choose one and the same person as an object of their love, and on the basis of this similarity they develop group emotions between each other.

Type 5: The Central Person as Object of Aggressive Drives

Illustrative Example, 1: A type of teacher similar to the one described under the heading of Tyrant is less intensive in his sadism, less superior in the rest of his personality traits. He is in charge of a group of rather problematic adolescents in a school setup which is so well regimented through an established system of suppressive rules that no one dares to rebel because it would be too futile. These children obey their teacher under the constant application of pressure. They behave sufficiently well to keep out of trouble, but they do so grudgingly. They neither identify with the teacher nor with what he represents. Their relationship toward him—with the possible exception of a "sissy" in the class—is one of intensive hatred, of piled-up aggression which is kept from exploding only by their reality-insight. And yet, although they do not identify with the teacher, the emotions they develop toward each other will be truly positive and strong. The amount of "comradeship" these children display is enormous—greater than in any of the other groups. He who dares to identify with the hated oppressor is an outcast—arouses a lynching attitude in the rest of the class. Their feeling toward him is one of moral indignation, but its content is different from the other examples. It is moral indignation "from beneath," to use one of Nietzsche's terms.

Illustrative Example, 2: Here is a group of children who have developed no special group structure. There is no person in charge of them with a sufficiently outspoken personality to encourage any of the previously mentioned types of group formation. A new youngster suddenly enters the class who differs from them in that he is a very outspoken type. This new youngster is especially narcissistic, defiant, lofty, and unskilled in handling other people's weaknesses. If he is intellectually superior, he need not even be of a different ethnic group. Everyone's aggression is immediately turned against him. At the same time one may observe that his entrance into the class has indirectly influenced group formative processes. The class moves closer together; their common aggression against him seems to "bind" them, and they become more of a "group" than they were before.

Explanation: This new youngster cannot be called a "leader." The others neither like him nor "identify" with him. They do quite the contrary; and yet, he does apparently become the focal point of their group formative procedures, much as the teacher did in Example 1.

Formula: The children choose one and the same person as an object of their aggressive drives and, through this similarity, develop group emotions about each other.

Type 6: The Organizer

Illustrative Example: In a class of approximately thirteen-year-old boys there are five who find clandestine enjoyment of the cigarette as a symbol of adulthood. And yet, all five are of the type who have decided worries about how they can obtain cigarettes. They have neither the money to buy them, the courage to do so, nor the impudence to steal them from their fathers. Preadolescent revolt against adult concepts of what a good child should be has not progressed far enough. A new boy for whom smoking is no great problem enters the class. He neither invites, instigates, nor encourages the others in this enterprise. They all know that he can get the desired cigarettes for them if they but ask. I have seen cases where hardly any other factor was involved. The boys neither loved nor admired this youngster; on the contrary, he was rather looked down upon as socially inferior. They did not fear him nor did he use any direct or indirect pressure upon them. Yet, by the mere fact of getting them the cigarettes, they suddenly eventuated into a regular "group," held together on the basis of their participation in the same forbidden pleasure.

Explanation: Perhaps this example seems more complicated–less credible–than the others because it is not customary to find this function of the organizer isolated. Usually, it is coupled with other roles which the central person assumes for the potential group members. Although there are not many clear examples of this type, they cannot be reduced to any of the other types because neither love, hatred, nor identification is involved.

Formula: The central person renders an important service to the ego of the potential group members. He does so by providing the means for the satisfaction of common undesirable drives and thus prevents guilt feelings, anxieties, and conflicts which would otherwise be involved in that process for them. On the basis of this service, the latent undesirable drives of these youngsters can manifest openly. Through this common conflict-solution, group emotions develop in the interpersonal situation.

Type 7: The Seducer

Illustrative Example, 1: In a group of thirteen-year-old boys, six involved in group masturbation are apprehended. The first superficial examination by school authorities reveals apparent unequal participation. Some were onlookers, none were mutually active; all agreed that one of them was the "leader" of the gang. After thorough investigation, the following situation was revealed. The obvious "culprit" was most "actively" engaged in masturbation. He was the "first to start it." However, he was not at all active in encouraging the others to join or to perform likewise. He was a little more developed than any of them; he masturbated freely at home without special guilt feelings. Masturbation meant something entirely different for him than for them, nor did he need the group from the standpoint of sex satisfaction. He gained nothing from the group situation except prestige. He was not homosexual in the usual sense of the term; more surprising, perhaps, is the fact that the others neither especially loved nor feared him. They were more infantile than he. They had sufficiently conquered their anxieties about sex curiosity to take the first step in active experimentation on a highly pregenital level. They might not have done so alone, however, since that would have made them feel guilty about it. Actually, they used this boy for the purpose of "seduction." They needed him, and the group situation allowed them to overcome their restrictions. Only after he was the "first one to do it" were they ready and able to join.

Illustrative Example, 2: A class of fifteen-year-old children, in high spirits toward the end of their morning sessions, wait for their teacher to arrive. He is somewhat late. He is the "leader" type, with a slight patriarchal tendency. Recently, at an examination period, a considerable amount of tension and dissatisfaction was extant. The relationship between them and their teacher was rather strained. He now enters the room. They stand at attention as was expected. Suddenly, one youngster, neither much liked, respected, nor feared by the others, starts yelling aggressively in a much more rebellious manner than anyone would have expected, especially toward this teacher. There is a moment of surprise. Before the teacher can react manifestly, they all join in. The whole class is in an uproar, more intensively so than any of them can afterwards "understand."

Explanation: Both examples beyond doubt represent group formation through the existence of a central person. In both cases the potential group members had much in common before the group formative processes began. It is also evident that they did not start before the central person committed the "first act." Apparently, what evoked the group emotional reactions was the fact that these central persons committed an "initiatory" act. Through this act, the satisfaction of undesirable drives became possible in others, who would otherwise not have openly expressed them. This concept of the initiatory act is not an invention, but the description of a procedure observed so frequently in school and adult life that it does not require proof. It needs, however, to be explained. Thus far, I do not attempt to show why the first act may have such magical power over other people's suppressed drives. I simply allude to the fact here and keep its explanation for a later presentation.

What occurred in these children is here described. There is a strong increase in the intensity of undesirable drives–sex in Example 1, aggression in Example 2. The personal superego of these children remains strong enough to suppress any possibility of the drives becoming overt. The ego of these children is in a predicament. Pressed with equal strength from suppressed drives and superego demands, it knows not what to do. Anxiety and uneasiness are the usual emotional accompaniments of such disturbances to balance. It is on the basis of such a situation that the effect of an initiatory act seems to take place.

Formula: The central person renders a service to the ego of the potential group members. He does this by committing the initiatory act and thus prevents guilt feelings, anxieties, and conflicts. On the basis of this service, the latent drives of these children manifest openly. Through this common conflict-solution, they develop group emotions.

Type 8: The Hero

Illustrative Example: This is the same tyrant-group described under Type 3–where all the children were fully identified with their oppressor–at a later interval. These children have developed further into preadolescent rebelliousness. Their reality insight begins to fade in important issues: yet, sufficiently frightened, they keep their defensive identification against rebellious wishes. The tyrant now begins to make deplorable mistakes. He chooses, for example, one child as the object of his sadism and persecutes him more and more persistently. The others almost pity the child, but pity would imply criticism of their

tyrant, and that would tend to revive their own danger-
ously rebellious feelings against him. So they hold as tightly
to their protective identification with the oppressor as they
can. However, one of them has more courage. Something
in his history makes him less able to endure this—or, perhaps, his insight into the real dangers implied by rebellion
dwindles more rapidly. In any event, he is one day unable
to tolerate the teacher's attack upon his victim. This boy
defends his colleague and is considered "fresh" and reckless. The whole class gasps with surprise. They expect
something fearful to happen. Surely the teacher will kill
that child, or lightning will strike out of the clear sky. But
no avenging stroke of lightning descends to quell the rebellion. The teacher is evidently too surprised, or frightened momentarily, to know what to do. When he
demonstrates his fury, it is too late. The "hero" has worked
his miracle. All the youngsters have altered their senti-
ments, at least secretly. Now they adore him and even start
to identify with him. He takes his punishment, but remains
victorious.

Explanation: The situation is similar to the one previously described, but events now move in the opposite direction. These youngsters suffer similarly from a number
of suppressed tendencies—such as just rebellion in favor
of a suffering colleague—however, they are too fearful of
the realistic consequences of such feelings. Their personal
cowardice hinders them from doing what they feel is right
but would have awful consequences for them. Again the
hero commits the initiatory act. Through his demonstration of courage the others suddenly discard anxieties and
dare—if not to act, then, at least—to feel what their own
standard of justice has long wanted them to experience.

Formula: The central person renders a service to the
ego of the potential group members. He does so by committing the initiatory act and thus saves them anxieties and

conflicts. The initiatory act, however, leads in the direction of moral values versus cowardly self-protection this time. On the basis of this service, the undesirable tendencies toward cowardly submission in these children are conquered. Through this common conflict-solution, group psychological emotions are evoked.

Type 9: The Bad Influence

There are children in many classes who are constantly being accused of being "undesirable elements" by all teachers, parents, and by the other children, too. And yet, they can scarcely be accused of "having an evil" influence. Usually, what they are accused of is unclear, but it is assumed that their mere presence in the classroom affects the others badly—"brings out the worst in them." But it would be embarrassing to say how they do this. Accusations made against them often have to be withdrawn, because no definite basis in fact exists. Nothing can be proved. Sometimes, admittedly, these children are not so difficult to manage; they are better than the influence they are accused of having on the others. Fundamentally, this is an accusation of seduction through magic. Apparently, belief in the infectiousness of something within these children seems absurd, and yet it is not. The background upon which the accusations are made is usually true. These children do affect the others, not overtly—quite in contrast to the Seducer type—but, by their presence in the same room, something happens to these youngsters which makes them unruly, full of "dirty" ideas, or just difficult to manage. What supports this?

Illustrative Example: In a botany class of eleven-year-old children, a word is mentioned which reminds those who "know" of a sex situation. About a dozen are preoccupied with associations of this sort. When the word is mentioned, they all look at one boy, then at each other. They grin. He grins back. The whole room, at this moment, is divided in two. The threads of this little clique are spread like a net over it. Next day, a nearly identical situation recurs. However, that one boy happens to be absent from class. Nothing happens. The children fail to make the same association as the day before. Their little "gang" remains submerged in the group without interruption.

Explanation: This type, again, is very similar to that of the Seducer; the difference, however, rests in the technique used for "seduction." Nothing like the initiatory act is implied here. The explanation has to be reduced to a more descriptive statement to show how the "bad influence" works. The dynamic explanation must be considered later.

With the inner constellation of the potential group members similar to that described in the seduction type, it can apparently be said that they possess a number of undesirable drives which seek expression; their superego is in command of the situation, so that satisfaction of these undesirable drives is impossible without the penalty of remorse and anxiety; and the ego of these children is in a "bad jam," squeezed between the urges of their drives and the demands of a strong superego.

The inner constellation of the "bad influence" type of a central person is different from that of the group members. In him there is no conflict. His drives in the same direction do not set loose conflicts and problems for him. He faces them and does not care. Alertness on the part of the others to this event seems sufficient encouragement for the expression of what they had just been trying to suppress. This really means the assumption of a definite process, which might best be described by saying that the "unconflicted" personality constellation has an infectious influence on the conflicted whenever they meet. This again is the description of an easily observable fact, which by itself provides no understanding of the process. However, it is enough to explain the group formative processes in these cases. It is important to realize that these examples of so-called bad influence are usually group psychological procedures.

Formula: The central person renders a service to the ego of the potential group members. He does so by virtue of the "infectiousness of the unconflicted personality constellation upon the conflicted one." Through this, he saves them the expense of guilt feelings, anxieties, and conflicts. On the basis of this service, the latent undesirable drives of these children can manifest openly. Through this common conflict solution, these children develop group emotions in relation with each other.

Type 10: The Good Example

Illustrative Example: The same class as the one mentioned in the previous example contains another group of boys who "gang up" with each other even more intensively than do the undesirable ones. Nevertheless, the teacher would hesitate to call them a gang or even a group. They are just a bunch of very good friends, he would say. However, one of them is the obvious center, and he "has a marvelous influence" upon the others. They are much nicer when he is around. If pressed, the teacher could hardly explain how that boy manages to influence them, for he obviously does nothing. In looking at this group more closely, the following situation is discovered. These children are not "friends" in the personal meaning of this term. All are at that stage where they are full of new curiosities of which they are afraid, because they would feel guilty in satisfying them. This one boy, however, is far removed from any undesirable thought or act.

Explanation: The inner constellation in the potential

group members shows a number of undesirable drives seeking expression; the superego is decidedly against this but scarcely able to maintain its position for long, and the ego is in a "bad jam" about how to maintain balance in such a situation. The inner constellation of the central boy in this situation contains no conflict of this kind. The mere idea of expressing undesirable thoughts in his presence is impossible. So the group moves closer to him; in his presence they feel secure. What they fear is their own drives; what they look for is some support for their endangered superego. The situation is the exact reverse of the Bad Influence example.

Formula: The central person renders a service to the ego of the potential group members. He does so by virtue of the "infectiousness of the unconflicted personality constellation upon the conflicted one." Through this, he saves them the necessity to face their own drives, of which they are afraid, and resulting conflicts. This time, however, the solution leads in the direction of moral values instead of undesirable drives. On the basis of this service, the children can suppress their undesirable drives according to the command of their own superego. Through this common conflict solution they develop group emotions in the relationship with each other.

SUMMARY

For the purpose of rapid summary, these ten types can be grouped into three main categories and tabulated:

THE ROLE OF THE CENTRAL PERSON
FOR THE GROUP FORMATIVE PROCESS

The Central Person as an Object of Identification
    On the Basis of Love
        Incorporation into conscience .... Type 1

DISCUSSION OF THE TEN TYPES

Group Psychological Speculations

The description of ten different group psychological patterns under "type" headings does not effect a compulsively logical separation between them. In fact, they are not rigid "types" of groups so much as they are typical *trends* in group formative processes. Simplification and abbreviation may have made the types seem much more final and exclusive than they are meant to be. The ten "types" are *auxiliary concepts for exploratory purposes* only. Holding them toward practical life situations should help to show certain trends in them that might not otherwise have been discovered. That is all they are good for. Nothing could be more wrong than to extrapolate practical group experience into any one of these "types," as though any one real group situation would ever be a clear exemplification of them.

Example: The "organizer" of a group usually combines leader or seducer functions, and vice versa–there is rarely a leader, tyrant, or seducer situation without some organizing activity linked up with it. Yet, there will usually be differences as to the degree to which the one or other type of relationship of central person to group is *basic*, or is *secondary* to group formation. Also, a person may start out by being the hero, seducer, or what not, and on the basis of this group formation he may later enter leader-organizer and other relationships, or even transform himself entirely from one to the other role. This seems to be the case where a person suddenly becomes central by a hero situation, then, on that basis, develops more pervading leadership functions for his group.

In establishing the ten "types" as auxiliary concepts for exploration, the question of their application to *historical, political, and educational reality* was neglected. This question is certainly a big temptation, for, no doubt, it would be interesting to know which type of group formation–or which mixture of them–is more frequently represented in any one cultural situation or at any one time in history or at any one socioeconomic, national, "racial" place. I am convinced, however, that it would be premature to try such speculations at the moment. There are two main handicaps. First, any decision about *frequency* and reality distribution of types or type mixtures can never be the result of speculation, but only of very specific research. Such research, carried out on the basis of the conceptual equipment suggested here, has not been undertaken yet. Therefore, it might be interesting to play with analogies, but scientific statements on such questions would be definitely out of place. Second, the real, psychoanalytic structure of any one group situation is very hard to ascertain. It definitely *need not be identical* with the terminology which that group chooses to express its allegiances. Nor can it always be guessed easily from a surface study of expressions of group life. In fact, the distance between the actual underlying group emotional constellation and the surface manifestations of overt group verbiage and group behavior may be as great, at times, as the distance between the conscious dream content and the latent dream thoughts.

Examples: Many a so-called "gang" situation—Type 7—may, upon close study, show up to be much more of the leadership type—Type 2; it only looked so undesirable because of the philosophy of the judging teacher. Many a group which proudly professes itself as believing in the "leader" ideal may upon closer inspection reveal itself as being nothing but a bunch of delinquents, indulging in reckless satisfactions of their destructive drives under the protection of a seducer who assumes the leader-title for the purpose of disguise. Equally, it would be deceptive to judge educational groups by the names of the political system in which they occur. Thus, for example, the idea that all school classes in a democratic state are free from the traits of "patriarchal"–or matriarchal–sovereign atmospheres, would easily prove to be an illusion if followed up by detailed research.

Mention of everything that happens in the groups illustrating the ten types is not even attempted. Only some of the *constituent* group emotional factors are presented. There is another side to this problem, which deserves at least equal attention. What types of emotion are being evoked in the members of any of these types of group formation; and especially, what type of character traits are being favored or inhibited under the pressure of any one of them? It would seem that Freud had purposely neglected this side of the picture. He describes what happens between the group members as "identification in their ego." However, there is no doubt that this can only mean the constituent situation. It is obvious that the group members, on the basis of that very identification, also do develop new emotions in relationship with each other. What are they?

Example: The groups on the basis of leadership—Type 2—will have to handle the danger of jealousy between the members as one of their crucial problems. For if every member loves the central person enough to establish strong identifications on the basis of that love, then it is apparent that the problem of demanded counterlove and the rivalry between the group members must enter the picture. A tendency for feelings of envy and suspicion against the other group members will be one of the handicaps of this situation. The group of Type 5—object of aggression—seems to be freer from this burden. The common hatred against the outside enemy engulfs all aggressiveness that might still be existent between the single members of the group. Therefore, from the outside, such groups look much more "comradely" than those of the straight leadership type, much more "united." This might even be suggestive of the idea that common hatred unites much better than common love. This, however, would again be a rash conclusion. For it would all depend on what is meant by "uniting better." If the momentary intensity of positive feeling of unity in the members is meant, it is true. Any expectation, however, that such sudden unity guarantees lasting changes in their interpersonal relationships would be disappointed. The unification on the basis of common aggression against an outside enemy does not seem to bind much longer than the open outside aggression lasts. Breaking up the fight situation, such groups may be seen to relapse into an aggressive free-for-all between all the members, unless, in the meantime, group psychological ties of a different structure have been built up.

While a positive application of my typology to any actual political or historical situation seems premature, I believe that I am ready to make one negative suggestion: The picture I have portrayed would make one highly suspicious of all attempts at *group psychological mysticism, of a too naïve rationalism*, and would also warn against what could be called *psychiatric individualism*.

Examples: The "strong-man theory," so frequently shared by even highly intelligent persons, aims at explaining the group formative effect of any one political leader by mentioning his "strong personality." On the basis of investigation, I could not see such a simple solution. On the contrary, I would expect that group psychological *flexibility* would be more effective than the "one-sidedness" of the strong man. The aims of Hitler, for example, seem to be furthered by an ability to become the "central person" for many reasons in different types of groups. There are distinct signs that wide areas of the more reactionary bureaucracy make him their "patriarchal sovereign"—much to the disgust of the younger, more adolescent, representatives of the Youth Movement. For some of the Youth Movement leaders he seems to assume the role of genuine leadership of Type 2, continuing the tradition of ascetic and idealistic glorification of the leader idea which was so characteristic of the German Youth Movement long decades before the Hitler Youth Movement began and which was so strong that it even urged definitely antitotalitarian movements, like those of social-totalitarian movements, like those of socialists, into patterns of "leadership cult." For many of the more aggressive storm troopers, the *Führer* or his representative does not seem to play this role of idealistic glorification, but more that of the seducer who allows the aggressive and destructive act and the satisfaction of sadistic impulses through his skill at exculpation magic. No doubt, many women "adore" their *Führer* as in Type 4, his nondescript role to the other sex definitely aiding them in this attitude. His most effective weapon seems to be illustrated by Type 3. By willfully playing the role of persecutor to one part of the population, he becomes the "tyrant" to the rest of those who would reject him; but the tyrant, not simply the object of aggression, which means that he leads them into genuine identification with his basic goals. Those who remain on the level of Type 5—choosing the head of the state as their object of common aggression and who are genuinely revolutionary enough not to be frightened into real identification—remain the only "realistic" problem to be dealt with by factual suppression and supervisory control.

Of course, this illustration only alludes to the "type" of process I assume is going on. In what frequency distribution any one of these group formative phenomena are taking place could not be reasoned by psychological speculation. One may be warned, of course, against the dangers of theorizing on the basis of superficial data—only the interpreted, not the overt, material could serve as basis for such a study.

Attempts at analysis of the complex group psychological pattern versus escape into theories of group psychological mysticism seem to be one of the negative consequences my theories could have on political thought.

The other negative application lies in the destruction of a widespread tendency toward a "rationalism" of the most naïve sort. Deep-seated powers of group psychological nature are at work; neither the talks nor the acts of leaders of totalitarian—and any other—states should be interpreted on their surface value and judged in the light of their rationality or purposefulness alone. Critics of Hitler, for example, repeatedly ridicule the extent to which totalitarian leaders emphasize the fact that they are going to take "all responsibility upon themselves." These critics argue that it is absurd to "assume responsibility" where there is no one to challenge them. The arguments of these critics are only logically correct. Group psychologically speaking, those leaders know the importance of the "magics of the initiatory act" and know, better than their critics, what dynamic power lies in it. A later section of this study will make this point clearer than it may now be.

The third theory which is frequently used by the sociologically and group-psychologically oriented layman is of special importance because it is shared by so many—otherwise highly authoritative—specialists in the field of clinical psychiatry and psychoanalysis. These specialists try to explain what happens in the world by demanding a clinical history of the persons who are currently in the limelight. Thus, many would be misled by the hope that if they only had a complete case history of Adolf, they would understand what is happening in Europe today.

Such naïvete cannot be condemned too strongly. A case history of Hitler could only explain why Hitler and not Schmidt or Huber is in his position, and some of the symptomatic paraphernalia of the European scene. It would not be correct to try and dissolve European events into a one-person case history—or even the case history of a whole inventory of persons. Such an attempt is blind to the socioeconomic as well as to the historical aspects, on the one hand, and—and this is what I want to emphasize—to the deeper group psychological mechanisms at work, on the other hand. It is by the nature of these processes that any person or group of persons in power anywhere manages to gain and keep control. The understanding of group psychological processes, therefore, is basic for any understanding of political events. This does not mean that I deny the highly stimulating value of clinical studies of leading persons—only the idea that they would suffice for an understanding of the group phenomena.

Which is first, the leader or the group, is a problem frequently raised in connection with discussions on leadership. Let me phrase it in a way which is less reminiscent of the futile hen–egg priority quarrel. Which is the more active factor in group formation, the influence of the leader or the readiness of the group?

From my way of centering the discussion around the role of the focal person, it might seem, at first glance, as though my types suggested that the group formative power emanates more or less from the central person. I cannot, therefore, stress emphatically enough that no such implications are intended. The degree of "active" or "passive" role of the leader or the members in group formative processes is entirely a problem of its own. In fact, there is no general answer to that problem. My suggestion is that each practical group situation contains both possibilities in varying degrees, with approximative values at both ends. In my experience with children I have found all these various situations.

Example: There obviously are situations in which members of a group who would otherwise not have entered distinct stages of group formation were induced to do so by virtue of the special type of personality who became their central person. A highly active "bad example" or Seducer type of a child among a group of youngsters who are still strongly involved in their latency-submissiveness, may perform miracles of gang formation where other youngsters could not possibly attain the role of central person. However, I have also observed situations in which the central person was almost forced into his role by virtue of the intensity of drive quantities within the group members which were ready to erupt at the first opportunity. Thus, many a youngster in the "seducer-role" may have been seduced by the group to become their seducer. It is sometimes the central person who is more "passive" than the group. This is an important item for which teachers should be on the alert. Practical considerations should, therefore, never enter the cul-de-sac of either-or propositions; defining the degree of activity and passivity on both sides should be the aim.

The question of the durability of group psychological effects upon each member has been raised in many contexts. I would be inclined to suggest that this is also a very complex problem which I would hesitate to ascribe to any one factor in group formation—like the degree of organization, or tradition—at first glance. I would further suggest that the problem be divided into the question of intensity of group influence while the group is together and into the question of postgroup situational effects.

Example: Some teachers of the "patriarchal sovereign type"–Type 1–have a strong group formational influence. While they are in charge of their classrooms the children are under their silent influence to a nearly hypnotic extent. The moment they leave the classroom, however, the children divide into a number of more or less delinquent gang formations, which previously seemed to have been submerged beyond recognition. Again, the leader may sway his students to high degrees of moralistic drive-control while he is with his Youth Movement group. In their private lives, these youngsters may be capable of leading a very different type of existence—the delinquent youngster, with much "boy scout" enthusiasm.

Nevertheless, I know of group situations which carry over into one's personal life, have a part in reshaping an entire philosophy of life, or even of interfering with a person's attitude to other group formative units while he is among them—when the youngster with "youth movement" enthusiasm of Type A comes home to his family who believes in political system Non-A, for example. The strength with which many seemingly "individual" reactions to situations and values are secretly colored by unspoken group psychological loyalties has often been described by sociologists–the dependence of many personal ideals upon the silent submission to class prejudices, national, and racial ideals. It is interesting to note how much repression is at work. Each social class, for example, seems just as defensive against the possibility of having its values recognized as an exponent of class affiliations, as it is keen in spotting such dependencies in the other classes.

Whether group influence will be limited physically to group members and central person, or whether it is capable of trespassing these limitations, is a problem of psychoanalytic interests. It seems that this problem is somewhat analogous to another with which the psychoanalyst is more familiar. To what extent are the actions of a child to be understood as reactions to the "real" persons around him, or to what degree are they the result of previously incorporated images of these persons? One might inquire as to the weight of manifest libidinal and aggressive relations in contradistinction to the effect of previous libidinal-aggressive relationships, now established for good or ill in the form of durable character traits and the result of identification. This is a question I am not ready to answer here. I hope that it may be kept in mind, since it promises new material from everyday work situations in schools and camp setting. Only one trend seems fairly obvious.

Whenever more lasting personality changes are wrought within the members of a group, there is a tendency to have an "idea" or "ideal" besides, sometimes instead of, the central person. In rare cases this ideal may assume the durable power of a guiding agency even without physical representatives. Experts in mass leadership usually do not rely on the group-formative and character-changing powers of the "idea"; they would rather maintain security by constantly re-enforcing the central persons installed. The theoreticians may eventually learn from this fact.

What is group libido? By group libido I mean libido aroused under group formational conditions. It is sometimes astounding what people can do on the strength of libido evoked in group configurations. Some persons will exhibit a degree of sublimation they never manage alone. Others will show libidinal intensities exclusively under group emotional conditions. For others, the barrier of individual differences disappears. While most discriminating in their person-to-person relationships, they are suddenly able and eager to love anyone if that person will but meet them in a certain group psychological situation. Others see their libidinal scope shrink to a minimum in the same configuration: capable of a relatively choiceless distribution of libidinal quantities in their personal life, they are approachable only by one type of leader-member-relationship in group emotional affairs. Briefly, if group libido means something entirely separate from what was originally intended, then I would advise against its use as misleading. If one agrees to think of it in terms of "conditions" under which libidinal quantities become usable, or blocked, then it might as well be used as a linguistic short form for what is quite a complex affair.

The problem of first interest to the analyst, as well as to the educator, seems to be the widespread assumption shared by many analysts that all group libido is homosexual. I do not have enough available clinical material to contest assumption, but I would like to present a few arguments against it.

The general statement about the homosexual nature of all group libido has developed from the fact that homosexual libido most apparently needs and finds outlets in group emotional forms. It is questionable, however, whether that statement can be so easily reversed. My argument assumes that group libido develops on the basis of identifications. At least one type of identification is the simple transformation of originally libidinal quantities. These libidinal quantities will be "reduced to" identifications if there is a strong reason why they should not come out in their original form. Such reasons exist if there is no chance for a libidinal countercathexis by the loved object, or, if the libidinal quantities engaged are under pressure of strong taboos and therefore exposed to repression. Rather than erupt through the repressive lines, the libidinal quantities seem to seek satisfaction on the level of oral —incorporative—identifications.

It is obvious that those two conditions will be most frequently given in connection with libidinal urges of the homosexual type–that they even may be the one way out for a certain surplus of unconscious homosexual tendencies in the overtly normal person; and that such drive elements are then used for the creation of social ties and group loyalties. However, it is probably not necessary that this be the fate only of the homosexual components of libidinal demands. While probably less often given, the situations for the repression of libidinal demands of the heterosexual type may occur in much the same manner, the incestuous for example. It ought to be an interesting challenge to the clinician to try to find clear traces of this in his detailed material.

Beyond this point, I would only like to draw attention to another tendency at generalizing that seems premature: the statement that group libido is originally of a homosexual nature is often made with that sweeping finality which puts an end to argument. I would suggest using such a statement as a starting rather than as the final point of an investigation. The problem is, which libido remains homosexual, and how much—and under what conditions–can it be used for the development of group emotional ties? For, while homosexual by origin, the libido does not necessarily remain close to homosexual satisfaction. Much of the group libido can be translated into further sublimative procedures–into the service of work for an enthusiasm about the group, while only some of it finds relatively direct satisfaction in personal contact and oral-symbolic ceremonies. The further destiny of the *desexualized* and *depersonalized* libido should become an item of much more intensive research. The educator is especially interested in this, since it is his task to invent new channels for the otherwise unusable libidinal quantities, and to discover the conditions under which energies become amenable to influence.

APPLICATION TO EDUCATION

The tremendous importance of group psychological investigations for the practice of education can best be suggested by the statement that school teachers never deal with persons as if they were individuals, but always insofar as they are imbedded in a particular group situation. Even more radically, it may be said that much of what they have to do does not primarily concern the group members, but are definitely tasks of handling the group; although they may want to influence the member by what they do, they really act in and toward the group.

This is why so many teachers complain that many of the insights gained about the development of the child seem difficult to "apply." Too long have such arguments been handled as though they were nothing but stubborn "resistance." They are more than that, in many cases. They are well-justified complaints about the lack of advice in one of the most tangible tasks of teaching–the task of establishing group psychological rapport with classes, and of creating the group psychological atmosphere most favorable for the educational process. There is also the necessity of reconciling guidance of the particular child with the definite demands of group leadership.

It is no wonder that innumerable group psychological problems are suggested the moment one begins to think of the teaching situation. Each one seems to be more urgent than the other. While this study cannot list each one, a few may be quoted for the purpose of illustration.

The most obvious implication of my "types" for teaching purposes is the fact that they do not all lend themselves equally well to the various educational objectives. The most apparent difference evolves from the fact that the role of the central persons as a Leader or Patriarchal Sovereign is very different from that as Object of Love. When neglected, this difference makes for educational trouble and disappointment.

Example: Only that kind of love which can eventually be translated into identification is of value for more lasting educational changes. Teachers, who are liked only, without gaining even temporary or partial identification of their children with them do not greatly extend their educational effect. How to elicit love which can be organized into identification, rather than respond to the children's appeal with too much direct countercathexis of a libidinal nature is one of the most vital problems of education.

The educational value of a group emotional atmosphere resides not only in the density and the nature of the relationship between member and central person, but also in the type of *secondary emotion* this group situation is liable to create.

Example: Cynicism against Johnny may increase the group density of the rest of the class, who may thus be seduced into identifying with the punitive teacher out of "fear of the aggressor." On that basis, it might be easy to

unify them. One might also force a more academic achievement and a more admirable, "goose-step" discipline. Ed-
ucationally, however, a very high price would be paid. At
the same time that the group was made more efficient, its
opportunities for character development would be distorted. It would become more snobbish; and outcast-lynch-
ing-mob-psychology would be encouraged. Most group
situations have a few advantages and a few disadvantages
for certain educational objectives I have in mind. Careful
appraisal of all the items, pro and con, would seem to be
a highly desirable improvement in educational planning.

At first glance, the educator will look with more favor
upon Type 1–Patriarchal Sovereign, and Type 2–Leader.
Some will enjoy the comfort of Type 3–Tyrant. Others will
mistake the chances of Type 4–the Central Person as Object of Love–with genuine educational influence. Type
6–Organizer–seems to be involved in most educational
activities. Types 8 and 10–Hero and Good Example–may
seem desirable or at least tolerable at times. Preferences
or rejections of any of these types will most strongly depend on the educator's philosophy of life, his personality
type, and a few other conditions. Still, most educators
would prefer any of these types to Type 5–Object of
Aggression. They would consider all attempts of children
to assume the role of Type 7–Seducer, and 9–Bad Example–a forthright challenge. This is natural, since Types
1 and 3 suggest the suppression of undesirable drives in
favor of moral values, while Type 5 is useless from the
beginning since it destroys educational influence. Types
7 and 9 seem evil in that they protect drive interests from
sublimation processes favoring maturity. Many educators,
therefore, have a tendency to designate all the other types,
except 5, group, and to correlate Types 7 and 9 under the
rejective term gang.

In fact, for purposes of quick demonstration one might

agree with this terminology, stating that groups aim at the suppression of drives and the protection of cultural aims, while the gang seems to serve undesirable drives in contradistinction to the development of moral standards and values.

However, such terminology would imply gross simplification, since the phenomenon called gang is usually much more complex than any one of the types I have enumerated. I would therefore prefer a classification into types of group formation which are basically friendly to the educative process, and those which have a tendency to become hostile to it.

In dealing with group or gang situations, educators tend to behave unwisely. They consider the creation of the right kind of a group atmosphere much too simple a task. They believe that they can destroy gang formations by simply fighting them or their symptomatic expressions. More detailed studies of the question of which educational task any one of these group patterns lends itself would be highly desirable.

Developmentally, children do not seem to be ready for all of these types of group formation at any one time during their growth. A very crude analysis leads me to suggest the following developmental parallel.

In earlier childhood they seem to be functioning naturally and fairly well in a more or less patriarchal or matriarchal sovereign-type of group pattern. This is also psychologically true for democratic political systems, according to the natural role of the adult and the parent for the child, although extremes in this line will be avoided in such patterns. During preadolescence, it seems normal for youngsters to be intensively attracted by the gang type of group relationship, a mixture of Types 6, 7, and 9. This is the age during which, in the language of some research experts, "peer culture" dominates the previous tendency toward submissiveness to the adult. Even very egotistic and spoiled persons may go through a phase of intense loyalty to a gang. It brings prestige. Acts of definite self-sacrifice for the "pal in danger" are the rule. A considerable degree of security is derived from this type of group relationship. Children of this age are desperately in need of expressing suppressed drives and urges. Many of them need drive protection more than drive sublimation. The adult is often quite upset about this phenomenon. The overt picture of gang life is anything but pleasing to aesthetic and moral hypersensitivities. However, it is important to realize that normal tendencies toward participation in some degree of gang-formation must be protected; that suppression of normal developmental needs will be paid for dearly by later difficulties.

The adolescent exhibits a growing preference for a more sublimated group formation–Type 2 is especially characteristic of most adolescent youth movements. The needs of youth seek outlet in the group, which also protects them from guilt feelings and anxieties, and leads into more mature patterns of life. The Youth Movement constitutes one of the most interesting problems and offers the richest materials for studies of group formation in the adolescent age. The delinquent youngster, however, retains his need for preadolescent drive protection against the educative process. This is why all so-called criminal gangs are obviously fixed at the preadolescent level of gang formation. An analysis of gang daydreams, which the movie and gangster fantasy offer, would corroborate this analogy in more detail than can be done here. This fact seems to be so clear that the preference of adolescents for more gang-like, or more grouplike, affiliations might be used for diagnosis. It would distinguish the more genuinely delinquent type from the youngster with simple growth problems. Which of the group formative types is more normal for the "adult" definitely depends on the philosophy of life the adult population of a certain age and place has developed. According to the "democratic ideals" of life, the following description seems appropriate.

The potential group members have enough in common to evoke group emotional relationships toward each other *without* the decided functioning of any one central person. On the basis of this "brotherhood" type of group formation, central persons may, secondarily, assume the role of organizers, or may begin to serve some of the emotional needs of the group members as leaders and patriarchal symbols, for example. The difference between genuine and pseudodemocratic patterns, however, is between a situation in which the central person is the basis of group formation, and one in which he is only allowed an organizing or secondarily supplementary function in the system.

This description of what might be considered the *idea* of an adult group formation type should, of course, not be mistaken for an attempt at describing the real structure of present-day adult society.

The educational problems that are raised on the basis of these developmental considerations are numerous. The most vital seems to be the recognition of the law for healthy growth. The value of a group formation for a certain phase of development should not be judged on the "idealistic" desirability of that type of group formation but on the basis of its fitness for the immediate task of growth. Thus, even the basically antieducational, gang-seducer type of group formation must find its place as a protective, hygienic institution to secure drive growth and expression during preadolescence.

The clinical importance of certain types of group formation, or of mixtures of such types, deserves as serious consideration as the strictly educational one. By this I mean that certain persons may have more difficulty than others in adapting to any one existing pattern of group formation and that this may constitute a problem in itself. Parenthetically, many so-called adjustment problems are the result of attempts to fit a person into a pattern of group formation that is developmentally not adequate for him.

For example, many school problems in preadolescence —sixth, seventh, and eighth grades—are due to the fact that these children undergo periods of rapid preadolescent development while they are expected to fit into earlier or later stages of group life. However, the clinical problem also comprises those cases in which the lack of group adaptation is due to some basic deficiency in the drive organization or the personality constellation. Thus, for example, some types of personality will always have trouble in transforming any libidinal relationship into identification. They will obstinately insist on "loving" their leaders and demand libidinal countercathexis with little concession to processes of sublimation. Others, again, will grasp the opportunity to transform any libidinal impulse into identification processes so that they seem more able to incorporate than to love, and to incorporate through identification without critical selection. Others react against certain group psychological conditions for identification and refuse to make any group psychological adaptation, unless these conditions are given. They refuse, for example, to identify with anyone except the tyrant type they had to identify with in early childhood. Briefly, there is a plethora of possible and practical complications.

I believe that I am justified in stating that too little attention has been given such group psychological data in connection with clinical work. People who handle group situations seem unaware of the fact that many children who have trouble in making their group adjustment need a change in their personal drive patterns before they can adapt effectively, although it is equally true that many children are only assisted in effecting personality developments under certain group psychological conditions. This fact has impressed itself upon me most clearly in three fields: first, the development of the normal preadolescent who is frequently mishandled unless in a group psychological situation suiting his developmental structure, which unfortunately is one that most schools and all parents are especially loath to consider; next, clinical work with delinquent adolescents who are capable of making certain identifications, but only under particular group conditions–never to an adult in a group psychological vacuum; failure of many otherwise excellently handled therapeutic interviews seem to fall into this category; last, the utilization of observations of a youngster in different types of group psychological media, for the purpose of diagnosing the degree of his delinquency or disturbance or the state of his growth at various points in his development.

The fact that schools, and especially institutions for difficult or delinquent children, know or realize little about the essential group psychological elements and their effect upon character growth and libidinal development is probably the one item on the list of desirable educational improvements that most needs attention.

One last item the educator should be taught is that a group may consist of only two people. These two-group configurations may seem strange, but they are frequent. There is a tendency to mistake the prevailing affect in such groups for genuine love, friendship, or lust–the homosexual type of relationship, in particular. Nevertheless the differentiation is vital. Attempts at dealing with such groups have to be modified accordingly. Anna Freud (1936) complained that adolescent love relationships seem astoundingly changeable, inconsistent, and short-lived–adolescents are faithless in their love and friendships. This observation can easily be corroborated. Most publications stress the fact of sudden intimate friendships, which endure intensively for but a few weeks, only to terminate with apparent forgetfulness shortly thereafter. I have often been puzzled by this. However, upon closer investigation of a few such groups, the suspicion grew that these short-lived intimacies were not genuine love-friendship relations. Some seem to fulfill the requirements for durable interpersonal relations, while others are revealed as groups consisting of the "good" example and his pal who seeks protection from temptations and desires, or of the "bad" example and his pal who seeks the opportunity of uttering thoughts his parent-ridden superego would never permit. Briefly, these groups are purposed for mutual—or one-sided—protection rather than for love or friendship. It becomes important for the teacher to recognize the two or three group type of relations, because the children who need this kind of security for their growth are not helped by being "guided into more social contacts with more people." Nor is it true that frequent homosexual pairing means a definite increase in homosexual versus heterosexual attachments. Quite a large number of heterosexually inclined youngsters may be found in "homosexually" paired group relations for mutual support in drive-superego conflicts.

Exculpation Magics Through the Initiatory Act

I have mentioned, without explanation, the guilt- and fear-assuaging effect of the initiatory act. This concept was used to explain the fundamental group formative power of the Seducer and Hero as central person. Seriously, I mean that this same process is basic to gang formation, and also that other group formative types make ample use of it.

I have admitted that my investigation postulates this process as an auxiliary assumption without which one obviously traceable fact of group life could not be understood. No completely exhaustive explanation of the initiatory act will be advanced, inasmuch as it involves problems far beyond the scope of the present article. I should, however, like to inquire if there is any other evidence supporting this assumption. There are three speculations which I believe may eventually indicate somewhat more clearly where the data may be found.

All children, up to a certain age, have a tendency to use the initiatory act of another child as an adequate excuse for what they have done. This is most intensively true in the years of preadolescence. Even very conscientious and intelligent youngsters will feel justified if only they can argue afterwards: "But *he* did it first." Here, their reasoning stops.

Most people think that this is easy to understand because they are so used to this occurrence; although, on second thought, they might find it rather difficult to explain. The naïvete of the argument is frequently quite incompatible with the sensibility, intelligence, or moral righteousness the same person exhibits in other situations. Another more startling point is the frequency with which adults fall victim to this projection technique of their children. Parents invariably seem to believe in the magical exculpating effect of another's deed. If their offspring can only demonstrate clearly that another's child "did it first," the one who "did it first," was, of course, the real culprit.

If parents think that way, should one be surprised if teachers start their investigations with the question: "Who began," or "Who was first to do that?" If the investigation threatens to become involved, they prefer to interrupt it. The "culprit" bears the full brunt of their punitive actions; meanwhile, nothing is done about the latent instincts of

the other children, which may have been basic for the
results effected by the seducer.

This situation is more ridiculous than is at first realized.
It seems that adults definitely do believe in magical exculpation through the initiatory act when it fits their plans.
The same is true for other superstitions which people believe only when they want to. There are potential superstitions for all. Remnants of these superstitions have
survived in this culture from primitive times.

Language has similarly developed its more logical form
of expression from naïvely magical roots. Most of the caus-
ative elements originally had but *temporal* meaning. Primitive thinking had no place for cause: the first thing was
the cause. This naïvete has been nearly eliminated in science. Only in the political field and in education do otherwise highly educated persons indulge in "logical
primitivism" without concern.

There were times when people clung more frankly to
superstitions. In medieval "gang" situations, thoughts
comparable to my illustration about the children were
openly expressed. When the ringleader was caught, he was
decapitated—sometimes he was the only one to be punished, or the others merely had a finger or a hand chopped
off. If men were needed, the others were set free, or even
selected for the army. Thus, it seems that some such "superstition" was at one time real. The leader of the gang
did take the punishment—all the "responsibility"—for the
others. He had the main share not only of profits but also
of danger and revenge. He was truly exculpating the members of the gang.

What was outside exculpation in the middle ages seems
to have been inner guilt assuagement. Even now, the unconscious still reacts parallel with primitive thinking in that
the one "who did it first" also has all the "responsibility
and guilt." Could not one also fall victim to this trick, as

it has been seen to happen in children and parents, *their* parents at least? Could some of the surprising declarations of political leaders that they take "all the responsibility upon them"–even where there is apparently nobody ever to make such suggestions real–be understood as one of the remainders of the magical exculpation beliefs, released by group or mob psychological conditions?

The primitive process of taking temporal priority for causation is reminiscent of another odd coincidence. The Latin *princeps* like the German *fürst* are called the "first people" and also were the "first." However, being the first of an aggressive, warrior group, has not always been connected with the privilege of staying at home in the event of war. The original situation was exactly reversed. These people became the first because they happened to be the first ones to charge into battle. Whether or not they continued marching into battle first determined the durability of the emotional relationship with other soldiers. What is so significant about being first? Some of the reasons are clear. Being first exposes one to the greatest danger threatening the group. This assuages feelings of envy among the group for various other privileges one may have enjoyed in peace time. However, it is doubtful if this rationalization explains the whole problem. There is another type of "risk" which the "leader" assumes. The one who commits the first aggressive deed is the murderer. All others are followers. For them, murder has now been transformed into holy aggression. For the first one it was not. Someone killed the father in the primal horde. Although the others identified with him–probably helped–one initiated the act and took risk *and* guilt upon himself by means of priority magics.

It seems that all the licence and romance about aggression and killing cannot render the unconscious at peace with the fact that it is murder. Hence, the institution of exculpation magics. The exculpation act is not repeated fully each time; no temporal priority is necessary in more highly organized groups. The temporary priority is replaced by a seniority of rank. The official state of authority ranks someone superior to others; through this they get their magic power of sanctifying aggression into a holy act. However, the yearning for the more primitive forms still lingers. Soldiers would like to see the real sanctification of murder re-enacted. This is why they still like their officer to be the first one in battle, even though there may no longer be so much "reason" for it. It is this thought which led me to suggest a thorough revision of Freud's (1921) theory of the group psychological nature of the army, and to discover trends that seem to suggest an entirely new theory concerning the nature of discipline. I intend to preserve these items for separate presentation.

My concept of magical exculpation through the initiatory act is parallel with these speculations. What makes the youngster feel better when someone else has "done it first" is the same old superstition that functioned in medieval law and still operates in many situations. True, it is "only" superstition. What I wish to establish is that it *is* superstition. The psychoanalyst, if anyone, should be most ready to see how *real* an explanation through the magic of superstition can be where the unconscious is concerned. The seducer renders the potential group a service: he does first what the others hardly dare to think of doing. If my speculations are correct, this explains what happens in group formation. The leader really does render a service merely through doing it "first": he destroys the magic expectation of punishment—through a magical act.

Spatial Repetition Cumpulsion: A Metapsychological Speculation

The other auxiliary assumption I introduced in this

paper needs justification even more than the theory of exculpation magics through the initiatory act–and I am even less able to present it. I refer to the concept of an original infectiousness of the unconflicted personality constellation on the conflicted one of the same drive pattern.

I used this principle as an explanation for Type 9–Bad Influence–Type 10–Good Influence. The power of this principle is easily documented. Johnny, who is afraid he might want to know about sex, is made happy when Jimmy is around because the latent goodness of the latter precludes such a wish. Or, Mary feels at ease in Joan's presence because she knows one does not have to feel badly if one thinks about sex. Joan has sexual curiosities and they do not cause her any guilt or fear.

The child is confronted by a dilemma in the field of the ego whenever the id demands something the superego decidedly rejects. The solution will be determined by the type of support the ego is able to obtain in its conflict. If this support tends to be in line with superego wishes, it will successfully manage the unruly drives. If the type of support it is given encourages the satisfaction of the drives, the decision will be in their favor. Of course, whichever way the ego decides depends on various factors in the situation. A transition from one type of solution to another is not only frequent but also normal in certain phases of growth and development. The trouble experienced by the ego in making a transition from superego support to drive support has been described by Anna Freud (1936, pp. 166-167) as one of the basic difficulties in early adolescence. I have noticed that children are obviously helped in their decision, either in favor of the drives or of the superego demands, by association with other children who definitely represent the one or the other solution. It seems that the ego insecurity of the conflicted child is somehow "magnetically" influenced by the already fulfilled solution in another person. I found, as a condition for this effect, that the first person must be on the verge of having to make either the one or the other decision. Moreover, the influential person must have definitely resolved his own conflict. It is upon this basis that I assumed there is a certain infectiousness of the unconflicted personality constellation on the conflicted one of the same drive-conflict pattern. By personality constellation, I here mean the relationship between the id, ego, and superego.

Without such an assumption there is no rational explanation for the reality demonstrated. The phenomena I described are facts of group life. The assumption would therefore be a group psychological postulate. But, is this a new assumption? I believe that this infectiousness of the unconflicted personality constellation on the conflicted one—which can be seen functioning so clearly in group life—is but another manifestation of Freud's (1920) famous assumption regarding the repetition compulsion.

Freud (1921) distinguished between two different types of identification in his paper on group psychology. The usual type—where identification is the result of what was object libido before it underwent repression—may be formulated: the children "love" their teacher. Part of this "love" is homosexual—never fully desexualized. It is therefore exposed to the forces of repression, and because this love must be partly frustrated by the demands of so many, these children will transform their love into identification. Freud also mentions another type of identification, which, he says, is even more primitive. He calls it primary identification. He says that it happens without a libidinal relationship having first been established—a process more primitive than has been ascribed to the libido. Methodologically considered, my assumption differs only in that I extend this primary principle of influence from the field of identification into the principle of infectious influence in the field of interpersonal relations.

Another speculation may fortify my assumption. Freud's assumption of repetition compulsion really means there is a basic principle that what was once shall be again in all living substance. The mere fact that certain events once led to the solution of a conflict is supposed to release a strong urge to return to this experience, to revitalize it, even at the expense of realistic considerations–including the pleasure principle. This word *repeat* is captivating. It has a double meaning. Something is repeated, if it is revived *in time*. The word also allows a spatial interpretation. One might also say that an ornament repeats itself, or that nature repeats itself if the same species were discovered on different planets. Time alone is not implied. The repetition also becomes one of space. Various events are *coexistent*–not after, next to each other. Repetition is for space, as well as for time. If the repetition compulsion is basic, why not extend the concept? A nice parallel may be offered.

A conflict solution that has once been effected by the ego tends to be repeated–temporal repetition compulsion. A conflict solution that definitely exists in one person tends to be "repeated" in another person in whom it does not yet exist–spatial repetition compulsion.

The precondition for this repetition effect is that the situation in both persons be strikingly similar, that the solution for the one really is a solution of approximately the same conflict, similarly organized, in the other. This would also explain why only certain children have such influential effect on certain others.

My theoretical problem would be simplified if there were but one basic auxiliary assumption instead of two. It would explain Freud's assumption of a primary identification as well as my theory of infectiousness.

A child may select an object for identification because the economic pattern of this other person represents what exists, merely as a trend, in himself–*Primary Identification.*

A child may effect a conflict solution because it notices to be *fait accompli* in the other what has been a strong trend in himself–*infectiousness of the unconflicted over the conflicted personality constellation.* Both would be manifestations of the same urge–the power of the existing solution over the one that is "not just yet" accomplished. There is no need to remind the reader how close these speculations are to Plato's assumption of the power of ideas over reality, a resemblance already noticed in Freud's other theoretical speculations.

DISCUSSION

In reviewing Freud's and Redl's contributions, it is especially noteworthy that they both, while denying any basic dichotomy between individual and group psychology, depicted group behavior as comprising the behavior of individuals in the context of group emotionality. Thus, unlike the ideas of Le Bon (1920) and McDougall (1920), there is no place in their theories for a "group mind" as distinct from the minds of the individual group members. This does not mean, however, that they thought that groups are not subject to being perceived as psychological wholes and as having, accordingly, such collective properties as organization, ideals, or *esprit de corps*.

As might be expected, both authors espouse the characteristic psychoanalytic duality of temporal (here-and-now) and of genetic (there-and-then) considerations. The latter are exemplified by the notion of reactivated sibling rivalry for the exclusive possession of the father-leader as well as by the phylogenetic themes from the prehistoric primal-horde theory. In this connection, Freud distinguished between each group member's personal *repressed* unconscious and his *archaic*, inherited unconscious.

In discussing group formative processes both Freud and Redl rely heavily on early psychoanalytic concepts of instinctual drives as quantities of energy moving in a certain direction. Freud, especially, went into considerable detail depicting aim-inhibited libidinal attachments, such as object ties and identifications, as crucial in fostering group cohesion and the related modification of individual self-centered conduct (narcissism) in deference to the wishes and to the opinions of others.

Insofar as these authors assume all groups to be subject to similar dynamics, they all tend to facilitate the expression of regressive attitudes and behaviors which are not necessarily pathological in character. Group regression is conceived as involving a loosening in the individual's ego control functions, which results in the freer emergence of covert emotionality. In a broader sense, the more "organized" (structured) a group, the greater the control over individual members' unconscious stimuli, the greater the resistance to forces of suggestion and of regression, and the stronger the preservation of personal identity.

The essence of group formation resides, according to Freud, in an emotional process wherein a shared tie of an assembly of individuals to a perceived father-leader leads to common attachments among the prospective group members (brethren) and a resultant sense of we-ness (cohesion). Freud mentioned also, in passing, that a shared ideology, abstraction, or common tendency was occasionally capable of taking the place of a leader in fostering such group formation. Redl enlarged on Freud's unitary formula for group formation by introducing the concept of a *central person*, by distinguishing between "constituent" and "secondary" group emotions, and by elaborating on nine additional constellations ("types") of group formation. These elaborations were very likely influenced by developments in psychoanalytic theory subsequent to the time that Freud's original essay was written, as well as by Redl's direct experience with children's groups in the context of education and therapy.

As for processes at work following group formation, Redl contributed the following three significant concepts, which he later elaborated on (Redl, 1949) and which have been adopted by many group practitioners: the concept of group contagion; the guilt- and fear-assuaging effect of the initiatory act; and the infectiousness of the unconflicted on the conflicted personality constellation.

While both Freud and Redl touch on the relationship between sexuality and group cohesion, they pay minimal attention to aggressiveness in groups. This factor, as well as their heavy reliance on the concept of libidinal energy in a quantitative sense, is readily contrasted with the material in Sections II and III of this book, where such notions are supplanted by ego psychological and object relations theories. Thus, Redl's questionable speculations about the homosexual components of group libido, or about "libidinal quantities" being reduced to "oral-incorporative" identifications have found little resonance in later psychoanalytic contributions on group psychology, including his own. A similar point can be made regarding Freud's hypothesis of the perpetuation of the memory of the primal-horde fratricide in the archaic unconscious of group members.

In general, the early Freudian propositions of group psychology covered in Section I are admittedly incomplete and spotty, with only threads of connections at many points. They do not even begin to cover the total field of group phenomena. Besides the limited range of the propositions discussed, there is also the problem of their clarity. Many of the terms considered basic to Freudian psychology had not and still have not been formulated in such a way as to exclude misunderstanding and ambiguity. To mention only two: the concepts of aim inhibition and of identification. The contributions which follow in Sections II and III fill at least some of these gaps.

Section II

The "British School" of Group Dynamics

INTRODUCTION

The term British School of Group Dynamics is used loosely here to connote certain group psychological formulations that have developed independently from American ones. As will be readily apparent to the reader, the following three contributions by Bion, Ezriel, and Foulkes share, to begin with, a strong emphasis on unconscious processes pertaining to the group-as-a-whole. Furthermore, the three were influenced in varying degrees by the British theories of "object relations" initiated by Melanie Klein (1948) and subsequently extended by Fairbairn (1952) and Guntrip (1971). These theories stand in contrast to the "classical" Freudian ego psychological approach advanced by Anna Freud in England and by kindred American psychoanalysts beginning with Hartmann (1939) and Rapaport (1959).

World War II gave particular impetus to the development of therapeutic group theory and practice in England, with the Northfield Military Hospital becoming the training ground for most of its future leaders in this field. Not only did Bion and Foulkes, for example, apply at Northfield their ideas about small groups to the treatment of war casualties, but broader concepts and practices pertaining to the therapeutic value of the milieu and of social networks also flourished in that setting.

As might be expected, since these contributions follow that of Redl's (chap. 2) by at least a decade, they are con-

siderably advanced in clarity, in sophistication, and in com-
prehensiveness. In a sense, while Section I depicts loosely
connected concepts pertaining mostly to large nontherapy
groups, this Section offers condensed presentations of
three distinct theoretical models derived largely from the
clinical study and practice with small therapy groups for
adults.

3

GROUP DYNAMICS: A RE-VIEW

W. R. BION

Using knowledge derived from his psychoanalytic studies, Freud (1921) attempted to illuminate some of the problems which had been raised by Le Bon (1920), McDougall (1920), and others in their studies of the group. In this article I shall briefly summarize some theories at which I have arrived by applying to groups in which I was participating the intuitions developed by present-day psychoanalytic training. These theories differ from many others, in merits and defects alike, in having been forged in the actual emotional stresses they are intended to describe, and they therefore constitute a different approach from that made by Freud. It will be noticed that I introduce some concepts new to psychoanalysis; this is in part because I am dealing with different subject matter and in part because I wished to see if, by making a start disencumbered by previous theories, I might reach a point at which my views of the group and psychoanalytic views of the individual could be compared and thereby judged to be either complementary or divergent.

I assume that every individual acts as if he believes that

Reprinted from the *International Journal of Psycho-Analysis*, 33:235-247 (1952), with the permission of the publisher and of the author.

the group has an attitude to him and that it is possible to put into words what this attitude is. Translation into precise speech of what I suppose to be the attitude of the group to me or to someone else, and of the individual to the group, constitutes the interpretations.

The conclusions that follow represent the distillation of some eight years of work. These are they:

In any group there may be discerned certain broad trends of mental activity. Every group, however casual, however idle it may appear to be, meets to "do" something. In this activity, according to the capacity of the individual, they cooperate. This cooperation is voluntary and dependent on some degree of sophisticated skill in the individual. Participation in this activity is a product of years of training, experience, and individual mental development. Since this activity is associated with the performance of a task, it is related to reality, its methods are rational, and, therefore, in however embryonic a form, scientific. It follows that its characteristics are similar to those attributed by Freud (1923) to the ego. This aspect of group mental activity I have called the Work Group (W).

The activities of W are obstructed, diverted, and on occasion assisted by certain other mental activities which have in common the attribute of powerful emotional drives. These activities, at first apparently chaotic, are given a certain cohesion if it is assumed that they spring from basic assumptions common to all the group. The first assumption is that the group exists in order to be sustained by a leader on whom it depends for nourishment, material and spiritual, and protection. This mental state I have called the basic assumption of dependence (D) and its leader the dependent leader (D.L.). The second basic assumption is that the group has met for purposes of pairing; I have called this mental state the basic assumption of pairing (P). It is suffused with messianic hopes and its leader (P.L.) can best be described as the unborn genius. The third basic assumption is that the group has met to fight something or to run away from it. It is prepared to do either indifferently. I have called it the fight–flight basic assumption (F) and its leader (F.L.). Participation in basic-assumption mental activity requires no training, experience, or mental development. It is instantaneous, inevitable, and instinctive. In contrast with W, it makes no demands on the individual for a capacity to cooperate, but depends on the individual's possession of what I call valency—a term I borrow from the physicists to express a capacity for instantaneous involuntary combination of one individual with another for sharing and acting on a basic assumption.

W function is always in evidence together with one, and only one, basic assumption. But though W may remain unaltered, the contemporary basic assumption that pervades its activities can be changing frequently; sometimes there may be two or three changes in an hour, sometimes the same basic assumption remains active for months on end. To account for the fate of the inactive basic assumptions I have postulated the existence of a protomental system in which physical and mental activity is undifferentiated and which lies outside the field ordinarily considered profitable for psychological investigations.

Many techniques are available, and are in fact daily used, for the investigations of W. For the investigation of basic-assumption phenomena I consider psychoanalysis, or some extension of technique directly derived from it, to be essential–a point I shall elaborate later. But since W functions are always pervaded by basic-assumption phenomena, it is clear that techniques that ignore the latter will give misleading impressions of the former.

The emotions that can be detected in the activities associated with a basic assumption may all be described by terms in common use, such as anxiety, fear, hate, love, and the like. Nevertheless, it seems to me that the emotions common to any basic assumption are subtly affected by each other as if they were held in a combination peculiar to the active basic assumption. That is to say, the anxiety in evidence in D has a different quality from anxiety which is evident in P, and so on with all other feelings which individuals exhibit.

Whatever basic assumption is active, the leadership of the group may be identical with the W.L. But D.L., P.L., and F.L. need not be identified with any individual in the group. The identification may in each case be with an inanimate object or with an idea (Freud, 1921; Le Bon, 1920).[1] It may also be identified with the history of the group, a phenomenon I have most often noticed in D. On these occasions the group, complaining of an inability to remember what took place in a previous session, has set about making a record of its meetings. This record then becomes a "bible" to which appeal is made if the leader proves to be refractory material for molding into the likeness proper to the D.L. Bible-making is an activity to which the group resorts when threatened with an idea the acceptance of which would entail development on the part of the individuals comprising the group. Such ideas must be regarded as deriving emotional force and exciting emotional opposition from their association with characteristics appropriate to the P.L. In particular, when D or F are dominant, a struggle takes place to suppress the new idea, or P.L., so that these basic assumptions should retain their dominance in the emotional life of the group. If the P.L. is not suppressed in its incipient stage, then a period of dominance by P in a group continues until feelings of

---

[1] Unless otherwise indicated, all references to Freud are to his "Group Psychology and the Analysis of the Ego" (1921).–Ed.

anxiety give way to feelings of persecution, whereupon a period of dominance by F supervenes. This in turn, after a similar sequence of emotions, gives way to a period of dominance by D. In my experience, this is the most common sequence of events.

The change need not be from one basic assumption to another, but may take certain aberrant forms depending upon the dominant basic assumption at the time of the increase in persecutory tension. These aberrant forms always lead to the involvement of an extraneous group. If D is dominant, the emergence of P.L., particularly in the form of an idea, is countered by provoking the influx or invasion by another group. If F is dominant, the tendency is to absorb or invade another group. If P is dominant, the tendency is to schism. This last reaction may appear anomalous unless it is remembered that the P.L. should be "unborn" or, in other words, nonexistent. The crux of the matter lies in the quality of the new idea to demand development and the inability of the basic-assumption groups to tolerate development. The reasons for this I shall educe later.

There are certain specialized W Groups whose task is peculiarly prone to stimulate the activity of a particular basic assumption. Typical groups of this nature are provided by a church or an army. It is possible to regard the church as a group peculiarly prone to interference by D phenomena and the army as suffering a similar interference from F. But another possibility has to be borne in mind, and that is that these groups are budded off by the main groups of which they form a part for the specific purpose of neutralizing D and F respectively and thus preventing their obstruction of the W function of the main group. If we adopt the latter hypothesis then we must regard it as a sign of failure in the specialized W Group if D or F functions either cease to manifest themselves within the specialized W Groups or else grow to over-whelming strength. In either case the result is the same–the main group has to take over the functions proper to the specialized W Groups. Something of this kind may underlie the evolution in church and D functions of the so-called Welfare State,[2] or, in army and F functions, outbreaks of war. In the small groups of which I have experience, these phenomena appear, in D as a tendency to form a small subgroup to interpret the D.L. to the group, or, in F as a tendency to find a pretext to send a deputation to some external group. In my experience, the formation of any committee or deputation can be seen as a response, not only to some need deriving from W function, but also to the rising pressure of a basic assumption.

I have not mentioned any specialized W Group analogous to church or army for P, but an aristocracy may be such a group.

There are two important inherent characteristics of basic-assumption mentality. Time plays no direct part in basic-assumption mentality; it is a dimension of mental function that is not recognized: consequently, all activities that require an awareness of time are imperfectly comprehended and tend to arouse feelings of persecution. Interpretation of group activity on the basic-assumptions level always lays bare a disturbed relationship to time. The second characteristic, which I mentioned earlier, is the absence of any process of development as a part of basic-assumption mentality. It is a point to which I shall refer later, but for the moment I concern myself only with the fact that stimuli to development meet with a hostile re-

---

[2] Freud here (p. 99) brings close together, without linking them, W and basic-assumption phenomena. For contrast I would put my view thus: If the State stimulates (and the Church fails to neutralize) D, its policy will show D characters; if a scientific group stimulates D, it will also show D characters. W changes, but basic assumptions remain.

sponse on the basic-assumption level. The fact that time is a component of all developmental processes tends to an exacerbation of hostile feeling, and it is the growth of this hostility which helps to produce the situation, described above, in which a specialized W Group fails in its function of neutralizing its basic assumption. It will be appreciated that this is a matter of importance in any group which purports, by the study of the group, to promote a therapeutic development of insight. It is the growth of hostility thus engendered that tends to determine that the reaction to the emergence of the P.L.[3] will take an aberrant form rather than spend itself in the cyclic change from one basic assumption to another. For, if a group wishes to prevent development, the simplest way to do so is to allow itself to be overwhelmed by basic-assumption mentality and thus become approximated to the one kind of mental life in which a capacity for development is not required. The main compensation for such a shift appears to be an increase in a pleasurable feeling of vitality.[4]

The defense which schism affords against the development-threatening idea (P.L.) can be seen in the operation of the schismatic groups,[5] ostensibly opposed but in fact promoting the same end. One group adheres to the D.L., often in the form of the group "bible." This group popularizes the established ideas by denuding them of any quality that might demand painful effort and thereby secures a numerous adherence of those who oppose the pains of development. Thought thus becomes stabilized on a level which is platitudinous and dogmatic. The recip-

[3] The messianic idea, or person, evokes destructive attacks in the group in which the messianic idea or person appears. The essence of P is that the P.L. is "unborn." Association of the P.L. with an actual idea or person heralds the breakup of P.

[4] The point is discussed by Niebuhr (1949).

[5] Interesting material on schismatic groups may be found in Knox (1951).

rocal group, supposedly supporting the new idea (P.L.) becomes so exacting in its demands that it ceases to recruit itself. Thus both groups avoid the painful bringing together of the primitive and the sophisticated, which is the essence of the developmental conflict. The superficial but numerous schismatics are thus opposed by the profound but numerically negligible schismatics. The result reminds one of the fear expressed sometimes that a society breeds copiously from its least cultured members while the "best" people remain obdurately sterile.

We have reached a point at which my description of the group is sufficiently far removed from that which Freud proposed; before considering in detail where the apparent difference lies, I would bring my views into juxtaposition with some earlier theories of the group.

In his discussion of society, Plato supposes that individuals are rational and that the governing consideration is the limitation imposed by reality. If the individual sticks to his task, if he cooperates with other individuals and lets them fulfill theirs, all will be well. In my terms this implies that group mental activity is wholly comprised in W functions and can be governed by reference to reality. But my contention is that W is only one part of group mentality and cannot be understood without reference to other mental phenomena. Aristotle indeed appears to criticize Platonic theory because it is deficient in its grasp of the reality of human behavior, but the real change comes with St. Augustine's formulations in the 19th Book of *The City of God*. He seems here to postulate a new dimension, and, by insisting that a right relationship with God is a prerequisite for a right relationship with individuals, to be predicating a state of mind similar to that which I describe as D. For in D, the individuals do not have a relationship with each other but only with the D.L. Since St. Augustine there has been no return to the classical view. The liberal view is that emotion and reason are easily harmonized, that is to say, that the operations of the W Group can be harmonized with the operations of the basic-assumption group. Nietzsche reacts against what he feels to be the arid intellectualism that this view would produce, seeming to suggest that a group achieves vitality only insofar as it releases the aggressive impulses. This would mean that a feeling of vitality could only be achieved by the dominance of the basic assumption, notably F. These and similar views are expressed in the group as ideals to be sought after as a solution of the problems of the group. But from what I have already said, it will be realized that in practice none provide any lasting solution. Group reactions are infinitely more complex than the foregoing theories, even in their full deployment, suggest. Freud expressly disavowed any but a superficial study of the group problem, making his observations in the course of a criticism, derived from psychoanalysis, of the work done by others.

In his "Group Psychology and the Analysis of the Ego," Freud points out that individual and group psychology cannot be absolutely differentiated because the psychology of the individual is itself a function of the individual's relationship to another person or object. He objects that it is difficult to attribute to the factor of number a significance so great as to make it capable by itself of arousing in our mental life a new instinct that is otherwise not brought into play. In my view no new instinct is brought into play—it is always in play. It is not necessary for a number of people to be brought together—the individual cannot help being a member of a group even if his membership in it consists in behaving in such a way as to give reality to the idea that he does not belong to a group at all. The psychoanalytic situation is not "individual psychology" but "pair." The individual is a group animal at war, both with the group and with those aspects of his personality that constitute his "groupishness."

It is necessary for a group to meet because the conditions for study can be provided only in that way. Freud, and others whom he quotes, such as McDougall (1920) and Le Bon (1920), seem to me to consider that group psychology is something which comes into being when there are a number of people collected together in the same place and at the same time, and in this respect I agree with Freud that too much significance is thereby attributed to number: I think he is mistaken in saying (p. 70) that a solution must only be sought in one or other of the two alternatives: (1) the possibility that the social instinct is not primitive, or (2) that its development begins in a manner such as that of the family. There is a third. I would say that the importance of the aggregation of individuals into a group is similar to the importance of the bringing together of analyst and analysand: it is necessary for an analysand to come to a psychoanalyst for the transference relationship to be rendered demonstrable: the group should come together so that the characteristics of the group may be demonstrated. There is no intrinsic importance in the coming together of the group; it must come together sufficiently closely for me to be able to give an interpretation without having to shout it. Therefore the number must be limited and the degree of dispersion of the group must be limited. This is necessary also because all individuals must have an opportunity of witnessing the evidence on which interpretations are based. The congregation of the group in a particular place at a particular time is important for these mechanical reasons, but it has no significance for the production of group phenomena. The idea springs from the erroneous impression that a thing must commence at the moment when its existence becomes demonstrable. No individual, however isolated in time and space, should be regarded as outside a group or lacking in active manifestations of group psychology merely because conditions do not make it possible to demonstrate it. The concept of the human being as a group animal would solve the difficulties which are felt to exist in the seeming paradox that a group is more than the sum of its members. The explanation of certain phenomena must be sought in the matrix of the group and not in the individuals that go to make up the group. Timekeeping is no function of any part, in isolation, of the mechanism of a clock, yet timekeeping is a function of the clock and of the various parts of the clock when held in combination with each other.

To sum up, there are characteristics in the individual of which the significance cannot be understood except as part of his equipment as a herd animal, nor can their operation be seen unless in the intelligible field of study—which is the group.

Freud does not recognize, in his discussion of groups, the importance of his own revolution in looking for an explanation of neurotic symptoms, not in the individual, but in the individual's relationship with objects.

The apparent difference between group psychology and individual psychology is an illusion produced by the fact that the group brings into prominence phenomena which appear alien to an observer unaccustomed to using the group.[6] Freud states that his contribution is visible only in his selection both of material and opinions (presumably from the standard works he cites in "Totem and Taboo," (1913, p. 75, n. 1). Explanations of group behavior are

[6] It is also a matter of historical development; the link between individual and group psychology cannot be forged until there has been sufficient understanding of Melanie Klein's work on the psychoses, and in particular of the papers on symbol formation (1930) and schizoid mechanisms (1946), to make its application to group work possible. I develop this point later.

derived from the psychoanalytic situation. It is possibly for
this reason that Freud's description of the group reads
strangely when compared with actual experiences in a
group. I attribute great force and influence to the Work
Group which, through its concern with reality, is compelled to employ the methods of science in no matter how
rudimentary a form; despite the influence of the basic
assumptions, it is the W Group which triumphs in the long
run. Freud himself considers—notably when he discusses
the part that the group plays in the production of language,[7] folk song, folklore, etc.—that Le Bon is unfair to
the group when he says it never thirsts after truth. Freud
discusses McDougall's view that conditions in the highly
organized group remove "the psychological disadvantages
of group formation." McDougall here approximates to my
view that the function of the specialized work group is to
manipulate the basic assumption to prevent obstruction of
the work group. Freud describes the problem as one of
procuring for the group "precisely those features which
were characteristic of the individual and which are extin-
guished in him by the formation of the group." He postulates an individual outside the primitive group who
possessed his own continuity, his self-consciousness, his
traditions and customs, his own particular functions and
position. He says that owing to his entry into an "unorganized" group, the individual had lost his distinctiveness
for a time. In my view the struggle of the individual to
preserve his distinctiveness assumes different characteristics according to the state of mind of the group at any
given moment. Group organization gives stability and per-
manence to the work group, which is felt to be more easily
submerged by the basic assumptions if the group is un-

---

[7] In view of my suggestions on pp. 101-102 of this article, it seems
significant that Freud picks the development of language as an example.

organized. Individual distinctiveness is no part of life in a group acting on the basic assumptions. Organization and structure are weapons of the W Group. They are the product of cooperation between members of the group, and their effect, once established in the group, is to demand still further cooperation from the individuals in the group. In this respect McDougall's organized group is always a work group and never a basic-assumption group. A group acting on a basic assumption needs no organization or cooperation. The counterpart of cooperation in the basic-assumption group is what I have called valency—a spontaneous, unconscious function of the gregarious quality in the personality of man. It is only when a group begins to act on a basic assumption that difficulties arise. Action inevitably means contact with reality, and contact with reality compels regard for truth and therefore imposes scientific method and, hence, the evocation of the work group.

Freud deduces group situations from his study of the transference. For reasons I have given, the transference is likely to be colored by group characteristics deriving from P, which are stimulated by the pair situation actually existing in psychoanalysis. Indeed, in the group situation we can find one source both of the prominence of sexual elements in psychoanalysis and the suspicions and accusations of the opponents of Freud that psychoanalysis was "sexual." He was able to deduce from psychoanalysis some of the characteristics of two specialized work groups, army and church, but was not led to a discussion of the specialized work group that attaches most importance to breeding and is therefore most likely to have to deal with P, namely, the aristocracy. If W characteristics were allowed to play a dominant role, the aristocracy would have a closer resemblance to the genetics department of a university, or to a stud farm, than it has. As it is, we cannot regard the interest shown in breeding as having the scientific aura which should be pathognomic of the work group. The reason is that it is not dealing with a W problem. It is a specialized subgroup split off to deal with P in much the same way as the army and the church have to deal with F and D respectively. Therefore, the relationship of this subgroup with the main group will not be determined by the fidelity with which it conducts its love affairs on strictly genetic principles, but rather on the efficiency with which it satisfies the group demand that the P should be so dealt with that it does not obstruct the W functions of the group as a whole.

Now, I have already said that in P, anxiety derives from the feeling that both group and individual are subservient to the unborn genius. The function of the aristocracy is sometimes to find an outlet for activity based on P without outraging the reality sense of the group; sometimes to prevent the reality sense of the group from undermining the institutions on the preservation of which the group depends for the neutralization of P.

Freud criticizes Le Bon's views on the leader of the group. Le Bon states that a collection of human beings place themselves instinctively under the authority of a chief; that the leader must fit in with the needs of the group in his personal qualities, and that he must himself be held by a strong faith in order to awaken the group's faith. Le Bon does not carry his view of the relationship between leader and group as far as I do by my description of the D.L., F.L., and P.L. The statement that the leader must fit in with the group in his personal qualities is compatible with my view that any leader of the group is ignored when his behavior or characteristics fall outside the limits set by the prevalent basic assumption. I also think that the leader must be held by the same "faith" that holds the group, though I do not believe that this is in order to awaken the group's faith. On the contrary, my view is that the attitude of the group and its leader alike are merely functions of the active basic assumption.

Freud (p. 85) discusses McDougall's distinction between the simple "unorganized" group and the "organized" group, and gives an account of two states of mind which, in my opinion, do not belong to different groups but can be observed to coexist in the same group. McDougall's simple "unorganized" group resembles the basic-assumption groups. I do not agree that the "unorganized" group is suggestible; I consider that it is very difficult to put over any view that does not fit in with the prevalent basic assumption. It is possible that the idea that the group is suggestible arises because any idea that is conformable with the prevalent basic assumption is automatically accepted.

Freud quotes one point in McDougall's conditions for raising the level of collective mental life to which I would draw attention, and that is his statement—"The first and fundamental condition is that there should be some degree of continuity of existence in the group" (p. 86). This convinces me that in the organized group McDougall is describing what I call the W Group. Meyer Fortes (1970), discussing Radcliffe Brown's views on social structure particularly the distinction between "structure as an actually existing concrete reality" and "structural form," says that the distinction is associated with the continuity of social structure through time. In my view the continuity of social structure through time is a function of the W Group. Meyer Fortes states that the time factor in social structure is by no means uniform in its incidence and adds that all corporate groups, by definition, must have continuity. As with McDougall's distinction between organized and unorganized groups, so with the incidence of the time factor. I do not believe that we are dealing with two different kinds of group, in the sense of two different communities, but rather with two different aspects, which coexist, of the same community. Continuity in time is an intrinsic quality of W Group activity, but is not a component of the basic group. All the functions of the basic-assumption group are in full activity before ever the group comes together in a room, although their observation may be difficult, and continue after the group has dispersed. There is neither development nor decay in basic-assumption functions and in this respect they differ totally from the W group. It stands to reason that observation of the group's continuity in time is likely to present anomalous and contradictory features if the operation of two different kinds of mental functioning within the group has not been recognized. It may help to clarify my meaning if I say that when an individual asks "When does the group meet again?" he is referring to W and W only, insofar as he is talking about mental phenomena at all. The basic-assumption group does not disperse or meet, and references to time have no meaning in the basic-assumption group. The apparent impatience of the basic-assumption group may therefore be read as an expression of anxiety aroused by phenomena associated with continuity, development, etc., which are intrinsically comingled with a dimension of which the basic-assumption group knows nothing. It is as if an organism devoid of organs of sight were to be made aware of phenomena that could only be understood by someone acquainted with the properties of light.

　　McDougall's principles for raising collective mental life to a higher level seem to me to be an expression of the desire to prevent the basic-assumption groups from obstructing W. His second condition appears to emphasize the need for individuals to have a clear knowledge of W aims. His fourth point, namely the existence of a body of traditions and customs and habits in the minds of the members of the group, determining their relations to one another and the group as a whole, comes very near to the platonic view of group harmony based on individual function which I have already described as a W phenomenon. It also corresponds to the views put forward by St. Augustine in the 19th book of *The City of God*. At first sight this would seem to contradict my statement that McDougall is describing W phenomena, but the discrepancy is resolved if it is remembered that in my view St. Augustine's theory is an attempt to postulate a specialized W Group for dealing with D.

Freud bases the next stage in his discussion on the statement that, in a group, an individual's emotions "become extraordinarily intensified while his intellectual ability is markedly reduced" (p. 88). From actual experience in a group I would say that this statement needs qualification. It will be appreciated that in the groups I have studied, the group naturally expects me to take the lead in organizing its activities. I take advantage of the position thus accorded me to lead the group in my own way—that is to say, in an exploration of group dynamics. This means that the desire for an organized group is frustrated. The group thereupon fears the emergence of the basic-assumption groups and expresses its fear by an attempt to produce a structure and an organization, thus doing its best to suppress all emotion, emotion being an intrinsic part of the basic-assumption groups. This produces a state of affairs which to the individual often appears as an intensification of emotion. Since attention is focused upon this, since, furthermore, the lack of structure promotes the obtrusion of the basic-assumption group in which intellectual activity is of the limited kind I have already described, it feels as if intellectual ability is markedly reduced. The belief that this is so is still further encouraged by the fact that the dominating position of the basic assumption causes the individuals to ignore all intellectual activity that does not fit in with the basic assumption. Actually I do not in the least believe that there is a reduction of intellectual ability in the group, nor yet that "great decisions in the realm of thought and momentous discoveries and solutions of problems are only possible to an individual working in solitude," (p. 83) although the belief that this is so is commonly expressed in the group discussion and all sorts of plans are elaborated for circumventing the supposedly pernicious influence of the emotions of the group. Indeed, I give interpretations because I believe that intellectual activity of a high order is possible in a group, together with an awareness (and *not* an evasion) of the emotions of the basic-assumption group. My behavior in doing this betrays, I hope, my indebtedness to psychoanalytic experience. If group therapy is found to have a value, I believe it will be in the conscious experiencing of group activity of this sort. Freud turns to discussion of something that crops up under a variety of names such as "suggestion," "imitation," "prestige of leaders," "contagion." I have used "valency" partly because I wish to avoid the suggestions which already adhere to the terms I have listed, partly because the term valency, as used in physics in reference to the power of combination of atoms, carries with it the greatest penumbra of suggestiveness useful for my purpose. I mean the capacity of the individual for instantaneous combination with other individuals in an established pattern of behavior—the basic assumptions. I shall not follow Freud's discussion in detail, but will pass on to his use of the term libido, which he takes from his study of the psychoneuroses (p. 90). At first sight it would appear that I conflict with him if he uses the word libido and I use valency. But in taking the word from his study of the neuroses, Freud is approaching his examination of the group through the technique of psychoanalysis, and psychoanalysis, in the light of my theories of groups, can be regarded as a work group most likely to stimulate P; that being so, the psychoanalytic investigation as a part of P is likely to reveal sexuality in a central position. Furthermore, it is likely to come under attack as a sexual activity since, according to my theory of P, the group must assume that two people can come together for a sexual purpose only.

It is natural, therefore, that if Freud uses the discoveries that spring from psychoanalytic investigation in order to elucidate the phenomena of the group, he will see the nature of the bond between individual members of the group as libidinal. An investigation carried out in the group itself shows that the libidinal component in the bond is characteristic only of P, and that the bond has a different complexion in F and D. I attribute it to the same cause that Freud (p. 94) describes the Commander-in-Chief of the Church as Christ. In fact, as I hope to show later, the Commander-in-Chief in this context is the Deity. Christ, or the Messiah, as I have already said, is the Leader not of D, but of P. The Messiah is an accidental feature in religion, the Deity, intrinsic. In P the Messiah is essential. It is significant that Freud makes this mistake, which should be obvious on purely theological grounds. The point is that, in psychoanalysis regarded as a P, the Messiah tends to occupy a central position and the bond between individuals is libidinal. The Messianic idea betrays its presence in the supposition that the individual patient is worth the analyst's very considerable devotion, and also in the view sometimes expressed that, as a result of psychoanalytic work, a technique will be perfected that will ultimately save mankind. Freud's description of the nature of the tie between individuals of the group I regard as correct for only one phase, though an important one in the group mental life, and feel the need for some more neutral term that will describe the tie on all basic-assumption levels (but excluding the tie in the W Group, which I regard as being of a sophisticated nature more aptly indicated by the word cooperation).

There is another reason for using the term valency: Freud's notion of the leader as important because the group depends upon him and derives its qualities from his personality is, I think, mistaken; the leader is as much the creature of the basic assumption as any other member of the group. That is to say, the leader does not create the group by virtue of his fanatical adherence to an idea, but is rather an individual whose personality renders him peculiarly susceptible to the obliteration of individuality by the basic-assumption groups' leadership requirements. That is, if it is true to say that in F, for example, the individual loses his distinctiveness, this applies to the F.L. as much as to anyone else. He only appears to have a distinctive personality because his personality is of a kind that lends itself to exploitation by the group demand for fighting or flight as the only two techniques its leader should require of it; the leader has no greater freedom to be a person than any other member of the group. This does not agree with Le Bon's idea that the leader must possess a strong and imposing will, nor yet with Freud's idea that he corresponds to a hypnotist. Such power as he has derives from the fact that he has become, in common with every other member of the group, what Le Bon describes as "an automaton who has ceased to be guided by his will." In short, he is leader by virtue of his capacity for instantaneous, involuntary (maybe voluntary too) combination with every other member of his group and only differs from them in that, whatever his function may be in W, he is the incarnation of the leader of the basic-assumption group.

Freud's view does not seem to me to make possible an understanding of the dangerous possibilities that exist in the phenomenon of group leadership. His view of the leader, and indeed all other views of which I am aware, is not easily reconciled with my experience of leadership as it emerges in practice. The usual description of the leader seems to me to be a mixture of different group phenomena, with the characteristics of the W.L. predominating. Now, for reasons I have already given, the W.L. is either harmless through lack of influence with the group or else a man who carries weight on account of his grasp of reality. It is likely, therefore, that descriptions of leadership which are colored mostly by the characteristics of the W.L. would tend to be optimistically tinged. My view of the basic-assumption group leader does not rule out the possibility of identity with W.L. function, but it allows for the existence of a leader apparently evoking the enthusiastic allegiance of the group, but devoid of any contact with reality other than the reality of basic-assumption-group demands. When it is realized that this can mean that the group is being led by an individual whose personality has been obliterated, an automaton, "an individual who has lost his distinctiveness," but who yet is so suffused by the emotions of the basic-assumption group that he carries all the prestige of a W.L., it becomes possible to explain some of the disasters into which groups have been led by leaders whose qualifications for the post seem, when the emotions prevalent at their prime have died down, to be devoid of substance.

We can regard Church and army either as work groups whose task is of such a nature that they are likely to have more experience than usual of D and F or, alternatively, as subgroups of the main group with the specific tasks of coping with D and F manifestations in such a way that the W function of the main group is, as far as possible, unobstructed.

I turn to Freud's views on panic. Freud says (p. 96) that panic is best studied in military groups. He does not appear to claim actual experience of panic in a military group. I have experienced panic on two occasions with troops in action and have on several other occasions in small civilian groups had reason to think that the emotional experience bore a sufficiently close resemblance to my military experiences to deserve the name panic. In some respects, to which I shall shortly refer, these experiences do not appear to me to bear out Freud's theories, though I think he is discussing the same phenomenon. I consider that McDougall's description of panic refers to an experience which is the same as mine. I am confirmed in this belief when McDougall says (1920, p. 24) "Other of the cruder, primary emotions may spread through a crowd in very similar fashion, though the process is rarely so rapid and intense as in the case of fear," and then describes in a footnote (p. 26) an instance he witnessed in Borneo of the almost instantaneous spread of anger through a crowd. McDougall has thus brought very close together, though without making the connection, anger and fear, and hence supports my view that panic is an aspect of F, and that there is no essential difference between panic flight and uncontrolled attack. But here is my difficulty: If it is argued, not merely that my theories offer a false description of the phenomena of the group, but that the experiences on which I base them were not panics at all, I do not really know what reply can be made, nor what steps are open to me to discover where my error lies, so long as the problem is approached as if it were an academic one, soluble apart from contact with the group itself.

Here, then, are my findings: Panic can never arise except in a situation which might as easily have given rise to rage: rage or fear in the given situation is offered no readily available outlet: frustration of the rage or fear, which is thus inescapable, cannot be tolerated because frustration is a function of time and time is not a dimension of basic-assumption phenomena. Flight offers a vehicle for expression of the emotion in F which is immediately available and therefore meets the demands of F for instantaneous satisfaction of impulse. The group in F will follow any leader and, contrary to all views hitherto expressed, retains its coherence in doing so, who will fulfill the characteristics of F.L., namely, give only such orders as are recognizable as licensing instantaneous flight or instantaneous attack. Provided that an individual in the group conforms to these limitations of the F.L., he will have no difficulty in turning a group from headlong panic flight to attack, or from headlong attack to panic.

The stimulus for panic, or the rage which I consider to be identical, must always be an event that falls outside the W Group functions of the group concerned. That is to say, that the degree of organization of the group is not relevant unless the organization, part of W function, is concerned with the actual external event as part of its *raison d'être*. In Freud's example of the fire in a theatre or place of amusement (p. 96), the W Group is devoted to the watching of a play but not to the witnessing of a conflagration, still less to the extinguishing of it. The essential point about organization is that it should be suitable both to the pursuit of the external aim of the group and to the manipulation of the basic assumption such a pursuit is most calculated to evoke. Panic in an army is not produced by a military danger, though military danger is, in the nature of things, very likely to be present. It is not likely to be produced by any situation in which attack or flight are appropriate to the operations of the W Group. If it appears to arise in such a situation it is because the actual cause is not observed.

Before I express further views about the causes of panic, it would be useful to consult early views that cannot be impugned on the grounds that they are tainted by theoretical psychological presumptions. To go to origins, the word itself derives from the belief that this fear was inspired by Pan, to whom is attributed the ability to induce in man terror like that of a frightened and stampeding flock or herd of animals. Pan is amorous and has as his chief function, originally, the making fertile of flocks. To him is attributed also the source of nightmares. He is formidable if disturbed at midday. There appears to be very little mythology about Pan, and, although there are comparatively late attempts to make him a universal god, these do not seem to have been very successful.

It seems from this that panic fear was from the first regarded as a group phenomenon in which fear possessed all members of the group instantaneously. It appears also that to the individual the fear is felt as something induced by an internal object in the sense in which I understand Melanie Klein to use those words. It is noteworthy that the power of evoking nightmares is attributed to Pan, because it would appear from this that the induction of panic fear was felt to be a quite different activity. My experience is by itself too limited to draw any conclusion from it, but it is worth remarking that such experience as I have had suggests that panic is in fact far more likely to arise in broad daylight or at least in a fully waking state. At any other time what occurs is not a panic but a nightmare, and this is an individual, not a group phenomenon.

It is now clear that between the theories Freud suggested, approaching the problem from the psychoanalysis of the individual, and the theories I have suggested, making my approach from the study of the group itself, there is a considerable gap. It is possible that the gap appears to be more considerable than it is because of my deliberate use of new terminology. I am disposed, however, to believe that more than a question of terminology is involved, and for this belief I shall now advance my reasons.

My first relates to the group's capacity for enduring almost endless periods of trivial conversation or none at all. There are protests, but endurance of this monotony appears to be a lesser evil than action to end it. When interpretations are made, they are, as likely as not, disregarded. Allowing for the possibility that the disregard is, as in psychoanalysis, more apparent than real, that the interpretations are faulty and on that account inefficacious, there yet remains a residue of inertia that is not explained by this or any suggestion that the F.L., D.L., and P.L. are so dominant that statements which lie outside the characteristic functions of these three are disregarded.

I have been forced to the conclusion that verbal exchange is understood only by the W Group. In proportion as the group is dominated by a basic assumption, verbal communication is important only as a vehicle for sound. In the *Germania* Tacitus gives a description of the operations of the bard in a German tribe—a description that might be prophetic of Hitler addressing a Nazi rally—which illustrates my point. The key to this is provided by Melanie Klein in her discussion of the importance of symbol formation in the development of the individual (1930). The W Group understands that particular use of symbols which is involved in verbal communication; the basic-assumption group does not. In the basic-assumption group the individual *is* the totem animal. He is not identified with it, or equated with it, he is it. Similarly he *is* the D.L., P.L., or F.L., or a function of those symbols (as a sense of reality demands that we should call them).

The language of the basic-assumption group is therefore a method of communication devoid of the precision that is conferred by a capacity for the formation and use of symbols. The basic-assumption group therefore lacks a powerful aid to development and remains fundamentally unaffected by stimuli that would provoke it. But the basic-assumption group has a means of communication that might well lay claim to the title of the Universal Linguistic which Croce (1921) conferred on Esthetic. Every human group instantaneously understands every other human group, no matter how diverse in culture, language, and tradition–but only within the limitations of the basic assumptions.

In the light of these speculations we may reread the biblical account of the building of the Tower of Babel (Genesis, 11:1-9).[8] The myth has these components: a universal language, a tower which is felt by the Deity to menace his position, a "confounding" of the universal language, and a scattering abroad of the people on the face of the earth. Using my theories to interpret this myth, I suggest that it embodies an account of the development of language, which development is itself an expression of the capacity for symbol formation. This capacity is exemplified in the myth by employment of the building of a tower to reach to heaven as a symbol of the increased potency achieved through the development of language. The inability to use symbols, which is shown even by recent commentators, is also suggested by the literal way in which the tower is mentioned. The growth of language would be a group event of the kind which I have mentioned as demanding development in the individual members of the group and would be opposed as an attack upon the D.L. The reaction to this development is the formation of schisms.

Melanie Klein (1930) has shown that the inability to form symbols is characteristic of certain individuals. I would extend this to all individuals in their functions as members of the basic-assumption group.

---

[8] This account is a part of the Jahvistic code and could therefore be regarded as an example of recording by a group with D dominant when threatened by the emergence of P.

We may now consider afresh a point that has struck many observers—namely, the loss in a group of the individual's distinctiveness (Freud, 1921, p. 86). The individual sees in the group a source of infinite frustration, but the psychiatrist will be impressed by the opportunity it affords for externalization of problems. One consequence is that the individual splits off his aggressiveness and projects it into the "leader." His wish to fight, to nourish, to choose a partner or his parents, all are in turn deposited in some external figure. Thus one source of the characteristics of F.L., D.L., or P.L. is activated. On this account, and because of the individual's feelings of guilt at being in possession of the group, which is equated with the breast, the leader thus formed arouses feelings of persecution, and steps then have to be taken to split off these feelings and to denude the leader of noxious persecutory qualities (Klein, 1946). This is done by a variety of complex mechanisms, which may for the moment be ignored while we notice that such activity, in which every member of the group participates—incidentally it is at this point that the therapist in charge of the therapeutic group must be most on his guard against becoming a protagonist of the idea that the "group" is "good for" the patients—must be felt by the group as a process of "curing" the leader. This feeling helps to explain one component in the belief that the leader is the patient to the welfare of whom all group energies must be devoted.

To turn now to the mechanisms employed in "treating" the persecutor. One is by reassurance which is directed toward allaying the anxieties of both the individual chosen to be the leader and the group as a whole. This process is, however, only a comparatively superficial one and is consequently easily observed. The leader is congratulated in a great variety of terms on his goodness, the group on its good fortune in having such a leader. It is in the course of these manipulations that ritual and ceremony come into their own, as do also the presentation of gifts or sacrifices. The sacrifices again may take many forms, the commonest being the abandonment by the rest of the group of all ambitions for cure or hopes of personal achievement. Their characteristics will vary according to whether the chosen individual is D.L., F.L., or P.L. For example, if D is prominent, the rituals and sacrifices bear a resemblance to the procedures of religious groups; if F, then the army; if P.L., then the privileges often associated with aristocracy.

A more profound movement in the group dynamics, which is implicit but not obvious in the superficies of reassurances and the like, is the attempt to rid the group of feelings of persecution by a shifting of the problems produced by projective identification from the basic-assumption group to the work group. In practice this means that the illest member of the group becomes the object of the group's attentions and becomes its leader, a situation I have described as the dual of D; the choice of descriptive term really depends on the emphasis the observer wishes to give to different components of the situation. It cannot be fully described as W because, in theory, the W Group is occupied with a real task, which in the groups of which I speak is the study of the group, although in fact this theory is an idealization that is never achieved. It cannot be justly described as a basic-assumption group because, in theory, the basic-assumption group is wholly characterized by an instinctual emotional absorption in acting on the given basic assumption—again not a state ever achieved in practice. Its interest for me lies in its resemblance to an incipient spontaneous development of psychotherapy. It is as if the group tried to cure itself by the concentration of its illnesses into one person and then to cure or expel the one person.

To sum up, "the loss of the individual's distinctiveness"

is a phenomenon indistinguishable from depersonalization. The link between my findings from the study of the group and those of psychoanalysis is provided by Melanie Klein's formulations in her "Notes on Schizoid Mechanisms" (1946).

I conclude with the following propositions:

(1) Individuals in a group must be considered to possess a capacity, called valency by me, for holding each other in involuntary and inevitable emotional combination. Activity arising from this is quite different from that which springs from cooperation, a term I reserve for describing voluntary combination.

(2) In every group two kinds of mental activity can be recognized as coexistent, W group activity and basic-assumption group activity, cooperation being a function of the former, valency of the latter.

(3) The individual, regarded as a participant in the basic-assumption group, is unable to form or employ symbols. This gives rise to the sense of "collective lowering of intellectual ability" described by McDougall and others. In consequence, the group, in its basic-assumption activity, does not, and cannot develop (Klein, 1930). What is more, the sense of intellectual deficiency produced by the interplay between the basic-assumption group, which is incapable of symbol formation, and the W Group, which constantly employs it, can be so strong as to pervade W Group function and inhibit intellectual activity in it.

(4) It follows that the employment of symbolism in a group is a W function only. In consequence, when a group appears to be employing symbols, especially if emotions are engaged, it is in fact doing no such thing–it is equated with them (Segal, 1950).

(5) From this it follows that words, if they are to elucidate basic-assumption-group phenomena, must not be interpreted in the light of their value as symbols (which

would only elucidate W Group function) but as sounds having preverbal significance. Their manifest content must be ignored and an attempt made to view them as identical, in their basic-assumption function, with the bizarre verbalizations of the psychotic. Their rational content must be ignored as accidental.

(6) Just as the psychoanalysis of the psychotic must be regarded as differing from the psychoanalysis of the neurotic, so, and for similar reasons, the interpretation of basic-assumption-group phenomena must be regarded as differing from the interpretation of W Group phenomena.

(7) The understanding of the emotional life of the group, which is a function of the basic assumptions, is only comprehensible in terms of psychotic mechanisms. For this reason, advances in the study of the group are dependent upon the development and implications of Melanie Klein's theories of internal objects, projective identification, and failure in symbol formation and their application in the group situation.

(8) Further investigation of group dynamics, and especially of basic-assumption-group phenomena, might be directed to the investigation of:

(a) depersonalization as the essential feature in the "loss of individual distinctiveness."
(b) failure in symbol formation and the use of symbols as an essential feature in inhibiting development of the basic assumption groups; and
(c) interpretation of basic-assumption phenomena in terms of psychotic, rather than neurotic, mechanisms.

(9) From these propositions follows a final proposition that theories of the kind I have proposed should be tested only against actual interpretation in a group at the moment when the phenomena are demonstrable.

History of life on this planet shows that decay of a species is often associated with overdevelopment of some portion of its organism. In effect such overdevelopment defeats its end and leads to the suppression of one species by the next. Is there a possibility of similar overdevelopment of mental function? The group may provide evidence of an opinion.

4

A Psychoanalytic Approach To Group Treatment

Henry Ezriel

Although the psychotherapy of patients in groups is a very recent method of treatment, there are already a great many techniques in use—almost as many, perhaps, as in individual treatment. Most scientific work has to be preceded by a phase in which adequate tools and skills are being developed, and it might be helpful, therefore, during this phase for therapists to report tentatively on their experiences and to examine what appears to them to be effective and useful. Indeed, the descriptions already written, for instance, by Bion (1959) have shown how stimulating such accounts can be. Following Bion's work at the Tavistock Clinic, a few members of the staff have tried to apply a strictly psychoanalytic technique to the treatment of patients in groups. So far we have not had an opportunity to compare our techniques directly, e.g., by sitting in at each other's groups, but discussions suggest that much of what we do is based on common principles. There are, however, some differences; hence, the following descrip-

Reprinted from the *British Journal of Medical Psychology*, 23:59-74 (1950), with the permission of the publisher and of the author.

tion, although representative in many parts, has features which are specific to myself.

My first group started a little over four years ago, and some of its original members are still under treatment. I can only say, therefore, that I have had a fair period in which to follow a few of these patients and to gain some impressions of the stability of changes in their behavior as a result of the method used. It must be emphasized that I do not for a moment consider that this strictly psychoanalytic technique is the only way of giving effective help to patients. It is merely one method of doing so, and it is not unreasonable to expect that future psychotherapists will have at their disposal a number of techniques which have been established as effective and economic for particular cases under particular conditions.

One often gets the impression that group therapy has been taken up mainly in order to make psychotherapy accessible to a larger number of patients and thus to make this time-consuming treatment less expensive. I doubt, however, whether this was the chief factor driving toward the development of group treatment. I think the reason psychoanalysts became interested in the application of their method to groups of patients was that the development of psychoanalytic theory and practice had reached a point where such a step was a logical consequence.

Two trends seem to be relevant in this connection: One is the development of the theory of "unconscious object relations" (Klein, 1932, 1946, 1948; Fairbairn, 1952; and others); the other is an increasingly "rigorous" technique of transference interpretations, originating from the work of Ferenczi (1926), elaborated principally by English analysts (Strachey, 1934 and others) and applied to groups by Bion. It is my intention to describe in a subsequent paper a theory of interpretation and of personality based upon concepts of object relations. In this paper, however,

I only want to show how I have tried to apply these two developments in psychoanalytic theory and practice to groups.

The basic assumption underlying an approach that makes consistent use of transference interpretations is that the apparently incoherent thoughts and actions produced by the patient one after another in a temporal sequence belong together dynamically. That is to say, there exists a common unconscious dynamic source, a need, which sets up a tension in the patient's mind and which tries to find relief through his establishing a certain kind of relationship between himself and his analyst in the "here and now" situation of the analytic session, i.e. through "acting out." This attempt is considered as one particular instance of a more general tendency, as one of many unconscious endeavors the patient makes to establish such a relationship between himself and his environment in general. Such needs are based on unconscious fantasies about his relations with unconscious objects (the residues of unresolved infantile conflicts) which are being transferred to objects of his present environment ("transference").

In this sense, transference phenomena are something that all of us show every moment of our lives to varying degrees. Our particular interpretations, and even distortions, of the external environment, whether physical or social, are influenced by our particular unconscious-need systems. Our behavior is therefore not only governed by conscious needs and environmental demands but also by unconscious needs. The individual tries to diminish tensions set up by such unconscious needs either in activities which serve *only* this purpose–e.g., symptoms, or sublimations like the enjoyment of works of art, or by activities *superimposed* on those which serve to gratify his conscious needs or the demands the environment makes upon him. Thus works of handicraft may both satisfy a practical conscious need and may have grafted on to them "artistic," i.e., unconscious, gratifications. Again, personality traits that find expression in the various ways in which different individuals try to fulfill the same conscious task represent such attempts to diminish tensions arising from unconscious object relations, superimposed on whatever conscious task the individual may try to solve.

In the analytic situation, which the patient enters to satisfy his conscious need for treatment, the adoption of a passive nondirective attitude by the analyst allows all these unconscious needs to emerge in the patient's attempts to establish appropriate relationships with the analyst. Strachey (1934) emphasized that it is only the analysis of this "here and now" relationship which represents a "mutative" interpretation, i.e., one which can permanently change the patient's personality or, as I would put it, his unconscious needs. Strachey expressed the opinion that extratransference interpretations (such as would not deal with the here-and-now situation) have a certain usefulness insofar as they may help to bring about a situation in which transference interpretations can be given. Since then, a number of analysts (especially Rickman, 1951, whose point of view I am following) have gradually tended to the view that none other than transference interpretations need be used.

To illustrate the application of such a technique, it might be helpful to consider, first, some clinical material from part of an individual psychoanalytic session. This material will also show how a person's apparently irrational behavior can be explained by making the assumption of unconscious needs arising from unconscious object relations.

The patient had been undergoing treatment for about two years. In the preceding sessions we had discussed his depressive fears arising out of his ambivalent conflict of both wanting to preserve a loving couple, a man and woman, whom he badly needed for the gratification of various needs, and at the same time wanting to destroy them since they aroused his jealousy by frustrating his sexual wishes and excluding him from their sexual life. It had also become apparent that in the transference relationship this couple, originally his parents, were now represented by my receptionist and myself.

The session started by his referring to my remarks about this transference relationship in the previous session. He said my deductions seemed "extremely logical," but that he just was not aware of any conscious desire for "my woman." He went on to recount an event of the preceding weekend when he spent an afternoon on the river with some friends. One couple, husband and wife, were rowing with their little son, who jumped about in the boat and nearly made it tip over. He added that he got a shock when he saw this. "It might have ended in a real disaster. She cannot swim at all, and he is a poor swimmer. Even if I had jumped into the water and saved the boy, how would he have got on in life if his parents had been drowned?"

After a short silence, he changed the subject and complained that recently he had been getting into difficulties with his married friends by apparently creating discord between husband and wife through what he called his perverted sense of humor. In a facetious manner he would make advances to the wife in front of her husband, for he was convinced that their relationship was such a good one that his behavior would be understood as what he meant it to be, namely, a joke. Often, however, he seemed to have an uncanny ability to hit upon some sore point in the relationship of these people, and thus he caused considerable embarrassment. While he spoke about this subject he was lying on the couch with his fingers interlocked, and he kept on pulling them apart. Then he mentioned that recently he had been worried by a ceremonial before going to sleep. He had always put his alarm clock on a little table next to his bed and his wristwatch on the same table a few inches away from the clock. Recently, however, he could not fall asleep without turning on the light several times to make sure that the clock did not touch the watch. He gave himself a conscious explanation for this behavior by imagining that the vibrations of the clock would spoil the watch, but he was well aware that this was not the real reason, for he became panicky time and again when he desisted from checking the position of the clock. In fact, he got worried about the compulsive nature of this checking as the number of times he had to do it kept on increasing. At this point in the session he started to smoke, and as he put the match into the ashtray he absentmindedly removed the book that was lying next to it. Finally, he asked me to get rid of my receptionist, whose "silly face" he did not like.

Starting with the assumptions mentioned above, I always ask myself, "What makes this patient behave (speak or act) toward me in this particular way at this moment?" In other words, what role does he unconsciously try to push me into, what sort of relationship is he unconsciously trying to establish between us?

If we try to discover some common pattern in this patient's manifest thoughts and actions, we can see that, with the exception of the two first thoughts, he seemed to be aiming at the separation of two objects—his two hands, book and ashtray, clock and watch, husband and wife, myself and the receptionist. Even if he had not made it so evident by mentioning the receptionist, I think it would have been justifiable to assume that he was trying to separate me from "my woman" (provided the above-mentioned basic assumption is correct, namely, that all his manifest behavior in the psychoanalytic session refers in some way to the here-and-now relationship).

The patient's first thought in the session referred to this relationship. He thus indicated that he was unconsciously preoccupied with the problems that jealousy, aroused by the presence of a loving couple, stimulated in him. The second thought portrays the disaster which might befall a child who gives in to wishes that endanger the lives of his parents. In the first two thoughts he thus describes an object relationship in which a person (himself) stands in front of a loving couple. In the first, he shows preoccupation with jealousy which he consciously tries to deny; in the second, he reveals the destructive attitude toward such a couple and its disastrous consequences. While the object relationship expressed in these first two thoughts, leading to the destruction of the couple, is something that must not materialize, he does allow the second object relationship, the wish to split the couple, to express itself in action. Linking these two object relationships dynamically, we may say that he feels a need to split a loving couple because seeing them united sets up feelings of jealousy in him and impulses to destructive actions with disastrous consequences.

We can thus explain this patient's need to separate two objects, a need for which he cannot give any rational reason, by assuming the existence in his mind of an unconscious fantasy about being confronted by a loving couple of whom he is jealous and who he wishes to destroy.

Common Group Tension and Individual Group Role

The previous incidents from an individual session are presented to illustrate the application of a technique based on rigorous transference interpretations, and the assumption that one individual meeting another will try to establish the kind of relationship between them that will *ultimately* diminish the tension arising out of object relations he entertains with unconscious fantasy objects.

What happens when several people meet, as when we put several patients together into a group? Each of them brings to the group meeting some unconscious relationship with "fantasy objects," which may be dominant in his mind at that moment and which unconsciously he wishes to act out by manipulating the other members of the group into certain positions, like pawns in a private game of chess. It has already been stated that in individual treatment, where the analyst (except when he interprets) takes up a passive, nondirective role, the patient will try to push him into roles that aim at relieving unconscious tensions. The situation in groups is in one sense different, for though the analyst assumes his passive role, the members of the group in relation to one another are by no means passive. What then does the behavior of a fellow patient mean to another group member?

Even in individual practice there are sometimes incidents that allow us to see how an occasional noninterpretative action on the part of the analyst becomes included in the patient's unconscious fantasies. An individual patient, when I once kept him waiting for several minutes, started the session by telling me that a relative of his had been kept on the waiting list of a hospital for rather a long time, and then embarked on a tirade against the administration of hospitals. Then he complained about having to wait for buses and how he was prevented by the conductor from getting on the bus when it arrived at last. He next told me that the night before he had had an anxiety dream in which he went out with a male friend of his and a young woman of their acquaintance who both of them thought rather attractive. Suddenly the two left him, saying they would be back soon; but he was kept waiting until he grew impatient and went out into the hall to look for them. He came to a door which was locked, and he heard the two giggling behind it. He got annoyed and shook the door handle, but suddenly he saw his friend behind him threatening him with a big pole. (I have left out of my account of this session various details which I think are not relevant to the illustration.) I pointed out that his desire to interfere with the sexual relations of another man and woman and his fear of doing so because the man might attack him seemed to have some bearing upon *our* relationship, since he had so strongly emphasized the jealousy-arousing waiting. Waiting played a part in his thought about hospitals into which one could not get, in his remarks about the bus one could not board because of the conductor's objections, in his dream, and, finally, in the fact that I had kept him waiting that day. Perhaps he was jealous of me but was afraid to give vent to his feelings for fear of what I might do to him. His reply was "I did think, when you came out with your female patient, what a good-looking girl she was. How nice it must be to be a doctor and have intimate discussions with such women." After a short silence, he said: "When I came in I hoped I would forget this thought, but I really wasn't annoyed with you today for keeping me waiting." After another short silence, he added: "Now when I think of it, I was annoyed with you when you kept me waiting last week, but I didn't tell you."

What I wish to emphasize here is that, although I had kept this patient waiting on several occasions, and although he had seen me come out with the same female patient many times before, these two actions on my part were taken up by him this time and given special meaning because of an unconscious fantasy which was now dominant in his mind and had found expression in his dream the night before.

The behavior of fellow patients in a group seems to

have effects similar to such noninterpretative actions on the part of the analyst. They act like the stimulus of a projective test, e.g., a Rorschach picture or a TAT, which elicits in the onlooker reactions born out of unconscious fantasies dominant in his mind at that moment.

The manifest content of discussions in groups may embrace practically any topic. They might talk about astronomy, philosophy, politics, or even psychology; but it is one of the essential assumptions for psychoanalytic work with groups that, whatever the manifest content may be, there always develops rapidly an underlying common group problem, a *common* group tension of which the group is not aware, but which determines its behavior. This common group tension seems to represent what I should like to call the *common denominator* of the dominant unconscious fantasies of all members. In the beginning of each session there is always some probing when a member of the group who seems to feel a particular urge to speak broaches one subject or another. Often a remark made by one member is not taken up by anybody, apparently because nobody can fit it into what is unconsciously at the back of his or her mind. If, on the other hand, it can be fitted in (as the incident of being kept waiting and seeing my female patient going out of my room was taken up by the patient just cited), and if it "clicks" with the unconscious fantasy of another member and then perhaps with that of a third, then gradually the subject catches on and becomes *the* unconsciously determined topic of the group until the next interpretation produces closure of this particular phase of the session. Apparently this is so because some aspect of the subject under discussion represents something relevant to the dominant unconscious fantasy in each member's mind. It is my view that in dealing with this common group tension (of a particular session or part of it) every group member takes up a particular role characteristic for his personality structure because of the particular unconscious fantasy of group-relations he entertains in his mind, and which he tries to solve through appropriate behavior in the group. It is by analyzing the role each group member takes up in dealing with the *common* group tension in the "drama" performed in that session by the group as a whole that we can demonstrate to each group member his particular defense mechanism in dealing with *his own* dominant unconscious tension, and we do this in the same manner as in individual psychoanalytic sessions.

To give an example: In the first part of a session, a female patient had made a remark about the group's behavior with which I agreed when I made an interpretation to the whole group later on. As soon as I finished speaking, a male patient immediately remarked upon my agreeing with that female patient and said that I was favoring her. Then there was a silence of several minutes, and one male patient suddenly suggested that they should discuss politics. Another man picked up the suggestion and started a discussion on the respective merits of socialism and communism, and, although such ideas were quite out of keeping with the usual view of the group members, in that particular session all the men and one woman seemed to turn communist. The main issue was that "political" democracy without "economic" democracy was really a disguised form of dictatorship. They pointed out especially that the owner of a factory could always sack people as he liked and even seduce his typist. The female patient I had agreed with remained silent, but looked worried and embarrassed. Another female patient agreed with the men. The third female patient, however, disagreed and thought that these communist views were only a disguised form of greed which one ought not to have, that all the misery in the world and all the quarrels and wars were only due to greed because people could not tolerate anyone else having something they did not have themselves. The discussion became more and more heated and suddenly broke off. After a short silence, somebody started to tease the weakest male member of the group, and this teasing very soon turned into a rather unpleasant attack on him.

What was the unconscious problem the group was dealing with in that session? When I asked myself my usual psychoanalytic question–What makes these people say these things at this moment?–the answer became obvious. The common group problem was what they felt to be my flirting with the "favored" female patient. The factory owner who could sack people and who could even seduce his typist was obviously myself "favouring," the female patient with whose remark I had agreed. This, by the way, was the same male patient who on many previous occasions had pointed out that one could not criticize me because I might refuse to treat whoever criticized me and even turn that particular person out of the group, and stop him from attending any further groups–in other words, sack him. The men obviously resented that I could, so they imagined, use my position as a doctor–as the "owner of the means of production," the man who could give or deny treatment–in order to make love to a female patient while they were apparently barred from doing the same. Moreover, the female patient seemed to prefer me as the "owner of the treatment factory" who had something to offer which they badly required. The female patient who had agreed with them had on many previous occasions openly expressed affection for me and was apparently very annoyed and jealous that I seemed to favor another woman in preference to herself. The so-called favored patient unconsciously seemed to have felt that the attack was directed not only against me but also against her and therefore remained in embarrassed silence. And finally, the female patient who accused the others of greed herself had considerable problems with regard to her own unconscious greed, which found expression in a symptom, an inhibition about eating in front of certain people. Her behavior was obviously a reaction formation, an attempt to deny her greed and to fight against that part of herself which she felt was so greedy and might get her into trouble. Finally, the attack against the weakest member of the group, after the political discussion, was obviously a displacement of hostility from me to the male patient they were less afraid to attack. When I made these remarks to the group, the woman who had agreed with the communist beliefs openly admitted her jealousy; the men, on the other hand, all turned against me and started to criticize my treatment, its "uselessness," my having been late at a particular session, and so on.

Before going further into theoretical and technical issues I am going to add another clinical example which will at the same time show the handling of a group at the beginning of treatment. The following report of a first session of a group[1] is based on fairly accurate shorthand notes taken by a secretary. It is abridged, but the content of the thoughts expressed in that session has not been altered in any way. This is the only group in which I started treatment by introducing the group members to one another and adding a few remarks in which I stated that our aim was to find out the causes of our difficulties and that no topic was barred from discussion.

My remarks were followed by a silence of three minutes.

(M1 *enters during this silence*)

F2. I suppose we are all waiting for somebody to say something.

---

[1] This group consisted of four men and five women. One man, M2, and two women, F2 and F5, were married, the others single.

M4. What do you want us to do? Do you want us to get everything off our chest, explain our own problems, our own difficulties, or should we not do that? If so, as a first thing, one of my problems is to be able to speak to a lot of people, to lecture. Do you want us to explain our difficulties, or are you already familiar with them? Does anybody else experience difficulty in speaking in front of a number of people?

M2. I think it is fairly common in most people—you don't like to push yourself forward.

M4. But you must admit it is a very bad thing. For certain jobs you have to master it somehow or else you don't get very far.

M2. Is there not a difference between talking about a technical subject and talking to people personally?

M4. I don't think the subject matters, as long as you know what you are talking about. If you don't know what you are talking about, it is more difficult. A person who is inclined to be a bit nervous in front of people does not really think of what he is saying. He is inclined to get a little bit confused—as I am doing now.

M2. Is your part, Dr. Ezriel, passive, or are we allowed to draw you in?

Dr. E. What do you think?

M2. I think it would be a good idea if you acted as a reference point. Then if we come to blows we can get you to arbitrate.

M4. It might ease the situation.

F2. I don't think he wants to. I think that if there are going to be any blows, he wants us to fight it out among ourselves.

(Somebody). Why should there be blows? This isn't the Peace Conference.

M2. I take it that in this group no subject is barred. Therefore we are likely to talk on subjects people don't normally discuss–subjects in which you are likely to get more disagreement.

(Short silence)

M2. I'm sorry. I have turned the discussion off.

M4. No, it all leads on, I presume.

M2. I don't want to alter it from the point of the difficulty of talking. I still think it makes a difference what one is talking about.

F5. No. Because you don't really think what you are talking about. You are thinking about yourself all the time, then you come home and think of all the things you should have said.

(Somebody). A sort of inferiority complex.

M2. Can we ask Dr. Ezriel what an inferiority complex is?

Dr. E. What do you think?

M2. When you say someone has an inferiority complex, you say it in the sense that they have a feeling of inferiority. But in what sense is one inferior? (To Dr. E.) Are we to regard it as a complex about associations with one particular thing, or not?

F4. The group don't know whether we are going to get guidance in the first part of the period. I feel as if I want to be dragged along the first few steps. [*Seems a little resentful.*]

[By refusing to answer the questions put to me and referring them back to the questioner, I had prevented the group from pushing me into a role they wanted me to play, i.e., that of a person in authority.]

I pointed out to the group that they apparently wanted the presence of such a person who would take responsibility for what happened, since they feared that without such a safeguard the free expression of their problems might lead to dangerous quarrels in the group. I added that they resented my not playing the part of this controlling figure. I then pinpointed M2, who seemed to fear the consequences of his hostile impulses even more than the rest of the group.

F2. We can't be expected to act spontaneously. From your earliest childhood on you are told that you must control yourself; that you must not speak before you are spoken to, and so on. Therefore when you grow up nothing you do is a spontaneous action, and it is much more unnatural in our civilization to say something just out of the blue. I am inclined to agree with Dr. Ezriel. There is a slight resentment against him. I feel you should have been talking to us for a little longer.

F4. I think we all agree that we have been rather left in the lurch, in the open.

M2. It may arise from the fact that Dr. Ezriel sits there and says nothing. As if we were all gathered in front of an altar.

[Other similar slightly anxious and teasing remarks about Dr. E.'s position, and laughter.]

M2 or *M3.* After all, I know that Dr. Ezriel knows a great deal more about these particular things than we do, and as a consequence we may resent his saying nothing, on the grounds that he is perhaps turning over in his mind what we are saying.

(*Short silence*)

F2. Should we find a subject to talk about, to give us a path to go along?

M2. I think that is quite a good idea. But I don't see how we are going to choose a subject.

(*Quite a long silence*)

F2. This is becoming an endurance test.

M1. Can anyone say what they are interested in? I came late and so don't really know what is supposed to be happening.

F2. We don't know any more than you do.

M1. I suppose we mustn't talk about politics.

F2. Nothing is barred . . . (to M1) Well, what are you interested in?

M1. Classical music.

These remarks were followed by about twenty minutes of discussion on music, how to classify it, whether or not jazz ought to be put on an equal level with classical music, etc. Three patients, F1, F3, and F4 remained silent throughout this discussion. Remarks which seemed to me particularly illuminating with regard to the personalities of those who made them came especially from M1 and M3.

M1 bowed to any man who cared to challenge him and tried to hide himself behind some powerful protector who was supposed to be responsible for M1's present attitudes; when, for example, challenged by M3 that his definition of classical music was equally applicable to dance music, M1 replied apologetically:

"I got it from my music master at school. You think this is the same? I have never really studied it sufficiently to be able to apply that definition to dance music."

Or, when asked in a provocative manner by M3, who stood up for jazz, why M1 preferred classical music, M1 said:

"My teacher put on a record of classical music before me at school when I was nine years old, a piece by Mozart which I enjoyed very much. That germ I got when I was nine stayed, and I gradually got to the other composers."

M3, on the one hand, kept on revolting against some "rulers" who were supposed to deprive the 'common people' of something good which they reserved for themselves as their privilege (he made, for example, several remarks about the restricted availability especially of classical music to the so called lower classes), and, on the other hand, he held up jazz against classical music as a means of expressing unrestrained emotion, especially by the "oppressed" with whom he identified himself: "The basis of jazz is that there is an orchestra and each member of the orchestra expresses his own feelings on his instrument. There is no special theme." And "You can look at music politically–jazz is the means of expression of the oppressed and proletariat, but in the average household they do try and develop the classical side."

Referring to remarks made by several people and in a particularly clear form by M1 and M3, I pointed out to the group that they had chosen to talk about music because they wanted to avoid any subject which might lead to hostility in the group; M1, for example, had said "We mustn't talk about politics." My drawing attention to this fear enabled M1 to express his feelings more clearly, and he interrupted me to say: "When I thought of politics, I thought we could go on for three-quarters of an hour or so and get nowhere, whereas music is not quite so controversial, we shall talk less loudly and keep our voices low and probably get somewhere."

I went on to say that perhaps music stood for something they wished to obtain for themselves, but which they thought they were prevented from getting by some authority (see, for example, M3's remarks about the "restricted availability of music to the lower classes"). They must feel that such a wish would arouse hostility among them and especially also toward me, the person in authority in the group. For these reasons they felt it easier to disguise their wishes as music, a socially acceptable pleasure, and perhaps their real wish was for something not so acceptable socially.

Finally I pointed out the particular attitudes various members took up in dealing with this problem, M3 and M1 as representing the two extreme poles, while others stood at various points between these two.

After M3 remarked that "A lot of that is very true," the discussion went on:

M1. In our music club we have a fellow who raves about Sibelius, and if anybody says he likes Tchaikowsky he immediately goes against them and says, "Oh, do you listen to that–do you call that music?" I can't talk as well as he can because I don't know anything about the technical side. That was the first point. The second point is, was it just that he had the "gift of the gab"?

M4. That is more important than knowing anything about your subject.

M2. We pay many people £5000 a year for talking a lot about things they don't understand.

M1. Are you thinking of the Socialist Government?

M2. No. They do sometimes know what they are talking about.

M1. I think a lot of people know a lot of different subjects and cannot say anything about them, and vice versa. In our office we have a man with an Oxford accent, and he can get away with it. A lot of people know as much as he does and can do as much as he does, but he just has that manner and it works with a lot of people. I have often found that if in a job you say "I don't know about this," people don't take any notice of you; but if you give an opinion as if you knew how, they let you do it. Not that I have been able to put that into practice myself. You may think I am just like that tonight; I talk too quickly. But we are here to say what we think, and Dr. Ezriel will let me, so there you are!

(Laughter)

M2. Are we free to continue our discussion from where we left off?

F2. We are free to do what we like.

M1. What are we here for? Are we here to talk about what we like?

M2. I feel Dr. Ezriel is an encumbrance on the group. He should be hidden behind the wall and watch us through a chink or something.

F5. We would still know he was here and listening.

F2. We would not have anyone to sum up for us then.

M2. That is what is so unfortunate, that he does do that.

M1. He had to. Otherwise he wouldn't be here.

M2. Well, we don't know that he really is here for that.

M1. He must be; otherwise he would be a member of the group, and someone else would be taking it.

M3. If we had a post mortem from Dr. Ezriel after everything that was said, then the people who did not talk would still say nothing and the people who did talk would be so astounded that they would not say anything more!

M1. What are we trying to get at? I know we have all got something wrong with us.

F2. Dr. Ezriel told us before you came in. [She repeated a summary of Dr. E.'s introduction.]

M1. In other words, we have to apply this group to our daily lives.

(*Remark here from someone about being abnormal*)

F2. I don't like the word abnormal. The doctor who referred me here said that probably 99 percent of the people who come to him are maladjusted, and psychiatric help is what is really needed.

M1. Do you think that is so?

F2. Yes, I think so. There are a lot of people like me, and worse, but they won't do anything about it.

M3. (*rather angry*). You are just trying to make excuses for being neurotic, and I don't see why we should have to make excuses for it.

M1. If I thought there were more people in the world worse than myself, but who did nothing about it, it would do me a lot of good.

F2. I knew the number who ought to be psychiatric cases was high, but I didn't know it was as high as 99 percent.

M4. Isn't all illness mainly psychological?

F4. It is the same with people's eyesight. In about 10 percent of the people who think they have normal eyesight, it is not normal in so far as "normal" is not "average."

M1. Aren't we here because if we were not here one day we will do something about it and jump over the bridge?

F4. That is why I am here.

M4. I have no ideas about jumping over bridges, but I thought by coming here I might become more efficient. You feel you need a little adjustment and want help.

F5. Do you mean to say that it doesn't worry you?

M4. Yes it does. But not all the time. I don't think I would ever jump over a bridge, though. I would just go off to a foreign land and live a meaningless life. There is no point in attempting suicide.

F5. No point at all.

M4. Therefore I say get away from it if you are scared of it.

F2. Has anybody come here because of a physical complaint?

M1. I have a state of nervous tension that has psychological causes at times.

M4. Mine is partly psychological and partly physical. Change of temperature has an effect on me. If it is muggy I often come out in a sweat. After having been to India it is even worse.

F5. That worries me too.

M4. You like a cool day with a breeze?

F5. Yes, that's right.

M4. As soon as you get hot and flustered you lose the trend of thought and you are lost.

M1. I thought it would be a good idea if we told each other why we have come here. Then we could get down to business.

M4. Yes, it might help.

M1. Nine-tenths think we are potty. I know people often tell me I am. If we all know, why worry about it?

F5. You think yourself that it's silly, but you can't overcome it.

M1. I had a nervous breakdown about three years ago and have been trying hard the last three years.

F5. You realize you are fighting all the time. That is the problem. Trying to fight all the time. If you could take your mind off it, it would be better.

M1. It doesn't help. I was in another job and hated the place. That brought it on. I don't mind telling you all this. I have a good job now, and it has made all the difference. I just want a little bit done to get me back to normal.

At this point I drew the group's attention to the dilemma in which they found themselves in their relations with me and from which they tried to escape into their neuroses. On the one hand, they felt envy, jealousy, and hostility toward me for being in an exalted leader position in the group, in a privileged position of authority which, as had been said before, was supposed to allow me to obtain certain pleasures and to deny them to the "lower classes," the average group member ("the man with the gift of the gab who forces people to listen to his speeches, the man with the strange Oxford accent who bluffs people," etc.)

On the other hand, this hostility leading up to the wish to remove me frightened them (F2: "We would not have anyone to sum up for us") since they needed me badly as their "doctor," the man whom they themselves wanted to be in charge of the group in order to give them help, protection, health–i.e., happiness.

Out of this dilemma, they literally escaped into their

neuroses by speaking about their symptoms. The guilt feelings about their neuroses and the emphasis they laid in the preceding discussion on the struggle against their symptoms thus seemed to be due to the fact that neurosis appeared as the cover for their aggressive impulses toward me arising from their wish to find forbidden gratifications for their ostensibly "antisocial" need; "antisocial" and "forbidden" because I, the man in authority, seemed to object, and gratification therefore appeared possible only after a struggle with me.

When I finished my remarks, the session had nearly come to its end. After a short silence, F2 said:

It has been such a long time before this group was organized.

(Laughter)

M1. I put my name down for this group, and after six months (I am not being rude to the Tavistock) I thought, "By the time they have started I will have cured myself." I think I had got halfway there on my own, but just need to finish it off.

M3. I have been waiting for nine months.

M4. I have been down for eighteen months, and I think I have improved tremendously since then. I was right down in March, 1947.

I then concluded the session by pointing out that the group was trying to diminish their guilt feeling about their neuroses and the underlying hostility toward me (as the representative in the group of "people in charge") by blaming me for frustrating their needs ("keeping them waiting") and for thus causing their neurotic aggressive attitudes. They thus managed to feel less guilty by displacing blame from their desire to gratify "forbidden" needs for which *they* felt responsible, to a subject for which they felt I was responsible.

RESTATEMENT OF HYPOTHESES AND
SOME PROBLEMS OF TECHNIQUE

I shall now list the hypotheses upon which my approach to groups is based and then raise some technical problems that arise from them.

(1) The "transference situation" is not something peculiar to treatment, but occurs whenever one individual meets another. A person's manifest behavior contains (in addition to any consciously motivated pattern) features that represent an attempt to solve an unconscious tension arising from this person's relations with unconscious fantasy-objects, the residues of unresolved infantile conflicts.

(2) When several people meet in a group, each member projects his unconscious fantasy-objects upon various other group members and then tries to manipulate them accordingly. Each member will stay in a role assigned to him by another only if it happens to coincide with his own unconscious fantasy and if it allows him to manipulate others into appropriate roles. Otherwise he will try to twist the discussion *until the real group does correspond to his fantasy-group*. The result of each member's doing this is that there will soon be established a "common denominator," a common group tension, out of each member's individual dominant unconscious tension. This unconscious group tension will lead to manifest interactions between the various group members, actions that aim at resolving or at least diminishing that aspect of their individual unconscious tension which is contained in the common group tension. Each member of the group adopts a particular role within the group, which corresponds to his or her specific way of defending himself or herself against unconscious fears set up by this group problem.[2]

---

[2] In the two examples quoted before, I essentially made use of a group (a "multibody," to adopt a term used by Rickman) as a medium

(3) It seems more effective to adhere strictly to a technique that uses *only* transference interpretations, i.e., interpretations of what is going on in the group *here and now*. In using such a technique, it appears best to follow the practice instituted by many English[3] analysts in recent years of leaving the patient free from rules and regulations. Instead, the unconscious meaning of everything brought into the consulting room verbalized or expressed in action, both in the session and with regard to his plans for outside activities, is interpreted. Such injunctions as not to read books about psychoanalysis, or not marrying, or not making important decisions during treatment, are not laid down before treatment; but when these topics come up, their unconscious significance is interpreted. What usually happens then is that the patient loses the unconscious need that is being gratified by the particular behavior that, formerly, analysts would have tried to deal with by making rules. I think that such rules in fact lead to the evasion of the analysis of the unconscious determinants of the patient's intentions. By allowing him,

---

for the solution of unconscious three-body problems of individuals who came to us for treatment *as individuals*. Such individuals require help because in their adult lives they find themselves hampered by the intrusion from their unconscious of unresolved infantile *three-body* conflicts, i.e., the Oedipus situation. During the last twelve months I have paid a good deal of attention to multibody dynamics, and, though my observations and theoretical views on this subject are still too incomplete to be presented in this paper, I have recently tried to include in my interpretations *specific* multibody problems, i.e., problems that can only arise in groups. My impression is that this, on the one hand, does more justice to the complexity of the behavior observed in a group and therefore widens the scope of treatment to a considerable extent; and, on the other hand, that the discussion of multibody problems does not make redundant the working through of unconscious two- and three-body conflicts, especially when the group members have originally come to the Clinic not as a group but as individuals.

[3] I am using "English" here to denote the fact that this technique has been developed mainly by analysts in this country.

through a nondirective technique, to display these in the transference, we get into the position of freeing him from the unconscious fantasies that determine, or at least contribute to, his behavior in outside situations. We thus enable him to make a decision based on an assessment of the real situation, free from the influences of unconscious fears. For these reasons I do not give any advice, and, indeed, I consider that every instance of reassurance or active interference in his so-called "real," outside problems arises from faulty technique–the result of my inadequacy in giving transference interpretations as consistently and as well as I should like to do.

It is in keeping with such a technique that I no longer ask any patient to tell me what comes to his mind in connection with any particular item but, on the contrary, take it for granted that all he displays are his "free" associations. Whenever I think that he is holding back something, I try to free his associations by means of interpretations. With one exception, I therefore started all my groups without any explanation, even though I was seeing them for the first time at the first group session. (The patients had had the general purpose of group therapy mentioned at the time of their individual consultations with other colleagues at the Clinic.) The initial tensions felt in such a group, in which the individual members have not been introduced to one another, silences, embarrassments, and so on, are the first material to be interpreted, and these interpretations lead to the unfolding of the individual difficulties and differences in a group. In one of my groups, the first session of which has been reported above, I saw the majority of the patients for a short individual interview before the group met, introduced them to one another at the start, and made a few introductory remarks. I cannot say that this had any particularly beneficial effect, an experience shared by several colleagues at the Tavistock Clinic.

(4) In carrying out such a rigorous "here and now" technique, interpretations are directed primarily to the "common denominator," the common group tension, and any particular patient's reactions are referred to only insofar as two things can be shown to him: (a) that his behavior represents his specific way of coping with this common group tension; (b) *why* he acts in this way in preference to other ways of dealing with this group problem. A patient in a group may, for instance, often try to obtain a "private interview" within the group session by offering "tempting" material to the analyst. He may recount a dream or some outside experience or his symptoms in great detail. On such occasions I pick out of this material only what seems to me to be relevant to the common group tension. A female patient, for instance, once reported an anxiety dream in which a train going through a tunnel had an accident. She mentioned many more details of this dream. In my interpretation I referred to this accident only as representing in symbolic terms a wish to destroy a couple in intercourse, namely, myself and a female patient who she thought was flirting with me. All the other details of the dream, the particular content of which did not seem to have a direct bearing on the group situation, were remarked upon as an attempt to seduce me into a private relationship with her to the exclusion of the rest of the group and especially of the other female patient. The essence of her recounting the dream in all its details seemed to be part of her reaction to a jealousy-arousing situation in that particular session when she felt that another female patient got on too well with me. To give another example, a male patient who in preceding sessions felt rejected by the women of the group gave a long narrative of difficulties with his wife. He then asked me to do something about it outside the group, since this was a "real" problem. In interpreting this material, I pointed out to

him only those features that seemed to me relevant with regard to the interpersonal relations prevailing in the whole group at that moment, namely, that he was trying to secure my help against the supposedly overpowering female members of the group. I did not refer to various other things he had mentioned on this occasion. Several difficulties he had with his children, if reported in an individual session, would no doubt have had to be interpreted as signifying something quite different, since they would then represent material elicited in a "two-person transference" relationship. I only took them up in the group session as demonstrating his wife's "badness." I think that, in this respect, my technique differs from that of many other group workers and also from the technique followed by many analysts who, as far as one can gather from published accounts of their group work, tend to interpret a patient's remarks independently of the common group tension. I use material only insofar as it finds expression in the "here and now" relations of the group members toward one another, i.e., as it forms part of the general group tension; I do not go beyond that.

Analysts experienced in individual psychoanalysis sometimes raise the question of what happens to the "tension" which a patient is supposed to feel in a group when he expresses some problem of his in great detail without getting from the group therapist an interpretation referring to these details. I think that his question misses the meaning of transference in a group (and, for that matter, sometimes even in individual psychoanalysis). In my opinion it would be a misunderstanding of the transference situation if the analyst took the verbalized material at face value, i.e., as the essential indicator of the tension which the patient experiences in the "here and now." I have tried to explain before that, for instance, the verbalized *content* of various details of my patient's dream did *not* indicate her tension, but that by enumerating them she was trying to capture my attention in an attempt to cope with her jealousy.

(5) From my experience I believe that, as long as we strictly adhere to the rule to interpret only what becomes apparent in the interpersonal relations of group members in the "here and now" situation, it is not only safe but essential to make conscious the symbolic or otherwise veiled sexual meaning of the manifest material. Analysts without group experience often doubt whether patients could express intimate sexual problems or that the therapist could give "deep" interpretations in the presence of other patients. Such a statement is even made by group therapists who do not follow a rigorous transference technique. I have seen anxiety reactions on the part of patients (like leaving the room or staying away from one or more sessions, or staying away and writing to me for an individual interview, or prolonged silence in many subsequent sessions) in the early months of my group work when I hesitated to give such interpretations, and I have seen only beneficial results from doing the opposite.

(6) *Some difficulties in the present technique.*

(a) *Silent patients.* One of the most difficult technical problems to which I have so far not found an adequate answer is the silent patient. We know that the silent patient is also a problem in individual technique, but it is much more baffling in groups, where one often finds one or two patients who may not speak for many months. Guided by the structure of the group on a particular occasion (e.g., subgroup formation), by the expression on their faces, etc., I try to deal with such patients by interpreting their silence mostly as an identificatory participation with what is said by others. Sometimes after such interpretations, the silent patient may make a short remark, such as, "I do not feel that." This indicates that such interpretations must have an effect upon the patient, and I therefore feel justified, on these few occasions when the patient does speak, to follow the remarks with a more adequate explanation of their behavior in the "here and now" situation. When, for instance, on one occasion I interpreted the group's behavior after they had expressed considerable dissatisfaction with me and thus showed a remarkable readiness to give up their idealizing attitude toward me, a usually silent woman apparently felt compelled to say that she did not feel like the rest of the group. In the particular setting of that session, this remark was enough to enable me to give a much fuller interpretation to that patient, namely, not only that she was afraid to give up her idealizing attitude toward me because of the imaginary dangerous consequences of such behavior, but also that she tried to ingratiate herself with me to the exclusion of other, especially female, group members.

Looking back over long periods, I think that there is no doubt that such silent patients do change in their symptomatology and behavior outside, but I cannot help feeling that the interpretations given to them are liable to be more of the nature of guesses.

Similar problems arise with patients who do not contribute enough in a particular session to allow the therapist to form a more adequate picture of what sort of interpersonal relations they are trying to establish in that session. I try to deal with them on the lines explained above with regard to completely silent patients. I have, however, the impression that, after such necessarily inaccurate interpretations, patients may tend to stay away for a session or two.

(b) *Choice of patients.* At the Tavistock Clinic my colleagues and I have so far not been able to formulate any definite criteria for the choice of patients, but are still in a stage of trial and error. In the course of treating a group one often has sessions in which some patients are absent and in which the particular composition of the group on that day seems to influence the behavior of one or another patient who is present and to facilitate the emergence of one of his difficulties. This would suggest that there might be definite compositions of groups optimal to the expression of certain of the problems of some patients and this indeed might hold for a considerable period of their treatment. At present, however, I think it is premature to say more about this topic and until we have gained more experience we are trying to keep our groups as 'homogeneous' as possible so as to make them into a projection screen which will be as neutral as possible for each group member. By 'homogeneous' we mean similarity in educational background and intelligence, and with ages (at least for the younger age groups) which do not vary by more than five or six years. For the same reason our groups consist roughly of equal numbers of each sex,[4] the total number varying between six and ten. If the groups get larger there is a tendency for more and more patients to become silent or almost silent members.

With regard to symptomatology, I am guided by the same considerations as would apply to the choice of patients for individual psychoanalytic treatment. My impression is that the type of patient who does well in individual treatment benefits from analysis in groups. Often, groups appear to be a less good medium to cope with severely ill patients, but it seems as if it were not the inadequacy of groups that leads to difficulties in such cases, but the fact that, as opposed to individual psychoanalysis, these groups meet only once a week.

(c) *Frequency of sessions.* The whole question of how fre-

---

[4] Some of my colleagues have been treating groups of different composition, e.g., a purely male group, as an experiment.

quently groups should meet is at present being considered by my colleagues and myself. I have myself had experience with groups who met once and those who met twice a week, and I think the results were very much better with the latter. I would at present tend to advocate even more frequent sessions. The duration of a group session is between an hour and an hour and a quarter, sometimes a little longer.

RESULTS

Work with groups at the Tavistock Clinic so far has been too much in the nature of pilot runs in exploring the technique of group therapy to allow a full assessment of the results of treatment. We have only now reached the point where we can select some groups whose members could be followed up carefully, e.g., by reports from external observers as well as by projection tests "before and after."

As is well known, the usual claims of therapeutic results in psychological medicine can be subjected to the most severe criticism in view of the absence of exact criteria to define illness or improvement, on the one hand, or the absence of an attempt to show that whatever changes can be observed are really the result of the therapeutic endeavors. My colleagues and I hope to report in later papers some work in this direction which we have recently started. I am therefore only stating some subjective impressions based on four years' experience with this form of treatment.

In the early stages of treatment I lost a number of patients owing to inadequacies in my technique. If the ability to keep patients in analytic treatment is taken as one of the criteria of the adequacy of one's technique, I should say that my technique has definitely improved, though it is naturally far below what one would expect in individual analysis. In terms of evaluation of results such "lost" cases would have to be classed as failures.

At the other extreme, there are cases who have attended for a few years, and, though some changes can be observed, there is no material improvement that would justify the expense in time and energy invested in their treatment. They are usually very rigid personalities, and my feeling is that it is not group treatment as such which has failed in these cases but the lack of intensity of treatment (i.e., seeing them only once a week) which may account for the therapeutic failure to break through their defenses.

A number of patients were discharged at their request since they felt "cured." Though they were subjectively improved, I would consider them far from cured if analytic criteria were applied, i.e., whether or not a material change of personality structure had been achieved. I think that in these cases the resolution of one or another unconscious fantasy has enabled these patients to deal more effectively (i.e., more in keeping with the real situation) with some problem in their environment, and once this problem has been overcome they become capable of carrying on life without further treatment and with more or less the same neurotic adjustment to it as before. There are some patients who have been attending for a few years, and, though definite positive changes can be observed in their behavior both within and outside the group (e.g., in our patients' club or in reports they give about their work, their social or sexual life), I find it difficult to assess in these cases to what extent this is the result of treatment or of changes in environmental conditions which may provide neurotic gratifications for the patient concerned.

In some cases remarkable change with regard to certain symptoms can be observed after a comparatively short time. In view of the fact that there was a working through in the group sessions of the psychopathology behind these particular behavior difficulties or symptoms, it seems justified to assume that these changes are the result of treatment. A patient, for instance, who started treatment on the verge of a psychotic breakdown with religious delusions, tortured by irrational guilt feelings and fear of being condemned to hell, was freed from his complaint in the course of several months during which we analysed in the group setting his infantile destructive fantasies toward his father as they appeared in the transference in his relationship with me, fantasies which seemed to underlie his religious problems.

I have several such cases, where I doubt whether individual psychoanalysis would have achieved more in a similar space of time. In fact, I wonder whether the experience of the transference situation is not more powerful in a group than in the two-person setting of individual therapy and whether in this respect the group is not a more powerful medium of psychoanalytic therapy.

Another factor which may account for some rather quickly achieved successes may be due to the fact that in groups, apparently sooner than in individual treatment, the patient can appreciate the reality of his hostile feelings toward his analyst which, in his ambivalence, he tries to hide behind an idealizing attitude. We can often notice how a patient may divert aggressive feelings from the person of the analyst to some fellow patient in the group toward whom he can experience such feelings in their full emotional content. (See, for example, the first group example quoted earlier.) When we then point out to such patients the displacement contained in their behavior, the preceding experience seems to be too convincing to allow the adoption of certain defensive techniques (like laughing it off, splitting of the ego, and so on), which we would commonly expect to appear on such occasions in individual treatment.

CONCLUSION

I have tried to give a short account of a psychoanalytic approach to group treatment and have discussed a number of problems arising from such a technique. Group research, in which several workers at the Tavistock Clinic are involved at present, is trying to investigate various aspects of these problems more systematically.

An additional result of such investigations, even though they are primarily directed toward therapy, is an increased understanding of group dynamics. Just as individual psychoanalysis undertaken as a therapy yielded considerable insight into the dynamics of the abnormal as well as of the normal behavior of the individual, psychoanalysis of groups seems to throw up similar insight into the *dynamics of group behavior*. I hope to report some observations on this topic in a later paper, and only wish to indicate at this stage that such knowledge of group dynamics may open up possibilities for therapy and for preventive work on a much larger scale than psychoanalytic group therapy could ever attain.

ADDENDUM[5]

When trying to understand a patient's behavior, I always ask myself: "What makes this patient say and do these things in front of me at this moment?" I make my interpretative comments as soon as I think I can distinguish in the material *three kinds of object relations* which, though pre-

[5] Dr. Ezriel, drawing on a more recent work (1973), added this Addendum in order to show the development of his ideas regarding group tension subsequent to the writing of the article included here.

sented by the patient as apparently independent of one another, can be linked up into a rational pattern by means of a "because clause," as just described. The three kinds of object relations are: first, one which the patient, consciously or unconsciously, tries to establish with the analyst. I call it the *required* relationship because the patient requires it in order to prevent the emergence in material reality of another, which I accordingly call the *avoided* relationship; he unconsciously fears to admit to consciousness the avoided because his unconscious fantasies make him believe that if it were admitted, and thus allowed to emerge in external reality, it would inevitably be followed by a third relationship, a calamity. . . .

Every individual has at any given time a certain level of *tolerance* for the *degree of manifestation of an avoided relationship* in external reality, and he will therefore not participate in any example of it unless it has a corresponding amount of disguise, that is, a certain admixture of a required relationship.

We can see . . . three ways of reacting to an avoided relationship particularly clearly in situations which are of no immediate practical significance to the individual in external reality, so that his reaction to them depends essentially on their meaning to his *Un*conscious. Examples of this kind are provided by the manifest contents of discussions to which a patient listens in a group therapy session. If, in such a discussion, some avoided relationship of a particular patient appears in a *more* disguised form than is required by his Unconscious, he will feel it to be of no interest. If it is disguised *just to the extent* needed by him, he will perceive it with interest and take part in it freely. If, however, it is less disguised than required by his Unconscious, it will cause some form of discomfort—for example, disgust or anxiety, and an urge to turn away from this disturbing experience or disguise it further until it comes within his present level of tolerance. In an earlier paper (1960) I described such attempts in group sessions as *"compulsive-reactive communication."* I quoted there a session in which first a man criticized me, and then a woman suddenly reported that her son always liked to hear a certain story of a kind doctor saving a sick boy. She then wondered why she had made this "trivial" remark, obviously not realizing that this was her unconscious way of dissociating herself from any criticism of me, since such a degree of manifestation of her own avoided relationship–that is, her own hostile feelings toward me–was more than she could then tolerate. . . .

In order to understand how transference operates in group sessions we need another hypothesis, i.e., that of the unconscious *common group tension* which, leading to the development of a *group structure*, determines the group's behavior. When in an individual session the patient tries to give expression to the three above-described object relationships, the analyst's passivity and his attempt to be nothing but a projection screen will facilitate this.

In the group, each patient wants, consciously or unconsciously, to express the three relationships currently dominant in his mind and more or less different from those of the others; even if in a particular session two patients, X and Y, have a similar avoided relationship dominant in their minds, their respective levels of tolerance for the manifestation of this relationship may be very different, so that when X raises the point disguised according to his unconscious needs, Y may find this by no means appropriate to what he requires. Each patient, therefore, tries to express something different and to impose his own pattern on the group, and this sets up a tension between the members of the group. *This unconscious common group tension* makes the patients react to one another, makes them select, drop, support, reject, modify, distort, etc. one an-

other's remarks, makes them push one another into different roles, or let themselves be pushed into certain roles:
all this has the result that gradually a certain *group structure*
develops. The group structure (and thus the role taken up
by each patient in it) is, therefore, the result of the individual contributions of all group members working upon
one another. It contains the dynamically essential features
of the three object relationships of each patient, and so
might be described as the *"common denominator"* of the
forces operating in the group. . . .

I shall now . . . refer to the two most important mechanisms that operate in this process. One I described above
as *compulsive reactive communication*; the other is what I call
communication by proxy, i.e., a patient does not say things
himself, but silently or even unconsciously identifies himself with a statement made by another patient in the group
and then treats it as if he had really said it himself.

5

PSYCHODYNAMIC PROCESSES IN THE LIGHT OF PSYCHOANALYSIS AND GROUP ANALYSIS

S. H. FOULKES

Group analysis is concerned with the total field of mental dynamics, whether these be better studied in an individual or group situation. In this chapter a selection will be made and particular attention paid to psychoanalytic equivalents.

Freud's contribution to group psychology was based on the findings of individual psychology, although he occasionally showed surprising insight in favor of the reverse procedure. In his book on the subject, he studied groups of an entirely different nature from those investigated by the present writer. He used two large, highly organized groups–the army and the Catholic church–as models from which to illustrate such concepts as, for instance, the ego ideal and identification. He did not attempt to explain the dynamic processes taking place in these groups as germane to them, but rather to show how the internal forces char-

Reprinted from *Therapeutic Group Analysis*, International Universities Press, New York (1965), with the permission of the publisher and of the author.

acteristic of individual life sought their expression through the group medium.

Classical psychoanalytic concepts can be used with advantage in a group setting, but the operative processes are not identical with those observed in the individual psychoanalytic situation. The wholesale transfer of psychoanalytic concepts to a new field is particularly inadvisable when they have lost their original precision and are exciting controversy in their own field of origin. Even such concepts as transference and identification are in the process of revision, or tending to become confused.

Our psychotherapeutic groups are, in principle, transference groups in the sense that members can use each other and the therapist as transference figures, as occurs in psychoanalysis between patient and analyst. However, the pattern of relationships develops with much more complexity in the group situation and cannot be explained by applying to it the term transference. On the contrary, the observation of classical transference processes within the group setting throws new light upon them as seen in the individual setting. In psychoanalytic literature the term transference is increasingly used to cover all interactions between therapist and patient. This development applies equally well to the corresponding concept of countertransference. The group-analytic situation could of course be termed a transference situation in this wider sense, but it is better to speak of a therapeutic, or "t"-relationship, -situation, etc., and reserve the term transference situation for its more specific and legitimate application.

Similar considerations obtain in the case of other terms, such as identification. Here again the group reaction seen as a whole cannot be understood simply on the basis of the psychoanalytic concept, whereas the understanding of the dynamics of identifications in an interpersonal situation helps us to discern new aspects of the process which escape observation in the psychoanalytic situation.

Group analysis views man's social nature as basic to him, and individuals emerging as the result of developments in the community, just as, in psychoanalysis, individual personality is viewed as emerging from and formed by the family. Conceiving the social nature of man as basic does not deny or reduce the importance of the sexual instinct in the psychoanalytic sense, or of the aggressive instinct. The infant-mother relationship is the first social relationship in the same sense as it is the first sexual and love relationship. Man's social nature is an irreducible basic fact. The group is not the result of the interactions of individuals. We conceive all illness as occurring within a complex network of interpersonal relationships. Group psychotherapy is an attempt to treat the total network of disturbance either at the point of origin in the root—or primary—group, or through placing the disturbed individual, under conditions of transference, in a group of strangers or proxy group.

When people are brought together in a psychotherapeutic group, conflicting tendencies arise, but, in spite of impulses to withdraw, the need of the individual to be understood by and related to the group prevails. This fundamental need to *relate* is shown with particular clarity even in our groups. (I add "even" because our artificial groups are in fact conglomerations of isolated individuals.) The social basis at once asserts itself. The idea of the group as the mental matrix, the common ground of operational relationships comprising all the interactions of individual group members, is central for the theory and process of therapy. Within this frame of reference, all communications take place. A fund of unconscious understanding, wherein occur reactions and communications of great complexity, is always present.

A principle which can be illustrated and supported by observation in therapeutic groups is that every event, even though apparently confined to one or two participants, in fact involves the group as a whole. Such events are part of a *Gestalt* configuration, of which they constitute the "figures" (foreground), whereas the ground (background) is manifested in the rest of the group. We have described as *location* the process which brings to life this concealed configuration; it is, however, not always a simple matter to locate this pattern of the group's reactions. Other important concepts for understanding the group-analytic process are those termed *mirror reaction, occupation,* and *translation.*

Mirror reactions are characteristically brought out when a number of persons meet and interact. A person sees himself, or part of himself—often a repressed part of himself—reflected in the interactions of other group members. He sees them reacting in the way he does himself, or in contrast to his own behavior. He also gets to know himself—and this is a fundamental process in ego development—by the effect he has upon others and the picture they form of him.

Occupation refers to the group's reason for coming together. In everyday life this may be for the purpose of study or work, to play bridge or golf. Such a declared manifest occupation is deliberately absent from a group-analytic group. In this it differs from a "free discussion" group. Observations of the group-analytic group makes it clear that such an occupation acts as a defensive screen to keep at bay intimate interpersonal reactions, thoughts and fantasies. This defensive or screen function makes the concept of occupation important for the understanding of the dynamics both of the group-analytic group and, by implication, of any type of group. There is a tendency for analytic groups to behave as if they had an appointed *occupation* such as "discussing our problems." An occupation can also be latent, and the group may not be conscious of it. This might be called its *preoccupation.*

Translation is the equivalent of the making conscious of the repressed unconscious in psychoanalysis. Interpretation refers to a special contribution on the part of the psychoanalyst to this translation. The whole group participates in this process, which ranges from inarticulate symptom to verbal expression, understanding, and insight, from primary process to secondary process, from primitive to logical, rational expression.

Group-analytic theory recognizes this translation as part of the process of *communication*. In a group-analytic group, all observable data are held to be relevant communications, whether they take the form of conscious or unconscious, verbal or nonverbal communications.

Characteristic nonverbal communications are those made in the form of behavior, either on the part of individual members or by the group as a whole. Appearance and dress may be communications; an exuberant tie or conspicuous shoes, provocative disorder or meticulous neatness may excite comment and lead to insight in the same way as verbal exchange. One person will press for more light to be put on in the room where the group meets, while another will prefer to sit in near darkness, or mislay his spectacles in order not to see. The group as a whole may communicate tension in the shape of silences or fitful, disjointed conversation. It may express a cheerful mood or relief or group gloom in which everyone sits and glowers darkly, some on the point of tears.

At one end of the scale is the inarticulate symptom: it may be nail-biting, excessive blushing, palpitation of the heart, or migraine headache; at the other lies its representation in verbal imagery. Between these two must be cut an intricate sequence of steps leading to verbalization. Many complex processes have to play their part before the mute symptom of a fellow member can attain linguistic expression and its meaning be grasped by the others.

It is the *process of communication* rather than the information it conveys that is important to us. In a group-analytic group, communication moves from remote and primitive levels to articulate modes of conscious expression and is closely bound up with the therapeutic process. The therapeutic group establishes a common zone in which all members can participate and learn to understand one another. Within this process, members of the group begin to understand the language of the symptom, symbols, and dreams, as well as verbal communications. They have to learn this through experience in order for it to be meaningful and therefore therapeutically efficient. The conductor strives to broaden and deepen the expressive range of all members, while at the same time increasing their understanding of the deeper unconscious levels. The zone of communication must include the experience of every member in such a way that it can be shared and understood by the others, on whatever level it is first conveyed. This process of communication has much in common with making the unconscious conscious and altogether with the concepts of unconscious, preconscious, and conscious in their topographical and dynamic sense. We will discuss these later.

Ego, Id, and Superego in the Group Model

Here we may pause to glance for a moment at the group-analytic group as a model of the mental apparatus. In what way do the psychoanalytic concepts of ego, id, and superego reflect in the group? The group is like a model of the mental apparatus in which its dynamics are personified and dramatized. A process analogous to this may be seen in the theatre where the characters not only represent themselves but also stand proxy for the audience both in their individual and community reactions. A very good illustration of the way in which this happens can be found in Friedman and Gassel's (1950) study of the Sophoclean tragedy *Oedipus Tyrannus*. Their paper is of no less interest to us because it was not concerned with the dynamics of the group in relation to group psychotherapy.

Oedipus, having commited patricide and incest, had to be punished in order to assuage the guilt feelings aroused in the audience by the activating of their forbidden wishes. The tragedy is played out between Oedipus, representing one wish, and the Chorus, representing the other. The authors write: "By remaining detached, it [the Chorus] absolves itself from responsibility. . . Actually, the Chorus maintains a driving demand upon the hero to fulfill what the community expects. . . Oedipus accepts fully the responsibility which the community is so eager for him to assume. . . The Chorus is not unlike a helpless community which is in the habit of throwing responsibility to the leader (father)" (pp. 214-216). The hero, Oedipus, here represents the id in that he stands for wishes and impulses inherent in everybody. He also embodies a kind of collective ego for the community (see Rank's description [1909] of the heroes of mythology as embodying "collective egos" who reflect the forces at work within the society that creates and projects them). Furthermore, he has to be punished for the crime he has committed in the name of the community and is thus in some sense a scapegoat. The conflict within the audience, within any given human being, is given expression by the conflict between Oedipus and the Chorus. The Chorus, which in present terms could delineate our group, plays the part of the superego; it remains detached and objective, but exerts a driving pressure on the hero to fulfill his destiny.

In another paper by the same authors (1951), also of interest to us, on the Orestes drama, the Chorus incites and drives Orestes to murder his mother. Orestes is tried and acquitted by a jury which gives its verdict equally for and against him, thus expressing the ambivalence of the community toward its wish to be rid of the maternal tie through matricide.

We find similar configurations in our own groups, though more often the leader or conductor is felt to be in the role of the superego. Group members may also play the part of the superego, ego, and id in relation to each other. A good example of the latter role occurred in one of my groups, when an older married woman registered considerable apprehension of a younger single woman in the same group. It later transpired that this younger member symbolized the maturer woman's fears of loss of control and impulses of an erotic nature. In other words, here was an incarnation of her own id functioning independently of her control and hence provoking anxiety. The group also manifests something in the nature of a collective ego.

I have repeatedly observed members functioning as scapegoats in place of the conductor. The group, angry with him but not daring to attack him directly or to show open hostility, will relieve and displace its emotion and fury onto one of themselves, usually a weak or absent member. The scapegoat thus chosen bears the brunt of a vicarious attack on the conductor. It therefore very often proves correct for the conductor to look for latent and repressed hostility directed against his own person under the guise of the scapegoat. Here is an interesting example of one variation of this process. One of my groups at various times repeatedly accused me of bias against a certain member. In such a case, I assume in principle that the group must have its reasons, however dormant my own awareness. I did not succeed in this instance in finding evidence of any bias either in my behavior or attitude. At a later stage, I had to defend the same patient against strong hostility on the part of the group. This made what had happened clear to me. The group, unconsciously wanting to make a scapegoat of the member in question, defended themselves against this tendency by first projecting it onto me and then accusing me of bias. These brief illustrations of clinical observations show how personalization, displacement, and location take place in our groups.

Multiple Dimensions in the Group

The group operates in many dimensions. How can we orient ourselves, bring some semblance of order into this chaos? In this connection I would like to draw attention to some old and very interesting concepts of Wernicke (1906). He thought the most important spheres in which psychosis could be placed were: (1) The external world, or allopsyche; (2) the *Körperlichkeit*, corporality or somatopsyche; and (3) the *Persönlichkeit*, or autopsyche.

A recent classification on developmental grounds is that used by Erikson (1950). He envisages three stages of childhood development that persist in some degree in adult life. These can be looked upon as corresponding at least roughly to Wernicke's spheres as I have indicated (in Table 1) in brackets. The first he called the *autocosmos*, wherein the world is experienced and reacted to exclusively in terms of the child's own body (somatopsyche). This stage is replaced by the *microsphere*. Here, object relations are formed, but the child endows the object with his own feelings and wishes, as, for instance, when the sofa becomes a boat or the doll an angry mother (autopsyche). Eventually the stage of the *macrosphere* is arrived at, object relations being now experienced in a world genuinely shared with others (allopsyche).

Among levels leading from surface to deeper and hidden aspects, four can be discerned in the group:

1. *The Current Level.* This is analogous to Erikson's (1950) macrosphere, and Wernicke's (1906) allopsyche. Here the group is experienced as representing the community, public opinion, etc., and the conductor as a leader or authority.

2. *The Transference Level.* This second level corresponds to mature object relations experienced in the macrosphere. It is the level most often envisaged by group psychotherapists of analytic orientation, for whom the group represents the family, the conductor, father or mother, and the other members, siblings.

3. *The Level of Bodily and Mental Images (Projective Level).* This level corresponds to primitive, narcissistic "inner" object relations in psychoanalysis. Here other members reflect unconscious elements of the individual self. The group represents as outer what are in truth inner object relations. The closest analogy here is with the concept of play analysis and its resultant psychopathology much associated with the name Melanie Klein. This is the level of the microsphere and also corresponds to Wernicke's autopsyche. Not only may individuals embody a part of the self, but the group as a whole may do so. The group often represents the mother image. The body image is reflected and represented in the group and its members. This phenomenon would correspond with Wernicke's somatopsyche, although the concept of a body image, owed in the main to Schilder (1935), was in no way thought of or familiar to Wernicke's generation.

4. *The Primordial Level.* This fourth level is the one in which primordial images occur according to the concepts of Freud and those particularly formulated by Jung concerning the existence of a collective unconscious.

Further illustrations of the functioning of all these levels is provided in the following table:

TABLE 1. LEVELS AND SPHERES IN THE GROUP-ANALYTIC GROUP

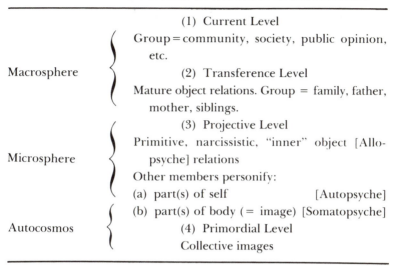

Macrosphere	(1) Current Level Group = community, society, public opinion, etc. (2) Transference Level Mature object relations. Group = family, father, mother, siblings.
Microsphere	(3) Projective Level Primitive, narcissistic, "inner" object [Allopsyche] relations Other members personify: (a) part(s) of self [Autopsyche]
Autocosmos	(b) part(s) of body (= image) [Somatopsyche] (4) Primordial Level Collective images

The conclusions arrived at by Schilder as to the close interrelationship between ego and outside world, the social nature of consciousness, and the relation between outer world and self as a fundamental human fact, come very close to our own. Schilder (1935) concluded that human existence consists of living simultaneously in what he called the three "spheres" of the body, the self, and the world, and that these spheres form an inseparable unit.

Arriving now at even closer equivalents of psychoanalytic concepts in the group than those already shown, we will first of all examine the unconscious, conscious, and preconscious in a group setting.

UNCONSCIOUS, PRECONSCIOUS, AND CONSCIOUS

We have already spoken of the systematic unconscious as used in psychoanalysis. This primary language in symbolic or symptomatic form, the language of the dream, operates in the group context. We do not merely see the distinction between primary and secondary processes as in psychoanalysis, but also many transition stages, and our process of communication and translation is closely linked with the construction of an ever widening zone of mutual understanding within the group. The concept of unconscious understanding, familiar in psychoanalysis, is one on which we build continuously. Every communication is understood unconsciously on some level and has to negotiate many levels before it can be grasped and shared in its full meaning.

Group Consciousness. Group equivalents of the topographical idea of conscious, unconscious, and preconscious, can also be clearly shown. To demonstrate this, we must recall Freud's metapsychological hypothesis (1915, pp. 201-202) that the process of becoming conscious is closely allied to or essentially characterized by the cathexis of word representation. This Freudian concept is of great importance for understanding the metapsychology of hysteria, schizophrenia, and various neuroses. The group equivalent of consciousness in terms of the group entity thus consists in any one member's *saying* something in so many words. If the group is ready and able to understand and assimilate what he says, the particular matter at issue can be said to be fully in its consciousness. The verbal cathexis assumed by Freud is here represented in the act of verbal expression on the part of any one individual.

The *preconscious* could be defined as something that remains unspoken, but potentially anyone could give utterance to this particular matter. The dynamic resistance between preconscious and conscious is perhaps well represented by the feeling that "certain thoughts are better not mentioned." Following these lines, it is easy to construe the group equivalent of the dynamic *unconscious* or *repressed*, but, for this to be of use, clinical illustrations would have to go into considerable detail.

Free Group Association

An equivalent of prime importance is that which corresponds to free association in individual psychoanalysis. "Free group association" evolved through my own approach and is significant for "group-analytic psychotherapy." An analytic approach to groups was made by Schilder (1936) and by Wender (1936), but my own differed from theirs in proceeding straight away to a spontaneous handling of the group situation. I instructed the patients who in the beginning had had previous psychoanalysis to "free associate" in the same way as in the individual situation. As expected, the associations that patients were able to produce were modified by the group situation. I then waited and observed developments over a number of years, eliciting the process to which I later gave the name of *free-floating discussion*. Then I became aware that it was possible to regard the group's productions as the equivalent of the individual's free association on the part of the group as a whole. Only at a much later date consequent on my studies in analytic groups did it become clear to me that the conversation of *any* group could be considered, in its unconscious aspects, the equivalent of free association.

Today I am beginning to fathom what elements in the situation of any given group of people approximate their conversation to free group association. Naturally the group-analytic situation itself is devised to encourage an optimum degree of freedom from censorship. The group association here is therefore the nearest equivalent to free association in psychoanalysis and plays a similar part. This can be expressed more concisely as follows. The more the occupation of the group comes to the fore, the less freely can group association emerge; if the occupation is a pretext, or can be completely scrapped as in our own technique, group association can emerge freely. Social groups can stand farther from or nearer to one or the other of these extremes. For example, in a casually thrown-together social group, such as is seen in a railway carriage, or on a conducted motor tour, though there is nobody to interpret, the ongoing conversation approximates to "free group association," the unconscious meaning readily shows itself to my own observation in such contexts.

In the group-analytic group, the manifest content of communication, broadly speaking, relates to the latent meaning of this communication in a similar way as the manifest dream relates to the latent dream thoughts. This matter is so important and so bound up with our concept of a *group matrix* that I shall once more take occasion to stress the group matrix as the operational basis of all relationships and communications. Inside this network, the individual is conceived as a nodal point. The individual, in other words, is not conceived as a closed but as an open system. An analogy can be made with the neuron in anatomy and physiology, the neuron being the nodal point in the total network of the nervous system which always reacts and responds as a whole (Goldstein, 1939). As in the case of the neuron in the nervous system, so is the individual suspended in the group matrix.

Looked at in this way, it becomes easier to understand our claim that the group associates, responds, and reacts as a whole. The group, as it were, avails itself now of one speaker, now of another, but it is always the transpersonal network that is sensitized and gives utterance, or responds. In this sense we can postulate the existence of a group "mind" in the same way as we can postulate the existence of an individual "mind." Whereas it is difficult for us to abstract from the concept of an individual in a physical, bodily way, it should not be so difficult to do so in the mental field, and to perceive that the matrix of response is indeed an interconnected whole. In the mental matrix, individuals also emerge, but the boundaries of these (perhaps they should be called by some other name such as *psyche-individuals*) do not run parallel with the boundaries of their physical persons.

EQUIVALENTS OF MENTAL MECHANISMS

We have already exemplified *displacement* in a group. Suffice it to add here that the group equivalent is seen when repressed tendencies in individuals emerge in the roles of others. The process of displacement should be strictly viewed in this context as occurring between individuals inside the group, not simply as a function of the individual mind.

Isolation occurs when an individual within the group is assigned tendencies, forces, or characteristics that are shunned in a phobic way by others. Isolation in the group is also manifest by punctuating silences, or by its abruptly turning from one theme to another at a certain point.

Splitting is another process clearly shown in the group. It takes the form in this context of subgroups, splitting into pairs, etc.

These few illustrations are given to underline the fact that even the processes akin to psychoanalytic ones should be seen as configurations in the group context. Clearly, the processes of *personification* or *impersonation* and *dramatization* are particularly stressed in the group and play a much bigger part than in individual psychoanalysis. All the models of processes described in this chapter incorporate this particular group feature, namely, dramatization and personification, in this as in other instances reminiscent of the dream process itself.

In conclusion, I would like to stress the difference in emphasis between psychoanalysis and group-analytic psychotherapy. Psychoanalysis, at any rate in its historical aspect, has laid great emphasis on the psychogenesis of illness. In group analysis we are more concerned with the outlook for change and the direction and means whereby to ensure it. We therefore work with operational concepts, formulated and applied in the therapeutic process itself and derived from immediate clinical observations. In our view, a dynamic science is needed which will incorporate and turn to good account the revolutionary idea that therapy is research and research in this field is therapy.

Group analysis as a method will then automatically fall into correct perspective as a powerful therapy, a stimulating theory, and a fertile source of information and discovery in the psychosocial field.

DISCUSSION

Bion's contribution as well as his other writings on groups (Bion, 1959) are difficult to understand without at least a minimal familiarity with Melanie Klein's theories regarding internal object relations with their inborn "psychotic" conflicts and anxieties, which, she believed, continue throughout life to exert profound influences on the personality. As Bion himself said in another version of this article (1955) " . . . in his contact with the complexities of life in a group the adult resorts, in what may be a massive regression, to mechanisms described by Melanie Klein as typical of the earliest phases of mental life. . . . Substance is given to the phantasy that the group exists by the fact that the regression involves the individual in a loss of his individual distinctiveness indistinguishable from depersonalization, and therefore obscures observation that the aggregation is of individuals" (p. 440).

In brief, according to Melanie Klein (1948), the infant is born with a rudimentary ego and with fantasies pertaining to the mother's breasts, which are perceived as both "bad" (attacking and attacked) and as "good" (gratifying and life-giving). There are also the defense mechanisms of introjection and projection which carry various unconscious fantasies and lead to fluctuating stages of perceiving "bad" objects as within or outside the self. Gratifying reality experiences contribute to a sense of security, while negative experiences add to the feelings of persecution. As noted by Yorke (1971) and by Greenson (1974), while in classical Freudian theory, psychic conflict is believed to occur between structures (i.e., id, ego, superego), the Kleinian conflict is essentially between the life and death instincts. Since the mental apparatus is indistinguishable from its contents and the ego is synonymous with the self, the Kleinians tend to depict objects and the self in concrete, almost literal, terms.

The *Basic Assumption* level of group process postulated by Bion, with its primitive "psychotic" fantasies appears to represent a reactivation of Kleinian psychic mechanisms in response to the stresses inherent in group involvement. Its search for a "pleasurable feeling of vitality," however, its opposition to notions of time, of rational thought, and of development, are reminiscent of Freudian portrayals of primary-process phenomena. Furthermore, Bion's concept of "valency," which he defined as " . . . a spontaneous, unconscious function of the gregarious quality in the personality of man," bears a resemblance to Freud's and Redl's concept of emotional "contagion" in groups. Bion's observation that the role of the Basic Assumption Leader is likely to be held by different people and only rarely corresponds to the more stable role of the manifest Work Group Leader, is also somewhat reminiscent of Redl's notion of the central person.

Bion's interchangeable use of the term group to connote a small therapy group, a large group (i.e., church or welfare state), or a level of group process (i.e., Basic Assumption Group) renders his material more obscure and more difficult to relate to the ideas of others. When he compared his group theories to those of Freud, he considered the latter incomplete, as well as anchored in "neurotic" rather than the "deeper" and more primitive Kleinian formulations. He thus criticizes Freud for failing to realize that his notions of libidinal group ties are appropriate for only the Pairing Basic Assumption kinds of groups, that an army and a church represent only "Specialized Work Groups" and that, above all, " . . . the individual is a group animal at war, both with the group and with those aspects of his personality that constitute his groupishness."

In the contribution included in this book, Bion makes only brief reference to some Kleinian mechanisms which he developed in much greater detail in his other writings on groups. These refer especially to "projective" and "introjective" identifications, which he believed are ever present in Basic Assumption processes. Not only are emotions such as aggression or fear readily projected onto the leader or onto the group-as-whole, but they can also just as readily be introjected by individuals. In this process, a group member or the leader can be easily swayed to actually behave in accordance with the projected emotions of others. As noted elsewhere (Scheidlinger, 1960), in this vein, Bion's following statements become understandable: "On this account, and because of the individual's feeling of guilt at being in possession of the group, which is equated with the breast, the leader thus formed arouses feelings of persecution, and steps have then to be taken to split off these feelings and to denude the leader of noxious persecutory qualities, (see p. 103, above). Or, " . . . the leader has no greater freedom to be a person than any other member of the group" (see p. 96, above).

Ezriel's contribution, being focused on the small group in the group therapy situation alone, is much less complex than Bion's. Much of his material deals with psychotherapeutic techniques, i.e., the rigorous "here and now" transference interpretations, which lies outside the scope of this book.

However, Ezriel's concept of the "common group tension" and of the way each group member's three kinds of object relations are reflected in it, are uniquely relevant to group psychology. Analogous to Bion's Basic Assumption level, Ezriel's Common Group Tension represents an unconscious group-level structure. Ezriel believes that this evolves through trial and error by accommodation and reflects each group member's unconscious conflicts via the "required relationship," which is a disguised rendition of a feared "avoided relationship" with its fantasied "calamity." In contrast to Bion's theory, which is in a sense wholly group-centered by virtue of his failure to deal with the issue of the individual group members' personalities, Ezriel's concept of the common group tension aims to account for both group-as-a-whole as well as individual-member considerations. While Ezriel refers implicitly to a conscious, reality-geared level of group activity wherein the group therapist's interpretations foster reality testing and development, he has no explicit concept analogous to Bion's Work-Group level. The closest he comes to it is when he juxtaposes the "real group" to the "fantasy group."

The clinical examples Ezriel cites suggest that in his adherence to British "object relations" theory he is closer to Fairbairn (1952) than to Melanie Klein. It is also noteworthy that, while Ezriel acknowledges having been a member of Bion's first group at the London Tavistock Clinic (where Ezriel also practiced), he makes no mention of Bion's group theories other than a citation in the references.

Foulkes' contribution, as is true also with his other writings, while primarily concerned with therapy groups, does at points transcend into the broader realm of group dynamics. When compared with the theoretical stances of Bion and Ezriel, Foulkes' model emerges as both infinitely more general as well as more eclectic. He employs many concepts drawn simultaneously from sociology, Freudian psychoanalysis (structural theory), and from Kleinian "object relations theory." He is quite close to Bion's ideas in his emphasis on the " . . . irreducible social nature of man" and in his conviction that with "the individual suspended in the group matrix," it is the group as-a-whole which " . . . associates, responds, and reacts . . . as a transpersonal network."

The eclectic character of Foulkes' theory is perhaps best reflected in his postulation of the four group-depth levels which incorporate concepts of Erikson, of Freud, and of Melanie Klein.

In comparing the three British theories from Section II with regard to their view of group formative processes, one is immediately impressed by their adherence to a group-centered position, wherein, from the very beginning, behavior within the group is believed to involve the group-as-a-whole. This is most evident in Bion's assertion that in the unconscious realm the group is *always* there, only waiting for its existence to be elucidated by the Work-Group Leader. Foulkes speaks of the individual's fundamental social need to relate to others, leading inevitably to the formation of the group as the mental matrix for interpersonal ties. In contrast to these two theoretical positions, which postulate an almost instantaneous group cohesion sparked by a common purpose, Ezriel's theory suggests a time lapse in group formation insofar as the *common group tension* is believed to evolve out of a trial and error accommodation of each individual's personal, internal tension states.

In Bion's and Ezriel's systems, the group members' conflict-laden relationships to the leader are considered basic to the group process and become the focus for therapeutic interventions via interpretations. Foulkes, in comparison, allows a more significant role to the other group members both as transference objects and as a source of support.

Some of these themes will be touched on further in the subsequent reprinted contributions and in the Discussion in Section III.

SECTION III

EGO PSYCHOLOGICAL GROUP THEORIES

INTRODUCTION

The term ego psychological in the heading for this last part of the book is employed in a broad sense. It is intended to help the reader to differentiate these papers from the contents of Section I on the one hand, and from Section II, on the other. As was already noted, the material in Section I is clearly anchored in the early Freudian topographical and "drive-discharge" conceptual model, while that in Section II is embedded in the context of the British "Object Relations" theories of Klein (1948), Fairbairn (1952), and Guntrip (1961).

The following five articles appeared during the period when ego psychology had emerged, in the United States at least, as a distinct subdiscipline of classical psychoanalysis. As might be expected, most of the articles relate to contemporary ego psychological notions in some fashion.

In brief, ego psychology views the ego as a conglomerate of functions relating to adaptation, in addition to defense, mediation, and synthesis. Hartmann's notion of a relative autonomy for some ego functions from instinctual drives and conflicts opened the way for a significant theoretical advance wherein these functions now comprised motivational elements on a par with those of the drives and of the outer social reality.

The concepts in the Whitman and Stock article (chap. 6) were subsequently further developed (Whitaker and Lieberman, 1964; Stock being Dorothy Stock Whitaker) toward an analysis of successive phases of interactions in therapy groups, with emphasis on the thematic expression of shared conflicts and of their resolutions.

As is well known, Erik Erikson (chap. 7) has made a number of seminal contributions to psychoanalytic theory in general and to ego psychology in particular. The relatively obscure piece selected for this volume is intended to highlight Erikson's dual concepts of *ego* and *group* identity, concepts which have smoothed the way for a meaningful linkage between individual and group psychological considerations.

My own contributions (chaps. 8 and 9) deal with the integration of the autonomous and affiliative aspects of a person's self in group belonging, with regression in small groups, as well as with the differentiation of conscious from unconscious levels of group interaction.

Saravay's paper (chap. 10) is aimed at updating Freud's model of group psychology within the framework of the Freudian structural theory, which encompasses the interaction between id, ego, and superego.

6

THE GROUP FOCAL CONFLICT

ROY M. WHITMAN AND DOROTHY STOCK

This paper presents an approach to the study of group interaction which is derived from both psychoanalysis and group dynamics. It is in part adapted from French's (1952) systematic interpretive method, which has proven so rich in clarifying individual psychoanalytic material and which is based on the assumption that behavior is problem-solving and that problems are dealt with one at a time. A primary concept is that of the *focal conflict* between a disturbing impulse and a reactive motive, which leads to varying solutions and attempts at solution. French defines the focal conflict as the most superficial conflict that can be constructed which explains *all* or *almost all* of the verbalizations, productions, and behavior of the patient in a given session. Thus, the idea of the focal conflict is similar to the idea of the focus of a lens. The impulses are condensed into a single conflict and then dispersed into the patient's verbalizations and productions. Topographically, the level of this conflict would be somewhere in the preconscious.

Examining group interaction in terms of the focal conflict has a number of advantages. One of these concerns

Reprinted from *Psychiatry*, 21:269-276 (1958), with the permission of the publisher and of the authors.

the codification of data, for progress in both individual and group psychology has been hampered by the lack of adequate methods of summarizing and abstracting the vast amount of data that accumulates in personal interaction. Condensation to quantifiable terms, such as counting interactions, fails to communicate the "feel" of the sessions. The approach outlined here offers a means of condensing the data generated in group therapy into smaller units which still retain the flavor of the original sessions. Another advantage is the hope which this approach offers for solution of the knotty problem of consensus in psychotherapeutic research. If only one problem is focal, the rationalization of various psychotherapeutic investigators–that, even though various formulations of data vary widely, "everyone is right" and consensus is therefore impossible–becomes invalid. This approach also, we believe, has advantages in the selection of patients for group therapy. If we agree with Harry Stack Sullivan that one task of the psychiatrist is to present alternative solutions to the patient, it might logically follow that a most fruitful group would be made up of persons with approximately the same focal conflicts, but with different sets of solutions. It should be added that, while the approach presented here was derived originally from a therapy group, it has implications for other groups as well, which we shall discuss later.

THE THERAPY GROUP

The group considered here comprised eight patients, six of whom were at the same time in individual therapy with other therapists than the group leader. They met with a therapist, R.M.W., and an observer, D.S., for fifteen sessions, each lasting one and a half hours. Participants included two patients suffering with ulcer, two from asthma, two from neurodermatitis, and two from headache. All were white adults with an age-group range of 20 to 40. All had above-average verbal ability and normal or above-normal intelligence. As a prerequisite, the patients had to be willing to consider the possibility that psychological factors could be contributing to their illnesses. Each of the sessions was recorded on tape.

All meetings were discussed by the therapist and the observer, and selected episodes which were considered to be crucial were typed up and examined intensively. These were episodes which seemed especially important in the historical evolution of the group and, on examination, were distinguished by a great amount of affective involvement and display. In addition, the group was manifestly different before and after these episodes, and group members frequently alluded to these occasions as being especially memorable for one reason or another.

What follows are data from three sessions of the group—the seventh, eighth, and ninth—in terms of the method of analysis we have used.

The Seventh Session

The seventh session constituted a crucial episode and illustrated the fact, observable also in other sessions, that during such an episode the members shared approximately the same *intra*personal problem but offered different and conflicting solutions. In this meeting, the members were dealing with the problem of whether the group could help them. Most of the members seemed ready to form a commitment to the group.

However, one member, Max, a particularly surly and bellicose peptic-ulcer patient, was very vociferous in his feelings that not only did he not need the group but that the whole thing was a "lot of crap." From his individual sessions and his behavior in the group, the following individual focal conflict was formulated as accounting for his behavior in this session.

Focal Conflict for Max

Disturbing Impulse		Reactive Motive
Need to be *dependent* on the group and be helped with his interpersonal difficulties	X[1]	Shame about his weakness and vulnerability, especially about having been psychotic

It is important to note that Max's dynamic conflict was not expressed in the very general terms of dependency-shame. Instead, the conflict was in terms of dependence *on* somebody—the group—for something—help with his problems–, and shame *about* something–inferiority and insanity–*in front of* somebody–group and leader. Here is an illustration of French's definition of the focal conflict as *the most superficial construct* which explains all or almost all of the behavior and productions of the patient in a given session. A formulation that is too deep loses its specific pertinence to the current situation and becomes too general while a formulation that is too superficial will account for only a part of the patient's behavior.

Thus, a focal conflict that is too deep for this patient might be: *Need to be dependent on his mother X shame about being a man.* Such a formulation is not necessarily incorrect, but it is too loosely stated to account for Max's *specific* behavior during the seventh meeting. Actually, this might be seen as the underlying *nuclear* conflict from which his current focal conflict and behavior were derived. Many other situations might be expected to call forth somewhat different focal conflicts derived from the same nuclear conflict.

Conversely, a conflict might be constructed that is too superficial. For example: *Need to be a group member X fear*

---

[1]The symbol X will be used to mean "in conflict with."

of having to talk about himself. Again, this conflict is not necessarily incorrect, but it does not account for *all* of Max's remarks. All of the data provided by the group and individual sessions must be consulted in order to construct a conflict at the right level—a tedious but nevertheless rewarding task.

Max's solution of his conflict was to engage in vigorous masculine protest—a not uncommon solution in ulcer patients—with loud protestations of his self-sufficiency, adequacy, and lack of need for the group. He therefore implicitly was against the continuation of the group.

Other members of the group had approximately the same conflict but with a different solution:

Group Focal Conflict

| Need to be dependent on the doctor and the group for help with their problems | X ↓ | Shame about needing to depend on others for help |

Solution: To accept dependency temporarily, as long as everybody is "in the same boat," and thus continue the group.

It is noteworthy that, while the general conflict of dependency X shame was elicited in most group members by the group situation, the focal conflict took a somewhat different form for each of the members. Max, on the one hand, and the rest of the group on the other, displayed different forms—both quantitatively and qualitatively—of this general conflict. Both the specific character of the focal conflict and the projected solution can be seen as products of, and consistent with, each unique life history. For example, Max had faced a somewhat similar conflict in many groups, and his persistent and excessive manifestations of masculine protest had led to his being frequently fired from jobs and had also led to several courts martial in the army.

It is clear that Max's solution and the solution acceptable to the rest of the group were in conflict. Max's solution, because of his inability to accept dependency, was to disband the group: "This group don't help nobody–you gotta talk to your own doctor." The group's solution was to accept the dependency, at least temporarily, and to continue meeting: "How do you know it won't help if you don't try it out?" At this point in the seventh meeting, the group as a whole was faced with the problem of resolving this secondary conflict. When one or two members are out of phase with the dominant solution of the group focal conflict, the secondary conflict between solutions may be referred to as a *group solutional conflict.*

Perhaps it would be useful to pause here to summarize the two kinds of group conflicts illustrated so far. The *group focal conflict* is that conflict which is closest to the surface and yet explains most of the material of the session. There is usually a fairly equal balance of forces between the disturbing impulse and the reactive motive, so that solutions vary between one side of the equilibrium and the other, and often end up including some of both. When a solution is reached which satisfies both sides of the conflict sufficiently for each member, it is accepted, and the group moves on either to personal material or to another group focal conflict.

Group solutional conflicts seem to be relatively infrequent because they require a strong and definite commitment to a unilateral solution of the group focal conflict. Most persons who wish to operate as "good" group members withhold commitment until the group has tried to work out a balanced solution of the conflict, which usually includes varying contributions from the members. However, when one or several persons commit themselves to a solution which the other members find unacceptable, a group solutional conflict is generated which requires that the deviant or deviants must be dealt with in order to preserve the group. It would seem that a person makes an unyielding commitment to a solution, generating such a conflict, when the solution of the group approaches his own nuclear conflict.[2]

The working through and integration of Max into the group was the sum and substance of the crucial episode of the seventh meeting. The group accomplished this by constructing an elaborate fantasy about Max's past life–for which some groundwork had been laid in previous sessions–which could account for his objectionable behavior and make it tolerable to them. This fantasy included seeing Max's "chip on the shoulder" as a response to a bad army experience, being neglected as a child, and so forth. While this was far from the reality of the situation, the positive affect of wishing to "include Max in" was nevertheless quite clear and was so interpreted by the therapist. In the face of the group's unequivocal expression of warmth and liking for him, Max's persistent perception of his interpersonal world as a hostile place momentarily yielded (Stock and Whitman, 1957). During the rest of this session, his behavior changed noticeably, and for the first time he participated in the group discussion without his habitual truculence and hostility.

Although this solution was different both from Max's personal solution and from that of the rest of the group, it in some sense incorporated and satisfied both. Max could still engage in some of his masculine protest behavior, which was afterward tolerated by the group. At the same time, the rest of the group could include Max as one of themselves by accepting him as something of an "exception" because of his difficult past experience. The fact that

---

[2] This type of conflict is seen most clearly in work groups and reaches its peak in the phenomenon of voting. Voting implies that the group has abandoned the hope of resolving the conflicting viewpoints into a compromise solution and wishes to decide numerically which solution will prevail.

this solution was generally acceptable was shown in Max's changed behavior and in the changed character of the group during the next session.

The Eighth Session

Following the integration of Max into the group, the members' trust of one another seemed generally to increase, and several were able to relate highly personal stories with much diminished shame. Jim told the group that he never allowed himself to be out in the open where anyone could slip up behind him, and recounted the incident that originally led to this phobia. He had been accused by an irate husband of seducing his wife and had always afterward had a constant fear that this man would spring at him, particularly from behind. He had not previously told this to anyone, even his wife, because of his expectation that he would be ridiculed, and had been carrying his fear all by himself for five years. Mike told the group about his first asthma attack, and for the first time really felt that emotional problems might be involved. Harry recovered an early memory and related it to some feelings about the therapist. This session seemed to be one without conflict; the group had worked through the focal conflict of the seventh session and could proceed with the task of individually-centered therapy.

It is important to emphasize the point illustrated by this session—that groups are not always in conflict. It seems that the working through of a group focal conflict or solutional conflict allows episodes to occur in which the members of the group are able to reveal and work through their personal problems on both a conscious and unconscious level. In the sense that psychoanalysis labels as resistance certain types of behavior which impede the flow of free associations and the production of unconscious material, the group focal conflict may be seen as a group resistance.

The Ninth Session

Another crucial episode, and a new focal conflict, appeared in the ninth session. Between the eighth and ninth sessions, Max had attacked Jim in the corridor by clapping him on the shoulder and saying, "Someone's following you," then laughing at Jim's panic and embarrassment. The incident was brought up in the ninth session.

Here another requirement that French laid down for the focal conflict was met—that is, there was a specific precipitating event. Generally, perhaps because of the number of participants, it appears more difficult to delineate the precipitating event in group therapy than in individual therapy.

The story of this attack was brought up in an extremely indirect and tentative way by the group. Finally, they asked for a general ruling by the leader without ever having mentioned the names of the two patients involved in the incident. They acted like a group of small boys, none of whom wanted to "tell on" the others. The following group focal conflict was formulated.

Group Focal Conflict

Wish for Max to be repri-manded	X	Guilt about tattling

Solution: Request for a general ruling without mentioning names.

The therapist blocked this solution by insisting that the incident be brought out into the open and examined fully and specifically.

Here is an example in which the group's solution was in equilibrium, but the therapist's intervention, stemming from his need to be therapeutic, did not coincide with their solution. This led to a group solutional conflict with the therapist as the deviant member.

Max's attack on Jim took the form of exposing his fear of being assaulted and then labeling this fear as ridiculous and "crazy." He attacked Jim in the same way that he himself feared attack in the seventh hour. It is interesting to speculate that Max's attack was an attempt to actively master his own anxiety by aggressive "kidding."[3] Probably the attack was also a way of retaliating for the needling that he had earlier taken from the group on the subject of his own "superiority and independence." This had been one of the group's unsuccessful efforts, prior to the seventh meeting, to get Max to admit to difficulty and become one of them.

Relation Between Focal and Nuclear Conflicts

Perhaps we have now, by our analysis of these three sessions, clarified our approach sufficiently to permit somewhat more general discussion. In describing the seventh session, we touched on the relation of focal and nuclear conflicts—a point that deserves fuller exploration. The type of conflict we have been describing is not an isolated problem which appears once, is dealt with, and is then never heard of again. Rather, successive and progressively modified focal conflicts relating to the same nuclear conflict are likely to appear. For the group, the specific character of succeeding focal conflicts is influenced by the particular solution the group achieves for each focal and solutional conflict, the kind of material the members have been able to bring up following the resolution of the conflict, external events between the members or in the gen-

---

[3] As Max's fear of his insanity's being revealed to the group became further elaborated in his individual sessions, he became progressively unable to tolerate further meetings of a therapeutic group he joined some time after this group was terminated.

eral hospital milieu, and other factors not yet understood. For each member, similar influences are operating. In addition, solutions proposed by one segment of the group often conflict with a single member's solution and may either force him to modify his solution or activate further related anxieties.

In the material presented here, such a series of related focal conflicts can be identified for Max. The pressure on him to reveal himself was one attempt on the part of the group to make him one of themselves by admitting that he had problems and needed help. This pressure, however, activated Max's anxiety that his having been "insane" would be discovered. As this anxiety came to the fore, it in turn came into conflict with his shame about such fears. This derived conflict led to his actively attacking Jim in order to master this fear. This can be diagramed as a series of related but changing patterns of conflict:

Nuclear Conflict

Need to be dependent on mother [1]	X ↓	Shame about not being a man

Derivative Focal Conflicts

Need to be dependent on the group and be helped with interpersonal difficulties	↓ X	Shame about his weakness and vulnerability
Requirement to reveal himself in order to become an equal and integral member of the group	↓ X	Fear of his insanity being discovered
Fear of his insanity discovered	X ↓	Shame about his fears

Solution: Actively attacks Jim and mocks his "insane" fear in order to master his own fear—a reversal of roles.

[1] An interesting speculation arose from this study and from an incident with a patient who was in simultaneous private and group therapy: the unconscious identification of the group with the mother. A female patient fled a therapy group which was daring her to defy them. She reported that she felt just as she did when she had to stand up to her powerful mother. If this speculation is valid, it provides a possible explanation of the strong need to be "at one" with a group.

The other possible solution, which the group accepted and which Max could not, was to trust the group and reveal his dread of being labeled insane. Max's shame about this was qualitatively and quantitatively so great that only compulsive mastery and masculine protest were available to him as solutions.

The group as a whole also had a series of focal conflicts which were the manifestations of a deeper nuclear conflict. Many data suggested that a number of the issues raised had to do with the conflict between the wish to depend on the group and leader for help, and the fear of self-revelation. The tremendous group affective response that occurred when Max, in his attack on Jim, carried material from the group out into the corridor is a good example of the preoccupation of all the members with the issues of trust, confidentiality, and shame. This and other material suggest a nuclear conflict fot the first ten sessions of the group:

Group Nuclear Conflict

Wish to trust the group and reveal oneself to the group	X	Fear of betrayal by other members

It is worth pointing out that this is a conflict which arises in all psychotherapy. The patient must rely on the professional ethics of the therapist to keep personal material confidential. However, it is an even more acute problem in group therapy where it is not so much the professional person who is doubted but the other members of the group. This might especially be so in psychosomatic patients, where the trauma is hypothesized as having occurred very early in the mother-child relationship and is related to basic feelings of trust and distrust or confidence.

The Timing of Focal Conflicts

The pacing or timing of a sequence of focal conflicts

is also an important issue. We have described crucial episodes occurring in the seventh and ninth meetings of this particular group. In the sixth, eighth, and tenth meetings, a great deal of personal material was revealed with increasing freedom. Thus the crucial episodes alternated with sessions in which there was no group conflict and which were given over to exploring personal problems. During meetings without conflict, the therapeutic benefits were analogous to those derived in individual sessions, with such added features as gaining the acceptance of peers and losing a sense of isolation and uniqueness. In the seventh and ninth sessions, therapeutic benefits involved learning about new ways of dealing with old conflicts and testing these out under the influence of pressures from other members. In the first crucial episode described here, for example, the group's acceptance of Max as one of themselves and his resulting more cooperative behavior was a new and useful experience for Max.

Thus sessions which involve the working through of focal conflicts can be seen as the working through of group resistances. Such sessions can then be followed by the deeper and freer exploration of personal problems, which in turn give rise to new resistances. As in individual analytic therapy, both kinds of sessions can be therapeutically useful to the patient. When the resistance is at the level of a group issue, it becomes important to focus on group dynamics rather than on individual dynamics only.

APPLICATION OF FOCAL CONFLICT THEORY
TO OTHER GROUPS

The focal conflict approach has been applied to other therapy groups and also to training groups such as those at the National Training Laboratories in Group Development at Bethel, Maine. For example, one such training group wished to examine the interpersonal reactions in the group as part of their training but were afraid of hurting someone's feelings, since discussion might involve criticism of certain members and their roles. Here, the group focal conflict was: *Wish to examine interpersonal relations of the group X fear of someone's getting hurt.* Most of the material in the session, according to the definition of focal conflict, could be seen as relating to this problem. Those members who wished to examine the interpersonal relations of the group suggested use of a sociogram, that is, specifying who each person liked most and least. The resulting diagram of acceptance and rejection within the group would then become a subject for group discussion. This was immediately countered by the members, who were most concerned about how those rejected would feel. The solution, after much discussion of the hurtfulness of hostility and people's vulnerability, was an anonymous sociogram, in which the leader collected the data and constructed the sociometric structure of the group by numbers rather than names. While there were many guesses as to the identity of the "stars" and "rejects" in the diagram, there was no way of breaking the code.

Thus the conflict was neatly solved; the wish to examine the interpersonal relations of the group was fulfilled, although on the superficial level of structure, and yet nobody was hurt. The universal acceptability of the solution, in contrast to many other suggestions blocked by the group, verified that it satisfied both sides of the focal conflict.

RELATION OF FOCAL CONFLICT THEORY TO FORCE FIELD ANALYSIS

Some of the parallels between focal conflict theory and Kurt Lewin's (1951) force field analysis are rather striking.

In both, a field of forces fairly equally opposed is hypothesized. Solutions usually represent a consolidation of the two conflicting points of view. Solutions may be derived, however, from either side of the conflict, depending on how the higher status members of the group behave, and, so far as therapy groups are concerned, most of all on which side the therapist chooses to favor.

Lewin examined attitudes, such as racial discrimination, which are often accepted as static. He suggested breaking down such attitudes into opposing forces. The interest of the white population in keeping certain jobs for themselves favors discrimination; the rebelliousness of the Negro population, if the discrimination is too great, opposes it. A level of discrimination is therefore established which Lewin called a "quasi-stationary equilibrium." This level may shift with the weakening or strengthening of certain forces; for example, if jobs become scarce, discrimination progressively increases.

Similar examples are "habits." Smoking is favored by such factors as relief of tension, social ease, and pleasantness of the taste of tobacco; it is opposed by fear of cancer, expense, and fear of being labeled a chain smoker. Thus the number of cigarettes smoked per day reaches a quasi–stationary equilibrium which may be disturbed in either direction; for instance, it may be increased by advertising or decreased by rising costs.

In group therapy, the opposing field forces are the two sides of the focal conflict. This is an emotional field of forces which may be changed in any direction. Max's attack on Jim increased the fears of the group that they could not trust the members with highly personal information. The therapist's intervention encouraging naming the people involved could be seen as a force acting toward openness, backed by all the prestige of the therapist.

INTERPRETATION

While the leader must aid the group to work through the group "resistance" generated by group focal or solutional conflicts, the most effective timing of his interpretations remains doubtful. If one again turns to Lewin's force field analysis, one gets the clue that most interpretations should be made of the reactive motive rather than the disturbing motive–that is, the fear rather than the wish–because it puts less tension on the system of forces. It might, for instance, be better to say, "It seems the group is afraid of hurting someone's feelings," rather than, "It seems the group should talk more about their feelings to each other." The therapist is then a freeing agent rather than a propelling agent. The whole question of the contribution these concepts can make to the therapist's interpretations is still, however, under study.

7

EGO DEVELOPMENT AND HISTORICAL CHANGE
CLINICAL NOTES

ERIK H. ERIKSON

Men who share an ethnic area, a historical era, or an economic pursuit are guided by common images of good and evil. Infinitely varied, these images reflect the elusive nature of historical change; yet, in the form of contemporary social models, of compelling prototypes of good and evil, they assume decisive concreteness in every individual's ego development. Psychoanalytic ego psychology has not matched this concreteness with sufficient theoretical specificity. On the other hand, students of history continue to ignore the simple fact that all individuals are born by others; that everybody was once a child; that people and peoples begin in their nurseries; and that society consists of individuals in the process of developing from children into parents.

Only psychoanalysis and social science together can eventually chart the life cycle interwoven throughout with the history of the community. To this end, the present

Reprinted in abridged form from *Identity and the Life Cycle* (1959), with the permission of the publisher.

189

collection of clinical notes offers questions, illustrations, and theoretical considerations concerning the relation of the child's ego to the historical prototypes of his day.

GROUP IDENTITY AND EGO IDENTITY

I

Freud's original formulations concerning the ego and its relation to society necessarily depended on the general trend of his analytic argument at the time and on the sociological formulations of his era. The fact that Freud, for his first group-psychological discussions, quoted the postrevolutionary French sociologist Le Bon has left its mark on consequent psychoanalytic discussions of "multitudes" of men. As Freud recognized, Le Bon's "masses" were society on the rebound, shiftless mobs enjoying the anarchy between two stages of society and, at their best and worst, leader-led mobs. Such mobs exist; their definition stands. However, there is a wide gap between these sociological observations and the material secured by the psychoanalytic method—namely, individual history reconstructed from the evidence of transferences and countertransferences, in a therapeutic situation *à deux*. The resulting methodological gap has perpetuated in psychoanalytic thought an artificial differentiation between the individual-within-his-family (or seemingly surrounded by projections of his family constellation on the "outer world") and the "individual-in-the-mass," submerged in an "indistinct aggregate" of men. The phenomenon and the concept of *social organization,* and its bearing on the individual ego was thus for the longest time shunted off by patronizing tributes to the existence of "social factors."

In general, the concept of the ego was first delineated by previous definitions of its better-known opposites, the biological id and the sociological "masses": the ego, the individual center of organized experience and reasonable planning, stood endangered by both the anarchy of the primeval instincts and the lawlessness of the group spirit. One might say that where Kant gave as the coordinates of the moral burgher, "the stars above him" and "the moral law within him," the early Freud placed his fearful ego between the id within him and the mob around him.

To take account of encircled man's precarious morality, Freud instituted within the ego the ego ideal or superego. The emphasis, at first, was again on the foreign burden which was thus imposed on the ego. The superego, so Freud pointed out, is the internalization of all the restrictions to which the ego must bow. It is forced upon the child (*"von aussen aufgenötigt"*) by the critical influence of the parents, and later, by that of professional educators, and of what to the early Freud was a vague multitude of fellow men (*"die unbestimmte Menge der Genossen"*) making up the "milieu" and "public opinion" (Freud, 1914).

Surrounded by such mighty disapproval, the child's original state of naïve self-love is said to be compromised. He looks for models by which to measure himself, and seeks happiness in trying to resemble them. Where he succeeds he achieves *self-esteem*, a not too convincing facsimile of his original narcissism and sense of omnipotence.

These early conceptual models have never ceased to determine the trend of discussions and the aims of practice in clinical psychoanalysis. The focus of psychoanalytic research, however, has shifted to a variety of genetic problems. From the study of the ego's dissipation in an amorphous multitude or in a leader-mob, we have turned to the problem of the infantile ego's origin in organized social life. Instead of emphasizing what social organization denies the child, we wish to clarify what it may first grant to the infant, as it keeps him alive and as, in administering to his needs in a specific way, it seduces him to its particular life style. Instead of accepting the Oedipus trinity as an irreducible schema for man's irrational conduct, we are striving for greater specificity by exploring the way in which social organization codetermines the structure of the family; for, as Freud said toward the end of his life, what is operating in the superego "is not only the personal qualities of these parents . . . but also everything that had a determining effect on them themselves, the tastes and standards of the social class in which they lived and the innate dispositions and traditions of the race from which they sprang" (1940, p. 206).

II

Freud showed that sexuality begins with birth; he has also given us the tools for the demonstration of the fact that social life begins with each individual's beginnings.

Some of us have applied these tools to the study of so-called primitive societies where child training is integrated with a well-defined economic system and a small and static inventory of social prototypes. Child training in such groups, so we concluded, is the method by which a group's basic ways of organizing experience (its group identity, as we called it) is transmitted to the infant's early bodily experiences and, through them, to the beginnings of his ego.

Let me first illustrate the concept of group identity by a brief reference to anthropological observations made by Mekeel and myself some years ago. We described how in one segment of the re-education of the American Indian, the Sioux Indians' historical identity of the–now defunct–buffalo hunter stands counterposed to the occupational and class identity of his re-educator, the American civil service employee. We pointed out that the identities of these groups rest on extreme differences in geographic and historical perspectives (collective ego-space-time) and on radical differences in economic goals and means (collective life plan).

In the remnants of the Sioux Indians' identity, the prehistoric past is a powerful psychological reality. The conquered tribe behaved as if guided by a life plan consisting of passive resistance to the present, which does fail to reintegrate the identity remnants of the economic past; and of dreams of restoration, in which the future would lead back into the past, time would again become ahistoric, space unlimited, activity boundlessly centrifugal, and the buffalo supply inexhaustible. Their federal educators, on the other hand, preached a life plan with centripetal and localized goals: homestead, fireplace, bank account—all of which receive their meaning from a life plan in which the past is overcome, and in which the full measure of fulfillment in the present is sacrificed to an ever higher standard of living in the (ever removed) future. The road to this future is not outer restoration but inner reform.

Obviously every item of human experience as lived by a member of one of these groups, and as shared or debated by members of both groups, must be defined according to its place on the coordinates of these interpenetrating plans.

Primitive tribes have a direct relation to the sources and means of production. Their tools are extensions of the human body. Children in these groups participate in technical and in magic pursuits; to them, body and environment, childhood and culture may be full of dangers, but they are all one world. The inventory of social prototypes is small and static. In our world, machines, far from remaining an extension of the body, destine whole human organizations to be extensions of machinery; magic serves intermediate links only, and childhood becomes a separate segment of life with its own folklore. The expansiveness of civilization, together with its stratification and specialization, force children to base their ego models on shifting, sectional, and contradictory prototypes.

III

The growing child must derive a vitalizing sense of reality from the awareness that his individual way of mastering experience (his ego synthesis) is a successful variant of a group identity and is in accord with its space-time and life plan.

A child who has just found himself able to walk seems not only driven to repeat and to perfect the act of walking by libidinal pleasure in the sense of Freud's locomotor erotism; or by the need for mastery in the sense of Ives Hendrick's work principle; he also becomes aware of the new status and stature of "he who can walk," with whatever connotation this happens to have in the coordinates or his culture's life plan—be it "he who will go far," or "he who will be upright," or "he who might go too far." To be "one who can walk" becomes one of the many steps in child development which, through the coincidence of physical mastery and cultural meaning, of functional pleasure and social recognition, contribute to a more realistic self-esteem. By no means only a narcissistic corroboration of infantile omnipotence (that can be had more cheaply), this self-esteem grows to be a conviction that the ego is learning effective steps toward a tangible collective future, that it is developing into a defined ego within a social reality. This sense I wish to call *ego identity*. I shall try to clarify it as a subjective experience and as a dynamic fact, as a group-psychological phenomenon and—in the bulk of this paper—as a subject for clinical investigation.

The conscious feeling of having a *personal identity* is based on two simultaneous observations: the immediate perception of one's selfsameness and continuity in time; and the simultaneous perception of the fact that others recognize one's sameness and continuity. What I propose to call ego identity concerns more than the mere fact of existence, as conveyed by personal identity; it is the ego quality of this existence.

Ego identity, then, in its subjective aspect, is the awareness of the fact that there is a selfsameness and continuity to the ego's synthesizing methods and that these methods are effective in safeguarding the sameness and continuity of one's meaning for others.

IV

While it was a step of inestimable import when Freud applied contemporaneous concepts of physical energy to psychology, the resultant theory that instinctual energy is transferred, displaced, transformed, in analogy to the preservation of energy in physics, no longer suffices to help us manage the data which we have learned to observe.

It is here that ego concepts must close a gap. We must find the nexus of social images and of organismic forces–and this not merely in the sense that here images and forces are, as the saying goes, "interrelated." More than this: the mutual complementation of ethos and ego, of group identity and ego identity, puts a greater common potential at the disposal of both ego synthesis and social organization.

When a Sioux Indian–at the height of his religious endeavors–drives little sticks through his breast, ties the sticks to a rope, the rope to a pole, and then (in a peculiar trance) dances backwards until the rope tightens and the sticks split his breast so that the gushing blood runs freely down his body, we find a meaning in his extreme behavior: he is turning against himself some first provoked, then energetically frustrated infantile impulses, a "fixation" on which we found to be of decisive relevance in the Sioux's group identity and in his individual development. This ritual puts "id" and "superego" in clear opposition, as do the abortive rituals of our neurotic patients. It makes similar sense when a Yurok man, having been with a woman, proceeds to heat himself by the fire of the sweathouse until he is supple enough to squeeze through an oval opening in the wall, only to jump into the cold river; whereupon he considers himself again pure and strong enough to net the sacred salmon. Here, obviously, self-esteem and inner security are restored by atonement. The same Indians, when indulging in promiscuous intercourse after having achieved the yearly communal engineering feat of bridging the river with a dam that yields a whole winter's supply of salmon, apparently experience the manic relief of orgiastic excess, which, once a year, throws atonement to the winds. But if we try to define the state of relative equilibrium between these better-known extremes, if we ask what characterizes an Indian when he does not do much more than just calmly be an Indian bent on the daily chores of the year's cycle, our description lacks a fitting frame of reference. We look for small signs of the fact that man, anywhere, anytime, betrays in minute emotional and ideational changes an ever present conflict manifested in a change of mood from a vague anxious depression through what Freud referred to as "a certain in-between stage" to heightened well-being—and back ("*von einer übermässigen Gedrücktheit durch einen gewissen Mittelzustand zu einem erhöhten Wohlbefinden*"). But is this in-between stage dynamically so unimportant that it can be defined by pointing out what it is not; by stating that neither a manic nor a depressive trend is, at the time, clearly noticeable; that a momentary lull exists on the battlefield of the ego; that the superego is temporarily nonbelligerent and that the id has agreed to an armistice?

The necessity for defining the relative equilibrium be-

tween various "states of mind" became acute in the need
to appraise morale in war. I had an opportunity to make
a few observations on one of the more extreme milieus of
human endeavor, namely, life on submarines. Here, emotional plasticity and social resourcefulness are put to a high
test. The heroic expectations and phallic-locomotor fantasies with which an adolescent volunteer approaches life
on a submarine are on the whole not verified in the small
chores and in the constricted space of his daily experience
on board and in the relatively blind, deaf, and dumb role
demanded of him in action. The extreme interdependence
with the crew and the mutual responsibility for comfort
and life under prolonged conditions of extreme hardship
soon supersede the original fantasies. Crew and captain
establish a symbiosis not governed by official regulations
alone. With astonishing tact and native wisdom, silent ar-
rangements are made by which the captain becomes sensory system, brains, and conscience for the whole submerged
organism of minutely tuned machinery and humanity; and
by which the crew members mobilize in themselves com-
pensatory mechanisms (for example, in the collective use
of the generously provided food) permitting the crew to
stand monotony and yet to be ready for instant action.
Such automatic mutual adaptations to extreme milieus
make "analytical sense" primarily where a seeming regression to a primal horde, and to a kind of oral lethargy, can
be traced. Yet, if we ask why men choose such a life, why
they stick to it in spite of incredible monotony and occasional nightmarish danger, and above all why they function
in good health and high spirits, we do not have a satisfactory dynamic answer. In psychiatric discussions it is not
infrequently suspected—on the evidence of mere analogies—that whole units, crews, and occupational groups are
regressive, or motivated by latent homosexual or psycho-
pathic tendencies.

Yet, what the submarine man on the job, the Indian

at work, and the growing child have in common with all men who feel at one with what they are doing when and where they are doing it is akin to that "in-between state" which we wish our children would preserve as they grow older; and which we want our patients to gain when the "synthetic function of the ego" (Nunberg, 1931) is restored. We know that when this is achieved, play becomes freer, health radiant, sex more adult, and work more meaningful. Having applied psychoanalytic concepts to group problems, we feel that a clearer understanding of the mutual complementation of ego synthesis and social organization may help us to appraise therapeutically a psychological middle range, the expansion and cultivation of which on ever higher levels of human organization is the aim of all therapeutic endeavor, social and individual.

EGO STRENGTH AND SOCIAL PATHOLOGY

I

Individual psychopathology contributes to the understanding of ego identity the study of its impairments by constitutional deficiency, early emotional impoverishment, neurotic conflict, and traumatic damage. Before we turn to examples of ego-damaging social pathology we may at least state a question, although its answer will have to wait for a more systematic presentation: What factors make for a strong normal ego identity? In a general way it is plain that everything that makes for a strong ego contributes to its identity.

Freud originally stated (1914) that the sources of human self-esteem (and thus an important infantile contribution to an individual's ego identity) are (1) the residue of childish narcissism, (2) such infantile omnipotence as experience corroborates (the fulfillment of the ego ideal), and (3) gratification of object libido.

Psychoanalysis came to emphasize the individual and regressive rather than the collective-supportive aspects of these statements. It was concerned with only half the story.

For if a residue of infantile narcisism is to survive, the maternal environment must create and sustain it with a love which assures the child that it is good to be alive in the particular social coordinates in which he happens to find himself. Infantile narcissism, which is said to fight so valiantly against the inroads of a frustrating environment, is in fact nourished by the sensual enrichment and the encouragement provided by this same environment. Widespread severe impoverishment of infantile narcissism (and thus of the basis of a strong ego) is lastly to be considered a breakdown of that collective synthesis which gives every newborn baby and his motherly surroundings a superindividual status as a trust of the community. In the later abandonment or transformation of this narcissism into more mature self-esteem, it is again of decisive importance whether or not the more realistic being can expect an opportunity to employ what he has learned and to acquire a feeling of increased communal meaning.

If experience is to corroborate part of the infantile sense of omnipotence, then child training must know not only how to teach sensual health and progressive mastery, but also how to offer tangible social recognition as the fruits of health and mastery. For, unlike the infantile sense of omnipotence which is fed by make-believe and adult deception, the self-esteem attached to the ego identity is based on the rudiments of skills and social techniques which assure a gradual coincidence of functional pleasure and actual performance, of ego ideal and social role. The self-esteem attached to the ego identity contains the recognition of a tangible future.

If "object libido" is to be satisfied, then genital love and orgastic potency must be assured of a cultural synthesis of economic safety and emotional security; for only such a synthesis gives unified meaning to the full functional cycle of genitality, which includes conception, childbearing, and child rearing. Infatuation may project all the incestuous childhood loves into a present "object"; genital activity may help two individuals to use one another as an anchor against regression; but mutual genital love faces toward the future. It works toward a division of labor in that life task which only two of the opposite sex can fulfill together: the synthesis of production, procreation, and recreation in the primary social unit of the family. In this sense, then, ego identity acquires its final strength in the meeting of mates whose ego identity is complementary in some essential point and can be fused in marriage without the creation either of a dangerous discontinuity of tradition or of an incestuous sameness—both of which are apt to prejudice the offspring's ego development.

The unconscious "incestuous" choice of a mate who resembles infantile love objects in some decisive feature is not to be considered necessarily pathogenic, as writers in psychopathology seem to infer. Such a choice follows an ethnic mechanism in that it creates a continuity between the family one grew up in and the family one establishes: it thus perpetuates tradition, i.e., the sum of all that had been learned by preceding generations, in analogy to the preservation of the gains of evolution in the mating within the species. Neurotic fixation (and rigid inner defense against it) signifies the failure, not the nature, of this mechanism.

However, many of the mechanisms of adjustment which once made for evolutionary adaptation, tribal integration, national or class coherence, are at loose ends in a world of universally expanding identities. Education for an ego identity which receives strength from changing historical conditions demands a conscious acceptance of historical heterogeneity on the part of adults, combined with an enlightened effort to provide human childhood anywhere with a new fund of meaningful continuity. For this task, the systematic investigation of the following strategic points seems indicated:

1. The coherence of the body image, and its possible basis in fetal experience, with special reference to the importance of the mother's emotional attitude toward pregnancy.
2. The synchronization of postnatal care with the newborn's temperament, based as it is on his prenatal and his birth experience.
3. The sameness and continuity of the early sensual experience of the mother's body and temperament, which nourishes and preserves a lasting fund of narcissism.
4. The synchronization of the pregenital stages and of the normative steps in child development with a group identity.
5. The immediate promise of tangible social recognition for the abandonment of infantile narcissism and autoerotism and for the acquisition of skills and knowledge during latency.
6. The adequacy of the solution of the Oedipus conflict, within the individual's sociohistorical setting.
7. The relation of the final adolescent version of the ego identity to economic opportunities, realizable ideals, and available techniques.
8. The relation of genitality to love objects with complementary ego identities, and to the communal meaning of procreation.

II

What has already been said concerning the collective space-time and the life plan of a society shows the necessity of studying the spontaneous ways in which segments of modern society strive to make a workable continuity out of child training and economic development. For whoever wants to guide must understand, conceptualize, and use spontaneous trends of identity formation. Our clinical histories help in such research, where they avoid being too episodic in type and where stereotypes such as "the patient had a domineering mother" (which are based on comparisons with a family image implied in classical European psychiatry) are further broken down into historically significant variations. During World War II, psychiatric and psychoanalytic attempts at explaining what childhood milieus cause or do not cause a man to break down under military stress, have, on the whole, failed for lack of historical perspective.

In our work with veterans discharged from the Armed Forces as psychoneurotics before the end of hostilities, we became familiar with the universal symptoms of partial loss of ego synthesis. Many of these men, indeed, regress to the "stage of unlearned function" (Freud, 1908). The boundaries of their egos have lost their shock-absorbing delineation: anxiety and anger are provoked by everything too sudden or too intense, whether it be a sensory impression or a self-reproach, an impulse or a memory. A ceaselessly "startled" sensory system is attacked by stimuli from outside as well as by somatic sensations: heat flashes, palpitation, cutting headaches. Insomnia hinders the nightly restoration of sensory screening by sleep, and that of emotional synthesis by dreaming. Amnesia, neurotic pseudologia, and confusion show the partial loss of time-binding and of spatial orientation. What definable symptoms and remnants of "peacetime neuroses" there are have a fragmentary and false quality, as if the ego could not even accomplish an organized neurosis.

In some cases this ego impairment seems to have its

origin in violent events, in others in the gradual grind of a million annoyances. Obviously the men are worn out by too many changes (gradual or sudden) in too many respects at once; somatic tension, social panic, and ego anxiety are always present. Above all, the men "do not know any more who they are": there is a distinct loss of ego identity. The sense of sameness and the continuity and the belief in one's social role are gone.

The American group identity supports an individual's ego identity as long as he can preserve a certain element of deliberate tentativeness; as long as he can convince himself that the next step is up to him and that, no matter where he is staying or going, he always has the choice of leaving or turning in the opposite direction if he chooses to do so. In this country the migrant does not want to be told to move on, nor the sedentary man to stay where he is; for the life style of each contains the opposite element as an alternative which he wishes to consider his most private and individual decision. For many men, then, the restraint and discipline of army life provides few ideal prototypes. To quite a few, it represents instead the intensely evil identity of the sucker; one who lets himself be sidetracked, cooped up, and stalled, while others are free to pursue his chance and his girl. But to be a sucker means to be a social and sexual castrate; if you are a sucker, not even a mother's pity will be with you.

In the (often profuse) utterances of psychoneurotic casualties, all those memories and anticipations appear associated that ever threatened or are expected to threaten the freedom of the next step. In their struggle to regain access to the nonreversible escalator of free enterprise, their traumatized ego fights and flees an evil identity which includes elements of the crying baby, the bleeding woman, the submissive nigger, the sexual sissy, the economic sucker, the mental moron—all prototypes, the mere allusion to which can bring these men close to homicidal or suicidal rage, ending up in varying degrees of irritability or apathy. Their exaggerated attempt to blame their ego dilemma on circumstances and individuals gives their childhood history a more sordid character and themselves the appearance of a worse psychopathy than is justified. Their ego identity has fallen apart into its bodily, sexual, social, occupational elements, each having to overcome again the danger of its evil prototype. Rehabilitation work can be made more effective and economical if the clinical investigation focuses on the patient's shattered life plan and if advice tends to strengthen the resynthesis of the elements on which the patient's ego identity was based.

In addition to the several hundred thousand men who lost and only gradually or partially regained their ego identity in this war and to the thousands whose acute loss of ego identity was falsely diagnosed and treated as psychopathy, an untold number has experienced to the core the threat of a traumatic loss of ego identity as a result of radical historical change.

The fact that these men, their physicians, and their contemporaries in increasing numbers turn to the bitter truths of psychoanalytic psychiatry is in itself a historical development that calls for critical appraisal. It expresses an increased acceptance of psychoanalytic insights insofar as they concern the meaning of anxiety and of disease in the individual case history. Yet this partial acceptance of painful unconscious determinants of human behavior has the quality of a concomitant resistance against the disquieting awareness of a social symptom and its historical determinants. I mean the subliminal panic which accompanied the large-scale testing of the American identity during the most recent period of world history.

Historical change has reached a coercive universality and a global acceleration which is experienced as a threat to the emerging American identity. It seems to devaluate the vigorous conviction that this nation can afford mistakes; that this nation, by definition, is always so far ahead of the rest of the world in inexhaustible reserves, in vision of planning, in freedom of action, and in tempo of progress that there is unlimited space and endless time in which to develop, to test, and to complete her social experiments. The difficulties met in the attempt to integrate this old image of insulated spaciousness with the new image of explosive global closeness are deeply disquieting. They are characteristically met, at first, with the application of traditional methods to a new space-time; there is the missionary discovery of "one World," aviation pioneering on a "Trans-World" basis, charity on a global scale, etc. Yet there also remains a deep consciousness of a lag in economic and political integration, and with it, in emotional and spiritual strength.

The psychotherapist, in disregarding the contribution of this development to neurotic discomfort, is apt not only to miss much of the specific dynamics in contemporary life cycles; he is apt also to deflect (or to serve those whose business demands that they deflect) individual energy from the collective tasks at hand. A large-scale decrease of neurosis can be achieved only by equal clinical attention to cases and to conditions, to the fixation on the past and the emerging design for the future, to the grumbling depth and the unsafe surface.

III

In studying the ego's relation to changing historical reality, psychoanalysis approaches a new phalanx of unconscious resistances. It is implicit in the nature of psychoanalytic investigation that such resistances must be located and appraised in the observer, and in his habits of conceptualization, before their presence in the observed can be fully understood and effectively handled. When investigating instincts, the psychoanalyst knows that his drive to investigate is partially instinctive in nature; he knows that he responds with a partial countertransference to the patient's transference, i.e., the ambiguous wish to satisfy infantile strivings in the very therapeutic situation which is to cure them. The analyst acknowledges all this, yet works methodically toward that margin of freedom where the clear delineation of the inevitable makes consuming resistances unnecessary and frees energy for creative planning.

It is, then, a commonplace to state that the psychoanalyst in training must learn to study the historical determinants of what made him what he is before he can hope to perfect that human gift: the ability to understand what is different from him. Beyond this, however, there are the historical determinants of psychoanalytic concepts.

If in the field of human motivation the same terms have been used over a period of half a century (and what a century!), they cannot but reflect the ideologies of their day of origin and absorb the connotations of consequent social changes. Ideological connotation is the inevitable historical equation in the use of conceptual tools which concern the ego, man's organ of reality testing. The conceptualizations of man's selfsame core and of reality itself are by necessity a function of historical change. Yet, here, too, our search is for a margin of freedom; our method, radical analysis of resistances to insight and to planning.

As philosophers would predict, the concept of "reality" itself, while clear in its intended meaning, is highly corruptible in its usage. According to the pleasure principle, that is good which feels good at the moment; the reality principle declares that to be good which, in the long run and with consideration for all possible outer and inner developments, promises most lastingly to feel good. Such principles, established by scientific man, fall prey easily to economic man. The reality principle, in theory and therapy, has taken on a certain individualistic color, according to which that is good which the individual can get away with by dodging the law (insofar as it happens to be enforced) and the superego (insofar as it causes discomfort). Our therapeutic failures often define the limit of this usage: Western man, almost against his will, is developing a more universal group identity. His reality principle begins to include a *social principle* according to which that is good which, in the long run, secures to a man what feels good to him without keeping any other man (of the same collective identity) from securing an analogous gain. The question that remains is: what new synthesis of economic and emotional safety will sustain this wider group identity and thus give strength to the individual ego?

A different sort of trend in contemporary conceptualization is typified in a recent formulation, according to which "All through childhood a maturation process is at work which, in the service of an increasing knowledge and adaptation to reality, aims at perfecting [ego] functions, at rendering them more and more objective and independent of the emotions, until they can become as accurate and reliable as a mechanical apparatus" (Anna Freud, 1945, p. 29).

Obviously, the ego as such is older than all mechanization. If we detect in it a tendency to mechanize itself and to be free from the very emotions without which experience becomes impoverished, we may actually be concerned with a historical dilemma. Today we face the question whether the problems of the machine age will be solved by a mechanization of man or by a humanization of industry. Our child-training customs have begun to standardize modern man, so that he may become a reliable mechanism prepared to "adjust" to the competitive exploitation of the machine world. In fact, certain modern trends in child training seem to represent a magic identification with the machine, analogous to identifications of primitive tribes with their principal prey. At the same time the modern mind, already the product of a civilization preoccupied with mechanization, attempts to understand itself by searching for "mental mechanisms." If, then, the ego itself seems to *crave* mechanical adaptation, we may not be dealing with the nature of the ego but with one of its period-bound adjustments as well as with our own mechanistic approach to its study.

Maybe in this connection it is not quite unnecessary to point to the fact that the popular use of the word *ego* in this country has, of course, little to do with the psychoanalytic concept of the same name; it denotes unqualified if not justified self-esteem. Yet, in the wake of therapeutic short cuts, this connotation can be seen to creep even into professional discussions of the ego.

Bolstering, bantering, boisterousness, and other "ego-inflating" behavior are, of course, part of the American folkways. As such, they pervade speech and gesture and enter into all interpersonal relations. Without them, a therapeutic relationship in this country would remain outlandish and nonspecific. The problem to be discussed here, however, is the systematic exploitation of the national practice of bolstering for the sake of making people "feel better," or of submerging their anxiety and tension so as to make them function better as patients, customers, or employees.

A weak ego does not gain substantial strength from being persistently bolstered. A strong ego, secured in its identity by a strong society, does not need, and in fact is immune to, any attempt at artificial inflation. Its tendency is toward the testing of what feels real, the mastery of that which works, the understanding of that which proves necessary, the enjoyment of the vital, and the extermination of the morbid. At the same time, it tends toward the creation of a strong mutual reinforcement with others in a group ego, which will transmit its will to the next generation.

A war, however, can be an unfair test to ego strength. During collective emergencies, all resources, emotional as well as material, must be mobilized with relative disregard for what is workable and economical under more normal conditions of long-range development. Ego bolstering is a legitimate measure in such days of collective danger; and it remains a genuine therapeutic approach in individual cases of acute ego strain, i.e., wherever the individual is emotionally too young or physically too weak to meet a situation bearable to the mature and the healthy; or if a situation is too extraordinary to be met even by a relatively adequate ego. Obviously, a war increases the occurrence of both types of traumatic discrepancy between the ego and situations not included in its anticipations. The indiscriminate application of the philosophy and the practice of "ego bolstering" to peacetime conditions, however, would be theoretically unsound and therapeutically unwholesome. It is, furthermore, socially dangerous, because its employment implies that the cause of the strain (i.e., "modern living") is perpetually beyond the individual's or his society's control—a state of affairs which would postpone indefinitely the revision of *conditions which are apt to weaken the infantile ego*. To deflect energy from such revision is dangerous. For American childhood and other manifestations of the specific American freedom of spirit are but grandiose fragments striving for integration with the fragments of industrial democracy.

The effectiveness of the psychoanalytic contribution to this development is guaranteed solely by the persistent humanistic intention, beyond the mere adjustment of patients to limited conditions, to apply clinical experience to the end of making man aware of potentialities which are clouded by archaic fear.

IV

In studying his subject, the psychoanalyst (so Anna Freud [1936] points out) should occupy an observation point "equidistant from the id, the ego, and the super-ego"—so that he may be aware of their functional interdependence and so that, as he observes a change in one of these sections of the mind, he may not lose sight of related changes in the others.

Beyond this, however, the observer is aware of the fact that what he conceptualizes as id, ego, and superego are not static compartments in the capsule of a life history. Rather they reflect three major processes, the relativity of which determines the form of human behavior. They are:

1. the process of organismic organization of bodies within the time-space of the life cycle (evolution, epigenesis, libido development, etc.);
2. the process of the organization of experience by ego synthesis (ego space-time, ego defenses, ego identity, etc.);
3. the process of the social organization of ego organisms in geographic-historical units (collective space-time, collective life plan, ethos of production, etc.).

The order given follows the trend of psychoanalytic research. Otherwise, although different in structure, these processes *exist by and are relative to each other*. Any item whose meaning and potential changes within one of these processes simultaneously changes in the others. To assure the proper rate and sequence of change, and to prevent or counteract lags, discrepancies, and discontinuities of development, there are the warning signals of pain in the body, anxiety in the ego, and panic in the group. They warn of organic dysfunction, impairment of ego mastery, and loss of group identity: each a threat to all.

In psychopathology we observe and study the apparent autonomy of one of these processes as it receives undue accentuation because of the loss of their mutual regulation and general balance. Thus psychoanalysis has first studied (as if it could be isolated) man's *enslavement by the id,* i.e., by the excessive demands on ego and society of frustrated organisms, upset in the inner economy of their life cycle. Next, the focus of study shifted to man's *enslavement by seemingly autonomous ego (and superego) strivings*—defensive mechanisms which curtail and distort the ego's power of experiencing and planning beyond the limit of what is workable and tolerable in the individual organism and in social organization. Psychoanalysis completes its basic studies of neurosis by investigating more explicitly *man's enslavement by historical conditions which claim autonomy* by precedent and exploit archaic mechanisms within him to deny him health and ego strength. Only the reinterpretation of our clinical experience on the basis of this three-fold investigation will permit us to make an essential contribution to child training in an industrial world.

The goal of psychoanalytic treatment itself has been defined (Nunberg, 1931) as a simultaneous increase in the mobility of the id, in the tolerance of the superego, and in the synthesizing power of the ego. To the last point we add the suggestion that the analysis of the ego should include that of the individual's ego identity in relation to the historical changes which dominated his childhood milieu. For the individual's mastery over his neurosis begins when he is put in a position to accept the historical necessity which made him what he is. The individual feels free when he can choose to identify with his own ego identity and when he learns to apply that which is given to that which must be done. Only thus can he derive ego strength (for his generation and the next) from the coincidence of this one and only life cycle with a particular segment of human history.

8

IDENTIFICATION, THE SENSE OF BELONGING AND OF IDENTITY IN SMALL GROUPS

SAUL SCHEIDLINGER

This paper is an extension of a discussion of identification in group psychotherapy (Scheidlinger, 1955), which explored the diverse ways in which the concept of identification has been utilized in psychoanalytic writings. Freud's initial depiction of the processes of "primary" and "secondary" identification in child development was considered, together with later attempts by others to distinguish between superego and ego identifications; Anna Freud's (1936) subsequent important distinction between identification as a kind of emotional tie between people and identification as a defense mechanism, i.e., "identification with the aggressor" or "altruistic surrender," was also discussed.

Psychoanalytic theories of group behavior were elaborated, with special attention to Freud's (1921) and Redl's

Reprinted from the *International Journal of Group Psychotherapy*, 14:291-306 (1964), with the permission of the publisher.

(chap. 2, this volume) views of groups as psychological units characterized by ego identifications among a number of people. These ego identifications are thought to be the result of each group member's having first established an emotional relationship to the leader (to the central person, in Redl's terms). According to Redl, this unifying relationship of each group member to the central person can be in the nature of a positive or negative object cathexis (love or hate) or of a positive or negative identification. Group ties can even be evoked if several individuals have used the same object (central person) as a means of relieving similar internal conflicts.

While a few papers have since appeared devoted exclusively to the subject of identification in group psychotherapy (Ziferstein, 1959; Briskin, 1958), the concern expressed nine years ago that almost all writings on group therapy treat identification in an ambiguous and too generalized fashion still appears justified. "There is almost always a failure to distinguish between its role in the group dynamic phenomena as contrasted with the therapeutic elements which are basically the same in *all* psychotherapy. Furthermore, identifications are also apt to be lumped together with transferences and object ties" (Scheidlinger, 1955, p. 666). This last-named problem is especially apparent in the writings on group psychology of such English authors as Bion, Ezriel, and Jaques, who follow the theories of Melanie Klein. As I have noted elsewhere (Scheidlinger, 1960), the Kleinian model of psychoanalytic group psychology places major emphasis on the idea of "projective" and "introjective" identifications. In this system, shared primitive ("psychotic") fantasies are believed to be "projected" outward by each group member or introjected, "taken in" from the here and now of the group situation. Jaques (1955, p. 479) asserted that "one of the primary cohesive elements binding individuals into institutionalized human association is that of defense against psychotic anxiety." Thus, Bion's (chap. 3, this volume) composite concept of "projective identifications" involves not only shared apperceptions of group elements, i.e., leader and other members, in line with irrational inner motivations, but also a spontaneous and involuntary *acting out* of these fantasies and "object relationships" as a group. It is a kind of "acting in the identification" not unlike the phenomenon of "acting in the transference" (Scheidlinger, 1955). As is true elsewhere, with Bion or Jaques there is, on the one hand, almost complete disregard of what we already know about the differences between primary-process and secondary-process phenomena, about intervening ego functions, and above all, about the difference between endopsychic processes and observable behavior.

My aim here is to subject to closer scrutiny a relatively neglected kind of identification in psychoanalytic group psychology, that involving the individual's relationship to the group-as-a-whole. Of the major therapeutic ingredients in group psychotherapy, the literature has tended to pay most attention to the patient's relationships to the central person-helper and to the patient's relationships to the other group members. While many therapists have also referred to the therapeutic value of such properties pertaining to the group-as-a-whole as climate, group code, group goals, structure, or cohesiveness, these have rarely been conceptualized with regard to the interplay of individual personality and group dynamic factors on various "depth" levels. It should be noted that Bales (1950), a sociologist, listed the "differential degree of solidarity or identification with the group as a whole" as one of his four universal kinds of differentiations between persons as units in small groups.

While there are many kinds of identifications, for my purposes here, identification will be viewed as an endopsychic process calling for a degree of individual involvement with a perceived object or its symbolic representation. I would agree with Alice Balint (1943) that, in the classical Freudian sense, identification brings into play such functions as adaptation to reality, reality testing, sense of reality, the self-concept (with its self- and object representations), and the capacity to form object relationships.

Contrary to the view prevalent among some writers, this kind of an identification does not necessarily involve a pathological engulfment of the personality by another object (Searles, 1951) or a regressive replacement of an earlier object cathexis. Rather, it would fall under the broader category mentioned by Freud of the capacity to share qualities, interests, or ideals precipitating identifications with others. According to Freud (1921), the capacity for forming such "desexualized, sublimated" group relationships springs from work in common.

The family not only constitutes the first matrix in an individual's association with other people, it is also a prototype of subsequent group relations. As Murphy (1947, p. 843) states, "... canalized and conditioned responses transfer to persons similar to those with whom the first associations were formed .... The deeper and more constantly reinforced responses to parents and to brothers and sisters will become the matrix from which the field of friendships and hostilities, dependent and autonomous social relationships will grow."

Children can be said to perceive the earliest shadowy ministrations to their comfort, the later more clearly emerging figures of mother, father, and siblings, as well as the total family atmosphere, differentially at various developmental stages. These impressions are retained as memory percepts, or, in psychoanalytic terms, as self- and object representations; such percept memories are always at play in the perception of contemporary situations (Sandler, 1960). In general, current stimuli tend to be perceived in terms of similar past stimuli. As L.K. Frank (1950, p. VII) has stated: "an active process goes on of transforming the world of situations and people into the forms, meanings, and values which the individual has learned selectively to perceive, by imposing upon them or investing them with the meanings they have for him." With regard to a therapy group, each member can be assumed to bring with him a complex patterning of conscious and unconscious attitudes toward himself, toward other people, and toward group experiences in general, i.e., toward groups as a *Gestalt*. Attitudes toward concurrent or antecedent group experiences are likely to be revived; in addition, under the impact of the tensions inherent in group participation, deeper and forgotten attitudes and levels of perceiving are also reactivated. These are broad in scope and have been amply covered in the literature; my interest in this paper is limited to the emergence in each patient of attitudes and perceptions toward the group as a collective entity. These attitudes and perceptions occur on two levels: contemporaneous-dynamic and genetic regressive. I have described elsewhere (Scheidlinger, 1960, p. 354) the contemporaneous-dynamic level of group interactions as pertaining to "the more readily observed momentary expressions of conscious needs and ego-adaptive patterns, the group roles, the network of attractions and repulsions, as well as the group structure. The behavior here is primarily reactive to realistic group-situational factors bringing into play the more external aspects of personality." The genetic-regressive level, in contrast, refers to unconscious and preconscious motivations, to defensive patterns and conflicts, to phenomena such as transference, countertransference, resistance, identification, and projection. The genetic-regressive type of phenomena is more apt to emerge in situations wherein the personality restraints (ego defenses) have been loosened (regression), with consequent freer expression of repressed emotionality.

On the contemporaneous-dynamic level the group-as-a-whole is likely to be viewed by the individual as an instrument for conscious-need satisfaction. The range here is broad, including needs of an educational or ideological nature or "to get therapy." Group associations are also sought to gratify less readily articulated needs for belonging, for emotional support, for protection, for sexual expression, or for assuaging guilt (Sandler, 1960). Bonner (1959) has referred to the close relationship between the need-satisfying power of the group and its attractiveness to the individual.

Cattell (1951, p. 19) went so far as to define a group in terms of this one element of individual-need satisfaction. According to him, a group "is a collection of organisms in which the existence of all (in their given relationships) is necessary to the satisfaction of certain individual needs in each." Schutz later (1958) evolved a research approach to interpersonal relationships with a basic postulate of three kinds of individual interpersonal needs: inclusion, control, and affection.

I have speculated that, on the deeper genetic-regressive level, the group entity becomes for the individual the symbolic representation of a nurturing mother (cf. such terms in popular usage as "mother earth" or "motherland"). In a broader sense, the hypothesis can be advanced that the universal human need to belong, to establish a state of psychological unity with others, represents a covert wish for restoring an earlier state of unconflicted well-being inherent in the exclusive union with mother, a theme I shall develop later.

In group treatment of people who have experienced marked early deprivations with resultant ego disturbances and "identity diffusions," we have observed that perceptions of the group-as-a-whole in a supportive and benign vein tend to be especially marked and fundamental (Scheidlinger and Pyrke, 1961). This observation assumes greater interest when we note that a young child's earliest perceptions appear to be diffuse and of a *Gestalt* nature. As Murphy (1947, p. 765) said regarding perception, "the preponderant tendency is from whole to detail, and usually from large detail to small detail. . . ."From hearing voices in general, the child at seven or eight months appears to distinguish between a "friendly" and "hostile" quality, to be followed by more detailed differentiation and integration of the parental figures. To quote Brierley (1951, p. 77), "Hence it is permissible to think of infantile relationships beginning as relationships to total situations but as relationships of sharply contrasted types: definitely affirmative or appetitive relations to gratifying pleasurable situations and unambiguously negative ones to conditions of pain and frustration."

In addition to this assumption that the child's first taste of a group includes an impression of its broader *Gestalt* (probably via its climate) is the related idea that this permits an early identification with the collective unity of the group. Such identification precipitates the individual's emotional involvement with the group and accordingly contributes to the group's cohesiveness.

I have already suggested that identification with the group-as-a-whole can be explored most profitably within the framework of the individual group member's perception, for, at any moment of his group membership, each individual can be said to perceive not only selected aspects of an existing social situation (i.e., interacting group members and a central person or central persons), but also the *Gestalt* of this social situation. These perceptions occur on various "depth" levels. They will vary, on the one hand, in line with individual personality factors such as the ego organization and the ability to deal with the inevitable stress involved in joining and interacting in a group, and on the other hand, with the nature of the specific group, which can range from a rational, structured assemblage of people to a highly volatile grouping with a seeming absence of structure.

Identification with a group entity goes beyond the mere perception of it and the investing of it with some emotional meaning, for identification in this sense also contains an element of responding or, more specifically, an element of individual commitment. To belong to or to feel part of a group (some people have used the term "ego involved") also implies a more or less transitory giving up of some aspect of the individual's self (or self-schema) to the group-as-a-group. "One literally 'loses' oneself in the group—not just in the crowd, but in the disciplined, highly integrated military or industrial, or religious, or artistic, or scientific unit" (Murphy, 1947, p. 766). Festinger et al. (1952) referred to a somewhat related process of deindividuation, wherein individuals act as if they were "submerged in the group." They hypothesized that the phenomenon of deindividuation brought about a reduction in inner restraint for the members.

In this connection, Bonner (1959) referred to the urgent need for investigating the role of the self in group behavior. This latter element has caused no end of confusion in group psychology literature. To begin with, Freud's attempt to explain mob phenomena in terms of the individual's susceptibility to emotional contagion by substituting the crowd leader's superego for his own was taken by some writers as an explanatory model for all groups. In all groups, then, there was to be found a labile emotionality, a pathological regression coupled with a loss of individual identity and a heightened suggestibility. In this vein, Bion (chap. 3, this volume), for instance, likened the loss of a person's individuality in a group to "psychotic" depersonalization. He and other followers of Melanie Klein asserted, furthermore, that the primary motivation in all group belonging relates to the individual's search for defenses against such loss of individual distinctiveness as well as against other "psychotic" anxieties.

In my view, only under special circumstances can individual group belonging be characterized by such pathological, regressive processes that involve the "introjection" of the leader's superego qualities and the concomitant relinquishing of personal identity and independence. Groups with autocratic leadership, moblike situations, and perhaps groups that comprise a membership with marked ego disorganization can approach this model; on the other hand, this is rarely the case in groups with a "democratic" climate where there is a balance between permissiveness and control, including analytically oriented therapy groups.

At any rate, the phenomenon of an individual's identification with a group entity, which is the concern of this paper, refers primarily to an ego and not to a superego manifestation. Insofar as it can occur on various "depth" levels, it can assume a regressive or integrative-adaptive character (Axelrad and Maury, 1951). (It should be noted that, in line with the concept of "regression in the service of the ego,"[1] regression is not necessarily synonymous with pathology.) Furthermore, the identification with the group-as-a-whole, being only one of numerous kinds of identifications at work in the complex dynamics of group life (Semrad et al., 1963), can accompany the superego iden-

---

[1] Schafer (1958), following Kris (1952), has defined regression in the service of the ego as a "partial, temporary, controlled lowering of the level of psychic functioning to promote adaptation" (p. 122). In this process the individual's access to preconscious and unconscious stimuli is increased without any major threat to the ego functioning. As a result, inner balance, interpersonal relations, and work are enhanced.

tification of the individual group members with the central person or with the group ideal or code. There is in fact some basis for assuming a close relationship, at least on the level of unconscious symbolism, between the group member's identification with the leader and his identification with the group entity. Freud (1921) amended his basic formula of group formation involving an ego-ideal (superego) identification with the leader to the effect that a common group ideology can also precipitate psychological group formation.

In trying to elaborate on the connection between the role of the individual's self-schema or self-representation and his group identification, Erikson's related concepts of an individual and of a group identity can be helpful. Erikson (chap. 7, this volume) spoke of ego identity as "a sense that the ego is learning effective steps toward a tangible collective future, that it is developing into a defined ego within a social reality." The sense of an ego identity is based on the common perception of an individual's self-sameness and continuity in time, together with the perception that meaningful people recognize this self-sameness and continuity. In other words, such basic human concerns as, "Who am I?," "What am I?," and "Where am I going?" are deeply anchored in the individual's group experiences from the family on. Erikson insisted that healthy ego development called for a synchronization of the stages in child development with a group identity. This group identity refers to the group as a social collective with a sense of shared human qualities, a communality with others, an ideology, goals, and, in a broader sense, to the group's basic ways of organizing experience. Although Erikson devoted a minimum of attention to the concept of group identity per se, he viewed ego identity as "a subjective experience, a dynamic fact, and a group psychological phenomenon." In the last-named connotation, ego identity refers to the "maintenance of one's inner solidarity with a group's ideals and identity." In this sense, it approximates quite closely our description of the dynamic-contemporaneous aspect of identification with the group-as-a-whole. There is an element of investing varying aspects of self in the collectivity as illustrated in the individual's sense of belonging, in his feeling so at one with the perceived group entity that it is theoretically not possible to speak of an ego identity apart from a group identity. The result of an individual's group identification is that he reacts to the attributes of the group as if these attributes were also his own. A striking illustration is offered by the many occasions when an individual reacts to a criticism or slight of his group as though he himself had been criticized or slighted.

Janis (1963, p. 227) studied the effect of external danger on group identification in the army. He defined group identification as "a set of preconscious and unconscious attitudes which incline each member to apperceive the group as an extension of himself and impel him to remain in direct contact with the other members and to adhere to the group standards." He offered repeated examples of soldiers who acted in the interests of their comrades, their groups, as opposed to their own self-interests.

It can be said than an individual's self-concept contains not only internalized representations of objects but also self-representations, which Hartmann (see Jacobson, 1964) defined as "the endopsychic representations of the bodily and mental self in the system ego." Sandler (1960) outlined the way in which the young child is believed to evolve a mother schema or imago, which in time becomes differentiated from his self-schema. The child experiences satisfaction when his mother or other persons approximate in their actual behavior his expectations of being gratified unconditionally as depicted in his internalized mother-schema; in contrary circumstances there is an experience of frustration and anger. Sandler distinguished between the individual's need for instinctual pleasure and his need to restore an ego state of well-being. Effects of the latter are seen in states of high self-esteem and feelings of being in a safe environment. Similarly, in identification with an admired object there is a rise in self-esteem. "The child feels at one with the object and close to it, and temporarily regains the feeling of happiness which he experienced during the earliest days of life." (1960, p. 151) Furthermore, people in the child's immediate environment become sources of "feeling loved" and of self-esteem.

The strong human need for restoring the original state of unconflicted well-being represented in the earliest infant-mother tie has been explained in terms of man's prolonged infantile helplessness. A related element is his persistent dread of abandonment. The fate of these factors has frequently been viewed as crucial in understanding the most serious psychopathological states. According to Rochlin (1959), even in psychotics the need for establishing a relation to an object is not actually relinquished. Some authors, such as Bowlby (1962) and Winnicott (1955), have made the early separation trauma from the mother the basis of a theory in which separation anxiety is an ever-present, powerful motivation in all behavior. As noted by Muensterberger (1955, p. 9), on the deepest levels all people are believed to seek a reunion with the maternal figure, with anxiety being generated through the awareness of one's basic aloneness: " . . . separation anxiety is one of the fundamental elements of our being human, of our being social and cooperative creatures. . . . We do not dare to give up our inborn need for maternal gratification. We cling to each other as if we were mothers to each other. . . ."

A study by M. Fried (1963) revealed some fascinating

findings in this connection. He reported continued marked feelings of painful loss, including manifestations of mourning and depression in a considerable proportion of resettled inhabitants of a slum neighborhood in Boston. It was as if this slum neighborhood, no matter how dilapidated and inferior when compared to these people's new domiciles, had somehow come to stand for a treasured maternal object. The reactions of mourning were almost identical to those manifested at the loss of a close human object. Fried's study suggests that not only one's group in a strict sense but also one's home or neighborhood can come to represent on the deepest levels a maternal image. This is especially likely with people who have already experienced considerable traumatization in childhood, as well as emotional and social deprivation throughout their lives. On another plane, these reactions of grief can be explained in terms of a kind of identity crisis, in Erikson's terms. In the old neighborhood, each individual and family had a clear identity. Everyone knew who they were, whence they came, and where they were going. When they moved, the few social ties, no matter how tenuous, with storekeepers, peddlers, or neighbors were broken. Uprooted themselves, uprooted with them was their sense of ego and group identity. It takes a flexible and well-developed ego and considerable resiliency to restore readily these kinds of relationships with complete strangers in a new locale.

M. Balint (1960) has posed a theory of primary love to supplant the concept of primary narcissism. Among the earliest object ties which are felt by the individual as vitally important for emotional support, he listed that to the mother, which can find expression in four archaic mother symbols: water, earth, air, and less frequently, fire. The question arises whether, in an extended sense, attachments to a group entity can come to serve similar ends, i.e., to symbolize an early child-mother tie, especially when the individual is faced with undue tension and anxiety. This would fit in also with Buxbaum's (1945) discussion regarding the supportive role of group associations in helping to solve young people's developmental crises at the termination of the oedipal phase and during adolescence. Anna Freud's (Freud and Dann, 1951) observations of very young concentration-camp children who had been deprived of mothering is of interest in this connection. These children's feelings of dependency and affection were initially centered exclusively in their own group; adults could foster relationships to themselves only after they had managed to become a part of the children's group.

The discussion so far has dealt with the concept of an individual's identification with the group entity and with the dynamic and genetic elements related to this concept. I have also suggested that such an identification plays a major role in the therapeutic process insofar as it promotes an individual sense of belonging, of enhanced self-esteem, and of ego identity. This latter factor would tie in with Erikson's notion that a healthy ego identity constitutes the end-result of many identifications and of a successful ego synthesis.

From the framework of group dynamics, this identification with the collective group is undoubtedly a major factor in strengthening a group's cohesive forces. In this connection, J.D. Frank (1957) has depicted how patients in the beginning phase of his groups have tended to foster cohesiveness, to seek "common ground on which the group may coalesce," which he relates to the general tendency, observed by social scientists, of individuals to perpetuate the existence of their groups. In line with the considerations advanced by Semrad and his co-workers (1963) the phenomenon of identification with the group entity may also play a major role in counteracting the divisive conflicts emanating from the group members' "desire for exclusive union or fusion with the central figure." Perhaps in addition to the role of the "central person" as an absorber of undue hostility, and of the "billets," as discussed by Arsenian et al. (1962), the individual's relationship to the group entity can be assumed to permit a degree of direct and of symbolic gratification, thus also contributing to the "limiting and binding of instinctual derivatives."

I have not dealt with the complex issue of how and when the individual group member's perceptions of the group-as-a-group become shared perceptions, which remains a subject for further investigation. The matter of such shared perceptions in small groups has been developed in contributions by Bion (chap. 3, this volume), Ezriel (chap. 4, this volume), Stock and Lieberman (1962), and by Kaplan and Roman (1963). The latter authors have also dealt with a further problem of delineating specific developmental phases in such shared perceptions as part of group development in an adult therapy group. Shepard and Bennis (1956), Schutz (1958), and Mann (1966) have outlined stages of group development for training groups.

One could speculate that as treatment progresses individual perceptions and attitudes toward the group-as-a-whole are likely to move in general from the irrational (genetic-regressive) to the more realistic levels (dynamic-contemporaneous). The assertion of some writers that broader group phenomena give way to an almost exclusive preoccupation with personal and dyadic themes in the final stages of therapy groups can be questioned. There is, to begin with, the readily observed idealization as well as realistic sense of solidarity and affection for one's therapy group in the final stages of group treatment. These come into full focus, together with expressions of anxiety, mourning, and depression, when issues of termination and of separation are tackled. There is also the observation by some writers that, if not discouraged by the therapist's theoretical bias, themes pertaining to the reality operations of the group-as-a-group are likely to emerge in the terminal stages of treatment (Martin and Hill, 1957).

Foulkes (1951) emphasized that, as therapy proceeds, "There is a crescendo move in the maturity of the group and a decrescendo move in the authority of the leader. Dependence upon authority is replaced by reliance on the strength of the group itself" (p. 327).

Similarly, according to Rashkis (1959), " . . . as the patients in a therapy group improve, their group identification increases: they become more of a 'group' " (p. 506).

I hope the discussion so far has served to underscore the fact that some form or level of the group member's identification with the group as a unit plays a significant role throughout the life span of the group, perhaps even after its dissolution. There are not only the related possibilities for direct or symbolic drive gratification, but also varied opportunities for ego strengthening and enrichment. The many growth-promoting elements inherent in group belonging are well known and do not require repetition (Scheidlinger, 1952). It might be of interest, however, to note that Freud, with his heavy emphasis on the libidinal factors in group relationships, also recognized the ego-strengthening aspects of group solidarity when he referred in his open letter to Einstein (1933) to the sense of personal strength derived by individuals from group involvement and solidarity.

What are some of the implications of these theoretical observations for the practitioner of group therapy? To begin with, there is in every therapy group the *experiential,* or what Foulkes and Anthony (1957) termed the "supportive" factor. When a therapist consciously fosters a climate of permissiveness, of acceptance, of belonging, he is in another sense promoting the development of a certain kind of group entity with a related sense of solidarity. With patients characterized by extreme ego pathology, such as hospitalized schizophrenics or markedly dependent personalities, the first (if not all) stages of group treatment might be centered on the promotion of a strong sense of identification with a small group. In line with the point made earlier, the wish for reunion with a nurturing mother is thus likely to be gratified on the deeper (genetic-regressive) level and on the here-and-now (contemporaneous-dynamic) level, thereby enhancing opportunities for ego repair and support. Such an identification with the group as a collective entity constitutes a bridge to mature object relationships and to reality. Group belonging and participation can be manipulated by expert group practitioners to promote the repair of a variety of ego functions ranging from reality testing through the self-concept (attainment of ego identity) to the control of drives (Scheidlinger et al., 1955). As noted by Polansky et al. (1957, p. 381) in their analysis of role images of patients in a mental hospital, "The degree of ego integration at any given time is probably always, in part, a function of the social situation since an essential part of what the ego must integrate is external reality."

I am reminded of an incident in which a group social worker had felt discouraged and exhausted while helping a reluctant small ward-group in a psychiatric hospital prepare for a party. They required continuous direction to the point where some individuals literally had to be led by the hand to help set the tables, decorate the walls, and put the sodas in the icebox. After the party was over, a number of patients exclaimed that it had been the most successful event they had ever had. Could they plan a more ambitious one? The group worker reminded them of the group's earlier reluctance and doubt, adding that perhaps as a group they could do more than they gave themselves credit for. The change in group morale was striking. The "group" and "we" were terms used repeatedly in the next week. A sense of collective pride, strength, and self-esteem noticeably "rubbed off" on everyone. It is doubtful whether such results could have been obtained had the group worker not placed major emphasis on the group's *esprit de corps* and self-image. The next party was an even greater success and infinitely easier to prepare.

The question arises here whether this outcome bears some conceptual similarity to a social science experiment reported by Cartwright and Lippitt (1957) wherein it was demonstrated in an industrial setting that members of highly cohesive groups exhibited less anxiety than members of poorly cohesive groups.

As for group psychotherapy in an outpatient setting, a variety of "hard-to-reach" patients with no motivation for seeking help were meaningfully involved in therapy through a group approach which relied on nonverbal communication, on reliving and experiencing, rather than on verbalizing and conceptualizing. The conscious fostering of an identification with the group-as-a-whole played a major role in enhancing attendance and group involvement in general (Scheidlinger, 1960).

In insight-focused group treatment, such as analytic group psychotherapy, group identifications can be utilized to enhance the cohesiveness required for developing a common sense of task or work orientation inherent in the job of therapy. In this connection, Nunberg (1951) went so far as to refer to the dyadic analytic situation as a "group formation of two persons," since helping the patient becomes a *common goal* of analyst and patient. In addition, if a therapist agrees with the validity of the notions depicted earlier regarding the symbolic perception of the group entity, or Erikson's twin concepts of ego and group identity, these themes would undoubtedly be especially noted in the group's free-associative deliberations as well as the therapist's interpretive comments. Some group therapists, steeped as they are in the exclusive importance of the individual in psychotherapy and psychopathology, are very likely either to ignore group-relevant behavioral phenomena, including group dreams, or to treat all of them as manifestations of resistance against "real" individual analysis and self-understanding. While I would be the first to agree that group identifications or dreams about the group can on occasion be utilized as individual or group resistances, this is not necessarily the case. The problem is not very different from the general observation that prolific dreaming by an analysand can at times represent resistance rather than an attempt to further the analytic process. Only a continuous process of diagnostic watchfulness by the therapist can ascertain whether any specific behavior on the part of individual or group is utilized primarily in the service of irrationality or in the service of growth. The basic therapeutic dynamisms are the same in all psychotherapy, individual or group. It is regrettable that some writers have gone so far as to find in practitioners' emphasis on group dynamic processes an attempt to cover up their alleged ignorance of the teachings of individual psychoanalysis (Schwartz and Wolf, 1963).

The broader implications of man's need for group involvement and identification as part of his quest for a stable and predictable environment was recently explored in an excellent paper by Peck (1963).

There is little doubt that in this day of unprecedented social change, with accompanying dissolutions of primary group ties, the need for finding self-esteem, coherence, and meaning in our environment has become a major concern of the behavioral sciences.

9

THE CONCEPT OF REGRESSION
IN GROUP PSYCHOTHERAPY

SAUL SCHEIDLINGER

The special relevance of the psychoanalytic concept of regression to group psychotherapy is undisputed. And yet the utility of this concept has been much limited by its complexity and by the ambiguity of its usage in literature and clinical practice.

In group therapy theory, regression has served to explain *group psychological manifestations* characteristic of all human groups as well as the *therapeutic process* entailed in clinical work with disturbed people. In other words, there are regressive phenomena rooted in group psychology in addition to those which are a part of all reconstructive psychotherapy.

In the broader context of Freudian psychoanalysis, the term regression was historically linked almost exclusively to individual psychopathology. Under the term were subsumed such varied behavioral manifestations as pathological defense mechanism, symptom formation, unconscious content, a mental process, or even the end-product of a

Reprinted from the *International Journal of Group Psychotherapy*, 18:3-20 (1968), with the permission of the publisher.

process. And it is this general view of regression which is still usually found in the dictionaries. English and English (1958) define regression as "a return to earlier and less mature behavior; or, manifestation of more primitive behaviors after having learned mature forms, whether or not the immature or primitive behavior had actually formed part of the person's earlier behavior" (p. 450). In the clinical literature, before the advent of ego psychology, regression–together with its sister concept, fixation–was couched in terms of the Freudian stages of psychosexual development, according to which psychological factors pertaining to any one phase are never entirely given up and the personality under stress reverts to earlier fixation points. Implicit is the notion that regression connotes maladaptation and that the further backward the move, such as to primary narcissism, the greater the psychopathology.

In a similar vein is Fenichel's (1945, p. 160) assertion that regression, unlike the other pathogenic defenses, is not brought about by ego activity. Instead, " . . . the ego is much more passive. Regression happens to the ego; in general, regression seems to be set in motion by the instincts."

Following a discussion of how the concept of regression has evolved in the group psychological as well as in the broader psychoanalytic literature, I shall advance a broader view which incorporates the most recent theoretical trends.

REGRESSION IN GROUP FORMATION

In his "Group Psychology and the Analysis of the Ego," Freud (1921) advanced a number of new concepts depicting group formation as the reactivation of an earlier kind of libidinal relationship of the group members with a "father-leader," with ensuing "sibling" identifications among them. Following the first appearance of this little volume, the psychoanalytic literature largely ignored the subject of groups.

The first group therapists, Schilder (1940) and Wender (1945), acknowledged Freud's formulations. Except for Redl, however, no one at that time questioned these theories or explored their relevance to work with therapy groups. In the scanty references to analytic group psychology, the implicit view of group emotionality as entailing each group member's regression to earlier stages of object ties, i.e., to identifications, prevailed. Even though when Freud discussed mob phenomena he referred to behavior akin to *ego regression* (reversion to earlier modes of ego functioning) as well as to *topographical regression* (shifts from System *Conscious* to System *Unconscious*), these distinctions were not mentioned in the subsequent literature. This failure was in keeping with the loose usage of terminology which characterized all early psychoanalytic writings. Similarly ignored but for different reasons, were Freud's speculations about *phylogenetic regression*, in which he viewed each group member's psyche as containing the archaic heritage of the drama of the "primal horde." In line with this now generally discarded speculation, he considered group psychology as being in a sense older as well as genetically more primitive than individual psychology.

As I noted in another context (1960), all of these Freudian postulates of group psychology were largely neglected in the American group therapy literature until the late fifties. Furthermore, with the latter steeped in the precepts of individual psychopathology and of the therapeutic process, the concept of regression was rarely employed explicitly, except with reference to multiple transference manifestations.

The writings of some English group therapists, such as Ezriel (chap. 4, this volume), Bion (chap 3, this volume), and Foulkes (chap. 7, this volume), challenged this state of affairs. Bion, for instance, posited regressive phenomena in therapy groups, which he viewed as being not only rooted in the dynamics of group life but also as considerably more "primitive" than those assumed by Freud's (1921) group theories. A proponent of Melanie Klein's (1948) ideas regarding the influence on personality of powerful fantasies from the infant's earliest months (prior to the onset of the classic Freudian neurosis), Bion suggested two analogous "depth" levels for therapy groups: Freud's level of "neurotic" family patterns with their associated conflicts, as well as his (Bion's) level of more primitive "paranoid-schizoid" and "depressive" anxieties.

In Bion's view, psychological group formation in a therapy group reactivates regressive levels of even greater depth than individual analysis. Thus, hand in hand with a work and reality orientation go patterns of functioning closely akin to primary process. Magical wish-fulfillment, splitting, projection mechanisms, persecutory anxieties, and condensation are part of this picture. The content of the fantasies pertains to perceptions of the leader as a positive, sustaining, and gratifying parent in Bion's Dependent Basic Assumption. He becomes a threatening parental image in what Bion terms the Fight-Flight Basic Assumption; and a Messianic symbol of the unborn genius in the sexually tinged Pairing Basic Assumption. The fantasied perceptions of the group entity encompass notions of the mother's breast and, at times, even contents of her body. What is noteworthy, too, in Bion's theory, relates to his preference for such concepts as "projective" or "introjective" identifications over the concept of transference. In projective identification, for instance, there is a splitting off of parts of the self with a projection of them into another person. These defensive mechanisms are brought into play in response to the marked anxiety engendered by intrapsychic conflicts with what Kleinians term internal objects and part objects, and by the threat of losing one's personal identity in the group.

One of the shortcomings of Bion's theory relates to his view of regression as primarily pathological and irrational. It fails to take into account modern ego psychology as discussed later in this paper. It is as though Bion refuses to give recognition to ego functions as intervening between impulse and actual behavior. Furthermore, he pays no attention to the individual differences in susceptibility to the regressive pull of the group. In his scheme, leader and group member alike are often powerless against the onslaught of unconscious stimuli which propel them into acting out of impulsivity. Rationality and control are a function he ascribes to the Work Group, a *group* rather than an *individual* manifestation.

Despite their limitations, however, Bion's theories have undoubtedly served to focus the attention of group practitioners and theoreticians on the concept of regression and on the broader issues of emotionality and of "depth" manifestations in group behavior.

Some Current Views of Regression in Individual Psychoanalysis

The concept of regression, while basic to general psychoanalytic theory, has been used in a variety of ways, frequently devoid of clear definition. Reference has already been made to four different kinds of regression: (1) *topographical regression,* wherein there is a shift of an individual's mental functioning from the System *Conscious* to *Unconscious*; (2) *drive or* instinctual regression, which is linked to the libido theory and involves a reversion to partial drives characteristic of earlier developmental stages; (3) *ego or genetic regression,* referring to the emergence of earlier, usually infantile, modes of functioning; (4) *phylo-*

genetic regression, connoting a reactivation of assumed archaic and innate memories common to mankind. As ego
psychological theory, with its emphasis on autonomous,
nonconflictual, and adaptive aspects of functioning gained
in popularity, the ideas of regression changed accordingly.
Not only did regression lose its earlier predominantly pathological taint, but, in addition, a new kind of "regression
in the service of the ego" (Kris, 1952) was postulated, with
the promotion of healthy adaptation as its primary aim
(Schafer, 1958). Regression has furthermore been increasingly viewed as a broad universal process characteristic of
personality functioning. Closely linked to general *genetic*
(when, why, and how) and *dynamic* (here and now) considerations, as well as to structural theory (id, ego, superego),
its nature and significance at any one time call for a simultaneous assessment of all these elements. As Rapaport
(1959) put it, "Psychoanalysis as a genetic psychology deals
with the genetic roots of behaviors, with the degree of
autonomy behaviors attain, and with the genetic roots of
the subject's relation to the reality conditions which cod-
etermine the appearance of a behavior at a given point in
a person's life" (pp. 45-46).

There is now increasing recognition that any or all of
the three structures of the psyche—id, ego, and superego—may contain primary-process phenomena. Thus,
regression from secondary-process functioning involving
control, delay, or modification in drive discharge, to primary-process functioning with its push for immediate
drive (libido, aggression) gratification, no longer necessarily connotes pathology. The most recent definition of
regression suggested by Arlow and Brenner (1964) is general enough to subsume the different major earlier meanings ascribed to this term: " . . . *re-emergence* of modes of
mental functioning which were characteristic of the psychic
activity of the individual during earlier periods of development" (p. 71).

If we were to accept this definition of regression for purposes of this discussion, we would have to assume that "modes of mental functioning" are meant to include ways of ego functioning as well as psychic content. Furthermore, we would conclude that the motivations for any regression can be varied, ranging from serving as a defense against intolerable threat from within the psyche (i.e., guilt) or fears of external objects to opening gateways for creative expression or freer communications with others. As Kris (1952) noted, control of regression is a part of the broader organizing function of the ego. Whether regression is pathological in a given instance depends less on its depth than on " . . . its persistent, irrevocable nature, the degree of conflict which it generates, and its effect on adaptation" (Arlow and Brenner, 1964, p. 74). Ego strength relates in part to the ego's ability to resist pathological regression at points of stress, whether the stress is due to intrapsychic conflict or to external pressure.

Before returning to the more complex issue of group behavior, it should be noted that I utilize the concept of regression in this paper as referring to an individual personality's mode of functioning. It can be asked: Since small groups and especially therapy groups abound in instances of regressive verbalizations or *acting out* of similar and perhaps even identical covert conflicts or fantasies on the part of many, if not all, members, are we not then dealing with a group regression? Or, can a mob scene or an incident of group hysteria be otherwise depicted? My answer would be that, despite the frequent use of such terminology, this is highly misleading. For, in the strictest sense, psychological processes such as regression or identification, or even fantasying or hating, operate in individuals only. Group members can maintain shared or common fantasies; they can even act in unison in response to group occurrences, such as the entry of a new member or the absence of the leader. But this need not mean that the group as a group now has a certain fantasy or acts in a certain manner. This view, that shared fantasies are far from being the same in each individual, has found some support in the few instances in which training or therapy groups have been subjected to systematic observation. A group can possess observable characteristics, can be perceived and reacted to as a whole, but this makes it a social and psychological reality, not a physical reality; it does not indicate a "group mind."

FORCES FAVORING REGRESSION IN GROUPS

When Freud (1921) ascribed to group formation "the character of a regression," he was impressed by the degree to which the individual group member's internalized controls, including his superego, were subject to relaxation and change. In considering the elements that facilitate regressive manifestations in a therapy group, an entity unknown to Freud, we would today pay major attention to such factors as the degree of structure evolving both from the style of leadership (directive versus nondirective) and from the broader group situation (permissiveness, degree of role definition, task orientation), for there is now general agreement regarding the inevitable anxieties due to "presence and contact" (Semrad et al., 1963) that characterize group formation in all face-to-face groups. With a membership weighted by personal pathology, there is the added lowered tolerance for situational frustrations, for "object anxiety," as well as for instinctual pressures from within. E. Fried (1965) suggested in this connection that the heightened climate of psychological stimulation enhances the regressive pull in therapy groups. Suggestibility and emotional contagion are undoubtedly a part of this picture. It would perhaps be no exaggeration to state that the therapeutic value, if not the very existence, of a group is predicated on maintaining an optimum regressive level. The same has often been said regarding the individual psychoanalytic situation.

The Role of Regression in Some Models of Group Formation: The Dependency Phase

Following Freud, and Redl (chap. 2, this volume), a number of writers have delineated the way emotional group processes evolve in analytic therapy groups with emphasis on the members' feelings toward the leader, toward the other group members, and toward the group entity. Some of these models center around hypothesized phases of development for the group, from its inception to its conclusion.[1]

My concern here will be limited to the question of how regression is handled in these models, with particular focus on the initial phase where, theoretically at least, in a developmental scheme, regression is at its height. I have already referred to Bion (1959) whose major criticism of the Freudian model of group formation was that the latter was not only incomplete but, above all, not "deep" enough. It might be of interest here to juxtapose Bion's view of the Dependency Basic Assumption with two parallel theoretical views of group formation. This is especially appropriate because almost all such models, beginning with Freud's, postulate an initial dependency phase: one connoting a regression of the group members to a dependent state in relation to a leader, followed by varied emotional manifestations in regard to the other group members and to the emerging group entity.

---

[1] Similar theories have been advanced with respect to training groups which lie outside the scope of this paper. Kaplan (1967) has recently compared the salient emotional issues in therapy and training groups. See also Horwitz (1964) and Frank (1964).

As already noted, in Bion's Dependency Basic Assumption, hand in hand with the group's conscious work and task orientation is a shared unconscious group fantasy which springs into being spontaneously. This fantasy evolves around a leader, a magical superior being who is there to feed, support, and protect. As part of the competition for the exclusive attention of this nurturing object, feelings of guilt for "being greedy in demanding more than one's fair turn in parental care" come to the fore. This fantasied relationship is an identification and could focus on the group therapist (the Work-Group leader) or on a symbolic idea, such as the group "bible." The Dependency phase also entails a defensive idealization of the group's history, which is accordingly utilized as a means of countering stimuli to individual growth and development. Bion does not allow here for relationships among the group members; the regressive tie to the leader is paramount. Except for stressing its greater "depth" as compared to the Freudian neurotic type of regression, Bion is not explicit on this point. One could assume, however, that the reactivated conflicts in this phase stem from the first six months of the infant's life, which in Melanie Klein's (1948) system are characterized by pregenital strivings and anxieties pertaining to part-object relationships. As noted earlier, Bion's fantasied group "culture" represents a defensive reaction against these infantile conflicts, symbolized, as they frequently are, by the group as a whole.

Foulkes considers his orientation closer to Bion's than to the American group therapists'. Nevertheless, he gives far greater weight to the "here and now" interpersonal relationships and goals in therapy groups than does Bion, enumerating four depth levels for the group interactions: (1) the *current level,* which refers to reality perceptions of the leader and of the group; (2) the *transference level,* wherein the group represents a symbolic family with the leader as parent; (3) the *level of bodily and mental images,* which contains aspects analogous to Bion's Basic Assumptions, including primitive "inner" object relations and projective identifications; (4) a *primordial level* containing elements of the collective unconscious (see chap. 7, this volume).

As for the earliest phase in group formation, which is my major concern here, Foulkes stresses its "leader-centered" character. There is a tendency at first to impute magical qualities to the therapist. In this infantile fantasy, he " . . . is put in the position of the *primordial leader image;* he is omniscient and omnipotent. . . ." In this phase, confessions, discussions of symptoms, and expressions of high hopes are intermingled. Again, not unlike Bion's Basic Assumptions, "deep and primitive" group fantasies, symbols, and mental mechanisms emerge without apparent causality. The therapist encourages greater activity in the direction of self-awareness and independence in his effort to move the group toward maturation and away from the earlier dependence on irrational authority. As for the depth of the regressive phenomena, while Foulkes does refer to the occasional reactivation of Kleinian pregenital conflicts, his preponderant preoccupation is with group psychotherapy as a transference situation in which true transference neuroses can be elicited, with the patients being encouraged to move toward society and the community.

A more recent formulation of a comprehensive group developmental model for adult therapy groups has been offered by Kaplan and Roman (1963). Their theoretical scheme, which includes a specific structure, theme, and interaction pattern, has markedly greater clarity than Bion's or Foulkes's discussions. According to Kaplan and Roman, at the group's beginning, the therapist constitutes the object of each group member's attention, and, on one plane, the members behave toward him in the traditional pattern of the patient to the doctor. The common covert concern, in contrast, is one of dependency on a magical leader. This general perception of the leader (a demigod in a shared mythology) fosters group formation to the point that the patients interact "as part of the group as a unit." Thus, an earlier desire for satisfaction of personal needs from the leader becomes reformulated in group terms. It is as if the magical therapist ". . . were withholding something precious which could magically cure them." The overall tone is one of enthusiasm, almost adoration, with no hostility or disappointment coming to the fore. These developments are followed by beginning signs of attention to other group members.

Kaplan and Roman do not deal with the concept of regression in detail. Instead, they refer in general to the psychological group formation as a defensive regression wherein anxieties related to the need for intimate contact in a new situation promote primitive identifications, fantasied perceptions, and patterns of magical thinking. Except for parenthetical references to child-parent manifestations as part of the *dependency* theme and of adolescent concerns during this middle phase, they do not touch on the issue of depth or specific fixation points in the regression. Their overall observation that ". . . individual transference reactions could be experienced and verbalized" only after some maturation had occurred, as expressed by a partial dissolution of the psychological group (the 86th session in their illustration), is especially noteworthy. It stands in close agreement with several descriptions of developmental phases for training groups (Bennis and Shepard, 1956).

For purposes of this discussion, the similarity in the way the theoretical models of Bion, Foulkes, and Kaplan and Roman portray the covert emotionality in the initial regressive phase in the therapy group is striking. All three emphasize the reactivation of early identification processes wherein group members in a shared fantasy appear to seek nurture and support from a magical parent-leader. In this dependency constellation, sexual or aggressive drive expression appears to be almost nonexistent, which is true as well for any concern with other group members. There are also, however, some differences in the way group formative processes are viewed by these authors. For instance, Bion, as well as Kaplan and Roman, place considerable emphasis on the marked degree of group cohesion, which is exemplified by the idealization of the group entity. This cohesion appears to serve defensive functions, standing in opposition to individual and group maturation. Foulkes, in contrast, does not deal with these issues in relation to the early phase in group formation.

As noted, in each of the theoretical models described, regressive manifestations constitute a basic element. However, these are either not discussed explicitly or, if so, as with Bion, they are portrayed in a manner markedly removed from the traditional psychoanalytic formulations.

Perception of the Leader in Group Formation

In addition to the three models depicted above, most of the other theories that deal with the formation of a psychological group also evolve around the shared perception of a leader or, less frequently, of a common idea or characteristic. Since these perceptions inevitably involve regression, it would be useful to list a few, albeit the writers presented them in a somewhat fragmentary manner.

To begin with, there is Redl's (chap. 2, this volume) formulation which both encompasses the theory advanced by Freud and extends it considerably. Using the broader term Central Person instead of leader, he lists three different kinds of relationships with the central person, each of which he deems capable of evoking group formation: (1) the central person as an object of identification on the basis of the group member's ego-ideal incorporation (as in Freud's model) or as a result of fear of the central person as an aggressor; (2) the central person as an object of the group member's libidinal or aggressive drives; (3) the central person as an object for the relief of similar inner conflicts.

While Freud and Redl referred to the perceptions of the leader as a father person, Money-Kyrle (1950) was the first to introduce the perceptions of a mother image in group formation. Extending the concept of a "good" and "bad" parent representation in a child's unconscious, he postulated three kinds of symbols: (1) the "good parents" (particularly the mother) representing the norms and ideals of the group; (2) the "bad parents" in the role of persecutors against whom the group values have to be defended; and (3) the "good parents," especially the father, who in his role as the mother's defender reappears as the group leader. Subsequently, Schindler (1951) advanced the view that transferences in every therapy group evolve on the pattern of a family. In this pattern, the therapist represents the father, the group members the siblings, while the group as a whole comes to represent the mother. In trying to conceptualize the group entity further, Schindler (1952) also refers to group formation as the development of a "group personality." He thought that this "common denominator" of the individual group member's characteristics could be divided into a group id, ego, and superego. The group id pertains to common needs such as security or pleasure. The superego refers to perceptions of the father-leader and mother-group, while the ego "registers" the id and superego functions and judges whether or not they serve the group's purposes.

Schindler (1966) followed Money-Kyrle in stressing the regressive unconscious perception of the group entity as a mother. Spanjaard (1959) observed that the regression in a therapy group composed of neurotic adults was less deep than that which he had noted in his practice of individual psychoanalysis. He thought that the group members perceived the leader both as a mother figure from the child's phallic-narcissistic phase and in terms of a leader image from adolescence.

In a paper on group identification (chap. 8, this volume), I suggested an outline for conceptualizing the individual group member's perceptions and attitudes toward the group as a whole. Viewed as an identification in the sense of an endopsychic process calling for a degree of individual involvement with a perceived object or its symbolic representation, it was distinct from transference. Such an identification with the group entity was believed to entail two related elements: (1) the ascribing to the group of an emotional meaning, as a conscious instrument of need satisfaction or, on the unconscious level, as the state of unconflicted well-being represented in the exclusive union with the preoedipal mother; and (2) the giving up of an element of "self" to the group.

Durkin (1964) has also advanced the idea of the group entity being perceived by patients in group formation as a preoedipal mother. Her formulation, however, differs from my hypothesis regarding the initial view of the nurturing, supportive mother-group. It also differs from the way the *dependency phase* was depicted in the three theoretical models described above. According to Durkin, the suggestibility and submission of the individual, noted by Freud, when groups come into being is due to a regressive fear reaction. She postulated two separate steps as transference manifestations: (1) the idea of a group, i.e., a large totality of unknown power, conjures up the harsh, preoedipal mother image, reactivating the individual's narcissistic fear of her, and (2) the individual perceives the group accordingly in distorted fashion and behaves toward it in a way that resembles his mode of reacting to his mother but in "modern dress." While a member is thus afraid of the group as a whole, the therapist in turn is perceived "in the image of the good all-giving omnipotent mother."

Because Durkin's ideas are clear and explicit, they can be readily subjected to validation by comparing them with the clinical findings of other group therapists and, above all, by exposing the group therapy process to independent observation.[2] On another plane, however, Durkin's theoretical position, in my opinion, makes for possible misunderstanding and confusion. She fails to distinguish between Freud's incomplete discussion in 1921 of *group formative regression* based on identifications in large groups, and *therapeutic regression* centered on transference in today's therapy groups. She went so far as to criticize Freud's failure to be aware that, in a *therapy group*, "the individual is not inactive and does not just take over the leader in place of his own ego ideal: a complicated transference is set up through which this occurs" (1964, p. 83). Had she kept in mind the historical factor, or had she addressed herself to Redl's contributions, which both include and extend Freud's formulations on group psychology in the light of more current psychoanalytic and group theory, her criticism might have been avoided. The tendency to lump together latent group formative processes, individual personalities in interaction, and transference manifestations is also apparent in Schindler's (1952) discussion.

---

[2] A promising method for such observations has been devised by Mann (1966) for training groups.

Some Thoughts for the Future

It is my hope that a systematic consideration of the concept of regression as attempted here will help further the much needed conceptual integration between intrapsychic, interpersonal, and group level phenomena in group psychotherapy.

The most recent psychoanalytic definition of this concept in ego psychological terms as the re-emergence of earlier modes of individual functioning could be readily adopted for theoretical and clinical purposes in group therapy. In viewing regression in this light, we must remember, as Bellak (1961) incisively illustrated, that the regressive process comprises two different, yet related, aspects: (1) the temporal regression of ego functions to modes that were characteristic in childhood, and (2) a topographical regression from primarily conscious to preconscious and unconscious levels of functioning, including the reactivation of primitive libidinal zones.

While not treated systematically, both of these aspects are included in the three models of group formation I have described. The *dependency phase* comprises such infantile patterns of ego functioning as magical thinking, poor reality perception, or an anaclitic relationship to the object. In addition, in each model there is an unmistakable air of primary process coupled with oral-libidinal features.

There is no agreement in the literature regarding the exact causes for the regression induced in group formation. While Bion and Ezriel appear to hold intrapsychic anxieties responsible, American writers such as Semrad et al. (1963) or Whitaker and Lieberman (1964) stress the influence of interpersonal tensions. Following a similar observation of Redl's, Arsenian et al. (1962, p. 432) believe that "regression from object choice to identification comes about because of the unavoidable frustration of the desire for exclusive union or fusion with the central figure."

Fenichel's assertion, quoted earlier, that regression generally "happens to the ego" and "seems to be set in motion by the instincts" exemplifies a historical tendency to ascribe pathology to this term. A new orientation is in order. In line with current concepts, including that of "regression in the service of the ego," preconscious and unconscious psychic contents as well as earlier modes of functioning can be precipitated in individuals for adaptive and growth-promoting purposes, as I discussed recently in relation to empathy in group psychotherapy (1966). Since there is general agreement that regressive elements are at work in all group formation, not only in therapy groups, it would follow that all group members are characterized by personal pathology unless we allow for non-pathological regression. To avoid such confusion, it is almost imperative to keep in mind the fact that the regression that accompanies group formation must be differentiated insofar as possible from the therapeutic regression that characterizes all analytic psychotherapy. Thus, all the major psychoanalytic hypotheses of group formation stress the preponderance of identification processes over transference manifestations in this initial phase. In line with the view of identification as a more primitive kind of involvement than object relationships, the group member is believed to perceive other people in the group in an undifferentiated way as representations of images rather than as complete objects. Furthermore, as part of this narcissistic orientation, objects are sought out primarily as instruments for the purpose of relieving inner tension. Insofar as transference reactions involve the unconscious reliving of powerful feelings of love and hate akin to more advanced stages of object relationships, these tend to emerge somewhat later, *after* group formation has taken hold.

In addition to analytic group psychotherapy's transference and resistance manifestations, a number of writers, including Foulkes and Anthony (1957) and Whitaker and Lieberman (1964), also assume that a kind of free association occurs in them. They believe not only that the manifest content contains derivatives of the unconscious meanings, but that diverse individual comments tend to cluster around shared group themes which encompass overt as well as latent levels.

Regarding the much-debated issue of which is "deeper," individual or group analytic therapy, a perusal of the wide range of regressive behavioral manifestations encountered in groups suggests that perhaps this is really not the issue at all. Whether or not one would agree with Bion's extreme view that every group phenomenon *always* reflects the deepest layers of unconscious conflicts, the fact remains that clinicians have reported free-associative productions and primary-process manifestations such as dreams from group members at least equal in "depth" to those encountered in individual psychoanalysis. Nevertheless, any comparison of the two treatment modalities, of individual and group analytic therapy, would have to address itself to a broader question: Does the totality of the therapeutic group experience, even if conducted along the classical Freudian line of the Fundamental Rule, and the Mirror Image, permit the kind of detailed and continuous *working through in depth* which is called for when structural personality reorganization is the aim? The claim that analytic group psychotherapy entails phenomena akin to free association, that there can be "depth" interpretations with reliving of repressed conflicts together with analysis of transference and of resistance, still does not place it on the same plane as classical individual analysis. Unless presented with compelling evidence to the contrary, I agree with those who believe that the copresence of a number of patients in a reality-geared experience makes the group therapy process, and especially the nature of the therapeutic regression, basically different. For, theoretically at least, the crucial issue in utilizing *therapeutic regression* in psychoanalytic treatment is not whether phenomena of the greatest "depth" can be elicited, but, rather, the degree to which the observing, synthesizing, and controlling functions of the ego can be helped over layers of resistance to accept and to master them. This is a tedious, and with some patients who have disturbances in using free association, an almost impossible task (Bellak, 1961). The observation of Spanjaard (1959), who is an individual and group analyst, is highly relevant: that though he could elicit a transference neurosis toward himself by maintaining the traditional analytic stance of detachment, the presence of others and, above all, his additional role as a source of suggestion and identification made it impossible for him to reach "the root problems of the personality and its structure." Group therapy's unique value for patients who either cannot utilize a dyadic, insight-geared treatment mode or who, in addition to insight, require the added dimension of a group's corrective emotional experience need not be repeated here.

I have already referred to the theoretical dilemma created by the well-known fact that as part of the regressive group climate, shared fantasies, similar emotional expressions and behavioral manifestations abound. This has led some group therapists to speak in terms of a group regression (Bion, 1959), others in terms of a "group personality" or "group ego." Pending data from careful independent observations of such group manifestations, I consider it sounder and less confusing to view a regressive group manifestation as the behavior of individuals. The fact that most, and perhaps on occasion all, group members appear to the clinician to share a fantasy or display an emotion as a result of identification processes does not, in the strictest sense of the word, make it a group manifestation. It is useful to remember here, in addition, that from a scientific standpoint, psychoanalytic concepts such as regression pertain to an inferred process which is utilized to explain certain kinds of behavior, not to an observable manifestation.

The three theoretical models of group formation which I have used for purposes of illustration allow for different depth levels in the group process. The phenomena described by these authors, as well as by others, could readily be subsumed under the two broader group process levels, a *contemporaneous-dynamic* and a *genetic-regressive,* which I have described elsewhere (1960). In this categorization, the *contemporaneous-dynamic* level pertains to "the more readily observed momentary expressions of conscious needs and ego-adaptive patterns, the group roles, the network of attractions and repulsions, as well as the group structure. The behavior here is primarily reactive to realistic group situational factors bringing into play the more external aspects of personality" (p. 356). The *genetic-regressive* level, in contrast, refers to unconscious and preconscious motivations, to defensive patterns and conflicts, to phenomena such as transference, countertransference, resistance, identification, and projection. The *genetic-regressive* type of phenomena is more apt to emerge in situations in which the personality restraints (ego defenses) have been loosened (regression), with consequent freer expression of repressed emotionality.

Faced with the challenge of differentiating among the plethora of therapeutic group approaches in mental health facilities, ranging from reality-geared and task-oriented groups to uncovering, analytic groups, I recently suggested a classification scheme (1968b) in which the degree of regression promoted consciously by the therapist constitutes a major criterion for differentiation. The following are the five broad categories that encompass the major group influence attempts depicted in the literature: (1) Activity-Catharsis-Mastery Focus, (2) Cognitive-Informational Focus, (3) Interpersonal-Socialization Focus, (4) Relationship-Experiential Focus, and (5) Uncovering-Introspective Focus.

It is my hope that, if nothing else, this discussion demonstrates the crucial nature of the concept of regression in any attempt to evolve an integrated theoretical framework for group psychology, one which would take into account the complex interaction of individual personalities and of group dynamic manifestations on different depth levels. Only through further systematic considerations of regression and of other concepts in this new field–so rich in creative hypotheses, yet beset by loose and often confusing use of terms–can high-level clinical practice and research flourish.

10

GROUP PSYCHOLOGY AND THE STRUCTURAL THEORY

A REVISED PSYCHOANALYTIC MODEL OF GROUP PSYCHOLOGY

STEPHEN M. SARAVAY

The psychoanalytic formulations contained in "Group Psychology and the Analysis of the Ego" (Freud, 1921) have exerted a powerful influence on all subsequent theoretical investigations into group behavior. Written more than 50 years ago, Freud's paper has remained the most effective bridge between individual and group psychology. It provided new insights into the nature of identifications, and further defined the ego ideal and superego through an examination of their function in groups.

Despite the durability of Freud's original formulations, the need has grown for revision and updating with newer structural concepts. In their current form, the original formulations cannot account for two recognized clinical features of small unstructured therapy groups: the initial regression of the members to an oral phase of organization

Reprinted from the *Journal of the American Psychoanalytic Association,* 23:69-89 (1975), with the persmission of the publisher, the author, and the Editor.

during group formation, and the gradual reversal of this regression during the group's subsequent development (Scheidlinger, 1968a).

Formation of a therapy group is usually accompanied by evidence of regression in all the members. This regression is partial and reversible and affects the members in varying degrees depending upon their personality structure. Subsequently, there is a gradual reversal of this initial regression; this takes place in a series of maturational phases resembling the stages of infant development (Powles, 1959; Kaplan and Roman, 1963). Proceeding from the oral phase reached in the regression during group formation, the group traverses the intervening phases to achieve the oedipal configuration described by Freud.

I shall begin with a review of descriptions of regression during group formation and the attempts to construct a workable theoretical explanation of this phenomenon. Next, Freud's account of regression in crowds will be examined. We shall see how Freud's use of topographic and narcissistic concepts to explain regression in crowds led to shortcomings in his explanation of regression in groups. From these considerations, a model of group psychology based upon the structural theory will be developed, and its advantages demonstrated.

Although it has been established that regression regularly occurs during the initial phases of small therapy groups, neither its cause nor the reason for its distinctly oral quality has been explained (Scheidlinger, chap. 9, this volume; 1968a). The oral derivatives mobilized during the regression are evident in the members' object relations with each other, in the unconscious wishes collectively directed by the group members toward the leader, and in the associated affects, ego functions, and defenses that determine the functioning of the group as a whole. Scheidlinger (chap. 9, this volume) has described the ego mechanisms, conflicts, and dynamics stimulated during this initial phase of group formation as derivatives of the first half-year of infancy.

The regression is evident in the functioning and behavior of the group as a whole. As a unit, the group functions at a level far below the average capacity of its members. The members deny the realities of their own capabilities in favor of the passive dependent wish to be helped by the leader (Appelbaum, 1963). Affects of helplessness, a growing despair of achieving satisfaction in the group, depression, defenses of passivity and withdrawal out of proportion to the real situation are provoked by the leader's frustration of the group's dependent wishes. The resultant disorganization and ineffectiveness, so profound at the beginning, stands in stark contrast to the sophistication, energy, and creativity evident in the later stages (Semrad et al., 1963; Scheidlinger, chap. 9, this volume).

Initially, members relate to each other as objects existing primarily for the relief of inner tension. Identifications made with other members are primitive and undifferentiated. Superficial similarities form the basis for a noncritical fusion (Sugar, 1971) prior to the development of a real personal relationship (Day, 1967). These primitive part-object identifications contrast sharply with the more advanced level of object relations and mechanisms of identification evident later in the life of the group (Scheidlinger, chap. 9, this volume).

Associated with the regression in object relations is a regression in the expression of the drives, as shown by the aim and libidinal zone represented: oral wishes assume predominance. In this dependent constellation, distinct heterosexual or aggressive drive expression between members is minimal, as is true investment in or personal concern with other members (Scheidlinger, chap. 9, this volume).

The establishment of a common unconscious identification based upon the wish for exclusive union with the leader serves to unite the members of the new group. Intragroup competition for the leader's favor is exchanged for membership in the group where, together, the members seek to merge with the leader for relief of tension (Durkin, 1964; Scheidlinger, chap. 9, this volume). Together, the members of the group as a whole wish to be nourished and cared for by the leader, to draw him into the body of the group and merge with him.

Fulfillment of this oral wish would be symbolized by the group's achieving union with the nourishing mother-leader. According to Anthony (1967) and Scheidlinger (chap. 9, this volume), this is precisely what transpires symbolically in the early phases. The group itself comes to represent the breast and body of the mother. Money-Kyrle (1950) and Schindler (1966) noted this symbolization but explained it differently. The unconscious representation of the group as the body or breast of the mother, as the symbolic expression of the members' collective wish to merge with the leader-mother, is a fundamental feature of the initial regression to an oral phase of group organization. The fantasied gratification of the wish for union with the leader produces euphoria and contentment (chap. 9, this volume); its frustration produces depression and withdrawal.

According to Durkin (1964), the organization of a group around an oral paradigm during its early phases contradicts Freud's historic formulation of an oedipal organization. Day (1967) summarized the problem as follows: "Traditionally, we have looked on the development of the group as following Freud's model of the group of brothers who wanted to be cared for by father and yet wanted to overwhelm and replace him. But these same phenomena can be viewed in another and more primitive way . . . . the intense fusion bear[s] witness to earlier determinants . . . having to do with the earliest relationship to the mother" (p. 445).

We shall see that Freud's theory of group organization postulated a regression to an ego identification among the members out of fear of the leader seen as the oedipal father, and was not compatible with the leader cast in the role of the mother. Money-Kyrle (1950), Spaanjard (1959), Schindler (1966), and others who describe the leader in the additional role as the representation of the mother did not address themselves to this contradiction with Freud's formulation. The oral quality of the regression that appears during small group formation is claimed to occur to a limited extent in all groups (Kaplan and Roman, 1963), but is most obvious in small unstructured groups designed to highlight the effects of unconscious factors on group processes.

Greenacre (1972) has come to an identical conclusion regarding regression in crowds (which correspond to a primitive stage of large group formation): " . . . the individual in a crowd uses the multiple contacts with those around him as a collective mother of many faces. . . " (p. 144). Whether the group is assembled for entertainment or for political or religious purposes, Greenacre believes a regression to "pregenital activity" is induced. A regression in object relations to mechanisms characteristic of the oral stage is evident in the reawakening of imitative "mirroring" as a primitive form of identificatory attachment. As in the early phases of a small group, the individual, when part of a crowd, functions at a level much below his capacity, with the "partial replacement of secondary process by primary process thinking" (p. 138).

Like other investigators, Greenacre recognized problems in reconciling Freud's original formulations based upon an oedipal psychology with recent clinical observations: "He discussed the relations of the leader to the individual members of a large group, essentially in terms of the libido theory, with the emphasis on the oedipal relationship involved. . . . ego psychology . . . had not yet been enunciated. . . . footnotes, however, make suggestions regarding the processes going on in individual members of large groups in terms of early identifications essentially belonging to the period of separation and individuation, but then referred to simply as characteristic of the oral phase" (p. 154).

Greenacre, Scheidlinger (1952, chap. 9, this volume) and Kaplan (1967) all emphasized the inability of existing psychoanalytic theories of group psychology to account for pregenital regression in crowds and groups. They believe the confusion over definition of terms and concepts produced by the separate evolution of different theoretical frames of reference, while not unique to the field of group psychology, has contributed to its current difficulties. In explaining regression, Freud used topographic, narcissistic, and structural frames of reference, which we will show to be incompatible with each other in important areas. Instead of identifying and resolving these problems, most investigators of group psychology have tended to apply Freud's formulations in their original state and have avoided any attempt at a fundamental reformulation.

Although Redl (chap. 2, this volume) proposed a revision of Freud's definition of the leader, few of the early small-group theorists in England did more than pay their passing respects to Freud's discussion of regression in groups (Scheidlinger, 1952; Durkin, 1964). In the late nineteen-forties, Bion (1959) re-examined the problem. According to Scheidlinger (chap. 9, this volume), his approach was influenced by the early belief that regression was pathological and was induced by fear of identity loss in the new group. Using a Kleinian frame of reference, he believed that group regression was a defensive reaction to psychotic anxiety caused by conflict between internal objects and part objects.

In the American group-therapy literature, Freud's formulations were acknowledged more out of respect than understanding until a resurgence of curiosity in the nineteen-fifties (Scheidlinger, 1952). In contrast to Bion's and Ezriel's (chap. 4, this volume) psychodynamic explanation of group organization using an intrapsychic frame of reference, Whitaker and Lieberman (1964) and Semrad et al. (1963) stressed the effect of interpersonal tensions in producing group regression. Arsenian et al. (1962) believed that "The regression from object choice to identification comes about because of unavoidable frustration of the desire for exclusive union or fusion with the central figure" (p. 432). In a similar vein Durkin (1964) espoused a theory using concepts of preoedipal psychology, that anxiety provoked by the leader or by the group itself—both of which initially may represent the preoedipal mother—was sufficient explanation for the regression observed during group formation. According to Scheidlinger (chap. 9, this volume) there was a prevailing belief among investigators that it could be accounted for by the existing psychoanalytic theories of transference. They likened group regression to the concept of transference neurosis. It was suggested that the cumulative effect of multiple transference reactions more quickly induced transference regression in a group than in the one-to-one situation of psychoanalysis. Arguing against this position and for a structural approach, Kaplan (1967) stated, "These . . . represent a special type of regression in object relationships which involve ego structures and functions that differentiate it from the instinctual, object-directed regression usually implied in transference relationships" (p. 497).

Both Kaplan (1967) and Scheidlinger (chap. 9, this volume) agreed that the neglect of structural concepts in group psychological theories was one manifestation of the cultural lag in psychoanalytic theory described by Arlow and Brenner (1964). They suggested that the study of regression in groups conforms to Arlow and Brenner's definition of the phenomenon: " . . . the *re-emergence* of modes of mental functioning which were characteristic of the psychic activity of the individual during earlier periods of development" (p. 71). Kaplan (1967) cited the need to explain the impact of group formative processes upon the psychic systems as well as upon the specific ego functions of object relations. He noticed an unexplained relationship between the regressive loosening of ego defenses and superego controls and the externalization of previously internalized self- and object representations. Scheidlinger (chap. 9, this volume) emphasized the effect of regression upon the mechanisms of ego functioning, the shift from secondary to primary process, and the predominant erogenous zone chosen for drive expression. Both believed that a definitive explanation of regression during group formation required the construction of a psychoanalytic model of group psychology based upon the structural theory.

Freud began his inquiry into group psychology with a study of the crowd. From earlier descriptions by McDougall (1920) and LeBon (1920), he selected two fundamental features of the crowd's effect upon the individual: regression and the merging of the individual's identity with that of the crowd. Regression in the crowd is evidenced by the weakening of rational influence and the proclivity for violent emotion. Deliberation gives way to impulsiveness; suggestibility and imitation determine decisions at the expense of moral and rational considerations. Rather than resembling the usual behavior of its participants, the crowd acts like an unruly child. Freud noted that the crowd was governed " . . . almost exclusively by the unconscious . . ." (1921, p. 177) having lost its "critical faculty" (p. 78).

The second essential feature of the crowd, the merging together of its members, Freud attributed to the heightened state of the emotions. The pleasure derived by the release of the passions was accomplished through the merging together in a group with the loss of the sense of individual separateness.

In addition to the regression and the individual's merging with the crowd, emotions may sweep through a crowd by contagion. The individual's suggestibility increases. He is more liable to imitate spontaneously the mass emotions that reverberate within him. It was recognized that the greater the number of people sharing a common emotional state the more powerful would be the crowd's effect upon a given member. The fewer the established rules of behavior of internal organization, the more profound the potential for regression.

These, then, were the properties of crowds that Freud attempted to explain with the theories available to him in 1921. We shall now examine how he used his topographic theory to explain the regression, and resorted to his then newly enunciated concepts of narcissism to explain the individual's merging with the crowd.

LeBon's explanation of the regression in crowds was quite compatible with Freud's topographic theory of the mind. LeBon had said that in the crowd the unconscious increases its influence over the conscious critical faculties. He offered the following intriguing explanation: In a crowd the influence of acquired heterogeneous characteristics is, by virtue of the dissimilarity among the members, canceled out, while the influence of what is held in common is enhanced. In the heterogeneous crowd, the homogeneous unconscious foundations of the mind, the affects, the instinctual inheritance common to all members of a crowd are intensified and therefore exert a greater influence. In other words, by summation, the common instinctual foundations of the mind are intensified at the expense of the more varied superstructure of the individual personality. "We see . . . the disappearance of the conscious personality, the predominance of the unconscious personality . . ." (Freud, 1921, p. 76). Freud reinterpreted LeBon's ideas as follows: " . . . in a group the individual is brought under conditions which allow him to throw off the repressions of his unconscious instinctual impulses" (p. 74) and, "As we should say, the mental superstructure, the development of which in individuals shows such dissimilarities, is removed, and the unconscious foundations, which are similar in everyone, stand exposed to view" (p. 74). The crowd thus will " . . . show an unmistakable picture of a regression of mental activity to an earlier stage . . ." (p. 117).

We can see, then, that Freud explained the regression induced by the crowd as a lifting of repressions in the individual in accordance with his topographic theory. This lifting of repressions was regressive because it thereby permitted the emergence of infantile material into the conscious.

However, the merging of the individual with the crowd, which occurred with the regression, could not be accounted for by the topographic model. Freud attempted to resolve this problem in the following way. He reasoned that, since the merging with the crowd occurred when the individual succumbed to the suggestive influence of the group and fell into a contagious imitation of affect and behavior, it must be that the contagion and imitation were produced by suggestion. By virtue of the crowd's powerful suggestive influence, the individual would be induced to relinquish his otherwise preciously guarded individuality and merge with the crowd. Hypnotic suggestion was, after all, included in a topographic frame of reference by virtue of its capacity to bring repressed material to consciousness. Freud, however, admitted his dissatisfaction with this proposal because suggestion, which was central to his argument, remained unexplained: " . . . there has been no explanation of the nature of suggestion, that is, of the conditions under which influence without adequate logical foundation takes place" (p. 90).

Freud recognized he had extended his topographic model to its limits to explain the regression, yet could not account for the individual's merging with the crowd. Also, his topographic model of crowds did not account for the role of the drives, and he could not ignore them, inasmuch as he considered them the forces binding the individual to the group or crowd. He then turned to his theory of narcissism to derive an explanation for the merging of the members of the crowd and to define the role of the drives.

Freud had to explain how joining a crowd could erase individual boundaries. According to his explanation of secondary narcissism, the ego attracts libido to itself, liberating aggression toward objects. Since object-directed aggression was important to the creation and maintenance of interpersonal boundaries, it should therefore prevent people from giving up their individuality and merging together in the crowd. He could not propose a regression to the stage preceding secondary narcissism because his theory could not account for a libidinal object attachment associated with the neutralization of aggression necessary to erase individual boundaries. Freud therefore postulated progression from secondary narcissism to object love. Thus, in the crowd, the individual was conceived as advancing from the stage of secondary narcissism (self-love with hostile depreciation of others) to the stage of object love where aggression was fused with libido, thereby permitting the erasure of individual boundaries. Individuals in a group or crowd " . . . tolerate the peculiarities of its other members, equate themselves with them, and have no feelings of aversion towards them. Such a limitation of narcissism can, according to our theoretical views, only be produced by . . . a libidinal tie. . . . Love for oneself knows only one barrier—love for others, love for objects" (p. 102). The proposal that maturation from secondary narcissism to object love explained the merging in the crowd was, however, in conflict with Freud's topographic formulation of regression. It also implied a deeper tie among members than the fleeting and anonymous character of the relationships that predominate in crowds.

Thus, the topographic theory was used to explain the regression in crowds, and concepts of narcissism to account for the merging of the individual with the crowd. The two accounts contradicted each other and neither one by itself succeeded in explaining both the regression and the merging in the crowd.

Let us now review those advances in the structural theory which we shall use to re-examine Freud's conclusions. Hartmann (1950), correcting an important aspect of Freud's theory of narcissism, showed that the self and not the structural system ego is the object of libido or aggression. Jacobson (1964) furthered this line of thought by demonstrating that the object representations that exist in the systems ego and superego become cathected with libido and aggression.

Jacobson's revised theories of preoedipal object relations and Kernberg's (1966) elaboration of them can account for a regressive merging of self and object in the absence of aggression. Ambivalent feelings and the associated object and self-representations may undergo splitting, with the fusion of the "good" self-representation and the "good" or loving object dissociated from the hateful or "bad" self-representation and the hated or "bad" object (Kernberg, 1966). The experience of merging with the crowd can thus be explained as a regression to primitive mechanisms in the ego function of object relations accompanied by regression in the expression of the drives. The structural explanation identifies the merging as a product of the regression induced in the crowd member and demonstrates thereby a distinct advantage over the topographic and narcissistic models by unifying the regression and the merging in one explanation.

However, an isolated regression in the mechanism of object relations cannot by itself explain the behavioral regression in crowds. We know that a regression in object relations need not produce a regression in function or behavior or revive the mechanisms of imitation and suggestion. Yet, this does happen in crowds.

Because mechanisms of identification play a large part in explaining regression in groups, the clarification in thinking about them permitted by Jacobson's formulations require mention. According to Jacobson, imitation, a characteristic of the individual in a crowd, is observable in the infant as a primitive, affective, oral-stage identification, and is a manifestation of the earliest form of object relation that involves perception of an object not as yet distinguished from the self. Imitation as well as suggestion are properties of the undifferentiated ego.

The structural identifications achieved during later development are accomplished by a partial and a temporary regressive merging between the self- and object representations that have achieved separate recognition in the differentiated ego. These structural identifications themselves produce the differentiation and growth of the ego and superego.

The temporary empathic affective identification (the kind made by the psychotherapist with his patient) Jacobson defines as an adaptive regression in the ego function of object relations to oral-stage mechanisms without regression of such other ego functions as reality testing, the concept of one's identity, and the like. As long as the regression in object relations is induced in the service of the ego and does not disrupt " . . . firmly established ego and superego identifications, they will not . . . affect a person's feelings of identity . . ." (1964, p. 41) or the reality-testing functions of the ego. If for any reason, however, an empathic identification produces a disruption of the structural identifications that have built the ego and superego, dedifferentiation of these structures would ensue, with the loss of such superego functions as moral attitudes, and with the loss of such ego functions as reality testing and the sense of identity. There would be a regressive shift toward primitive functions of the undifferentiated ego, and we would expect such mechanisms as suggestion and imitation to reappear. Such a regressive dedifferentiation of the ego and superego would occur if the structural identifications that built them were weakened in any way. Therefore, if we postulate a partial regression and dedifferentiation of the ego and superego along with the regression of the ego function of object relations, we can account for the poor reality testing, impulsivity, and moral weakening characteristic of individuals in crowds.

The use of structural concepts thus provides one explanatory theory that includes both the regression and the merging of the individual's self with the crowd. It provides, in addition, a satisfactory rationale for the appearance of the crowd properties of suggestion, contagion, and imitation. The affective tie to the crowd is explained by the regression in the ego function of object relations, while the behavioral regression and the appearance of suggestion, imitation, and contagion are explained by a parallel regression of the psychic agencies. We have yet to explain, however, why the regression in object relations should occur and why this should induce a regression in the ego and superego.

One might ask if the regression that has been described in crowds and beginning small groups occurs in a new dyadic situation as well. A regression and subsequent development similar in kind to that postulated for the individual in the group, has been postulated by Sutherland (1951) to occur in all new significant dyadic attachments. Anthony (1967) has proposed that the beginning one-to-one relationship of individual psychotherapy produces a process analogous to that described for groups. Schutz (1958) believes all interpersonal relations, dyadic or group, follow the same basic sequence. If this is true, why, indeed, should the extent of the regression in a crowd be so sweeping and profound?

From the structural point of view we know that significant objects are represented intrapsychically by the attachment of drive cathexis to a set of object representations, and that by this process identifications may be formed. In a fresh relationship, object representations for the new acquaintance do not exist within the psychic apparatus. It is likely, therefore, that the individual will sift through the reservoir of object representations accumulated from previous identifications and, by a process of reduction and resynthesis, attempt to adapt them to the new object. In fact, the clinical equivalent of such a process has been described in the early phases of small group formation by Martin and Hill (1957) and Day (1967). According to them, members attempt to decrease anxiety by fitting new people into previous molds until they emerge as distinct objects.

If a new acquaintance resembles a prior object, if he evokes reactions similar to those of past acquaintances, if he holds familiar attitudes and ethics, then pre-existing structural identifications composed of prior object and self-representations and the cathexis of neutralized drive energy contained within them can more easily serve to represent the new object and will facilitate the new attachment. More disruption will be produced in the pre-existing structural formations when a profound emotional bond is required with a new acquaintance who differs markedly from one's prior experience. With a less successful fit between object representations and the new object, a greater proportion of the total quantity of drive energy required for the new relationship will not be able to be channeled and neutralized through pre-existing structural identifications. Until new structural identifications are formed that can accommodate drive discharge in relation to the new object, drive discharge must be partially achieved through less differentiated channels. Withdrawal of the neutralized energy from the structural identifications in the ego and superego would result in their partial and reversible dedifferentiation, with a regressive loss of ego and superego functions. A more primitive quality of drive expression would reflect the by-passing of the previously established ego and superego identifications.

This process is greatly intensified by the demands that the crowd or new group place upon the psychic apparatus. The individual must form an intense attachment to a heterogeneous mass of people simultaneously. The psychic structures lack the specific object representations stabilized in previous structural identifications through which the drives can achieve discharge in relation to the crowd. It is proposed, therefore, that, under the pressure for drive discharge in the crowd, the ego function of object relations will undergo an equilibratory regression to the earliest form of object tie. This regression proceeds to that period of infantile development before a distinction of self- from object representation has been achieved and before object specificity as well. In this manner, drive discharge is accomplished in relation to the crowd through a merging of the self with the crowd. Regression to an object tie lacking object specificity is more consistent with the anonymous nature of the tie to the crowd than is a progression to a tie based on object love. The ensuing shift in the distribution of drive energy away from previously established structural identifications to the more primitive form of object relations required in the crowd produces the regressive dedifferentiation of the ego and superego.

This formulation provides a structural explanation of LeBon's observations of crowds from which Freud drew support for his topographic explanation of regression in crowds. LeBon had said that the heterogeneous acquired characteristics of individuals are canceled out in a crowd, while the influence of the homogeneous inherited instinctual elements is intensified. According to the structural model, in the crowd, the partial regression of the psychic systems proceeds to the undifferentiated condition predating the acquisition of those structural identifications unique to each individual which shape his particular personality. In the crowd, there is thus a partial regression of the psychic structures to that stage of infancy dominated by the instinctual drives homogeneous in the species, where personality differentiation produced by internalized identifications has not yet been achieved.

McDougall's and LeBon's laws of crowd behavior which Freud had cited are also explained by the structural model. They had shown that the greater the size, heterogeneity, and emotional intensity of a group or crowd, the greater the regression. In accordance with the structural model, each of these factors would increase the shunting of drive energy away from the specific object representations internalized within structural identifications, and increase the regressive dedifferentiation of the ego and superego.

The extent of the systemic regression produced in a

given individual will depend, in accordance with Hartmann's (1950) view, on the prior stability of the structural identifications that have built the psychic systems. For example, sports fans with poorly integrated personalities are more apt to exhibit extreme behavior in the crowd and after the game than the healthy spectator who can lose himself in the experience adaptively, yet maintain behavior appropriate to the situation.

Membership in larger organizations is accomplished with a minimum of transitory regression, experienced as a sense of uncertainty, hesitance, and strangeness in the new organization. As Freud indicated, the established functions and role differentiation within an organization, the aims, rules, and regulations defined by and represented in the position of the formal leader, all inhibit the initial regression induced in new members and may assist them, in time, to achieve a level of functioning surpassing their experiences outside of the organization.

In the preceding discussion, the regressive effect produced by the common ego identification among the members upon their psychic systems has, for heuristic purposes, been emphasized relative to a consideration of the leader's role. How the leader contributes to regression in groups or adds to its stability and development is essential to any consideration of groups and is a topic that will be treated in depth in a subsequent paper. A brief account, however, is pertinent at this time.

Freud (1921) offered his classical description of the structure of a group as follows, " . . . *a number of individuals who have put one and the same object in place of their ego ideal and have consequently identified themselves with one another in their ego*" (p. 116). In this formulation Freud attributed the stability of such organized groups as the army to two vectors acting upon each member: the substituation of the leader for the member's oedipal ego ideal, and an ego identification with the other members. According to Freud, the members' collective representation of the leader as ego ideal produced the ego identification among the members, which was accomplished by a regression in the mechanism of object relations from object love to an oral-stage identification based upon empathy. However, the structural model shows that this same ego identification may occur among the members of a crowd that has no leader.

A charismatic leader may certainly serve as a stimulus for group or crowd formation. In such a case the leader may contribute to spontaneous crowd formation by effecting in each of the individuals a potential or actual ego and superego regression with the release of powerful affects. However, the coalescence of the members into a functional crowd requires drive discharge through regressive fusion of their own selves with the other members of the crowd. We may say, then, that the attachment of the members to each other is achieved through a regression to a common ego identification, which may occur without a leader—but that a leader, by potentiating a systemic regression in each of the members, facilitates the regressive shift in drive energy required for the ego identification among the members.

Thus, whereas Freud explained the regressive ego identification among the members as resulting from their common attachment to the leader, the structural model proposes a dynamic and reciprocal interaction of both these factors upon the members' psychic systems. This model allows for preoedipal as well as oedipal paradigms of group organization as follows.

The regressive dedifferentiation of the ego and super-ego produces, as I have said, a disruption of previously established structural identifications. Those object representations previously internalized within structural identifications disrupted during the systemic regression will be reprojected or externalized. By virtue of the group member's systemic regression and the temporary dissolution of structural identifications by which parental ideals and prohibitions were originally internalized in the ego ideal and superego, the leader becomes the object around whom these previously internalized object representations are reprojected and toward whom the associated instinctual wishes are redirected. He occupies the same position vis-à-vis them as did the parent before the development of a stable ego and superego. The leader will serve as a substitute for those ego and superego functions lost to members during the group-induced systemic regression (Redl, chap. 2, this volume; Semrad et al., 1963). The leader as the externalized oedipal or preoedipal ego ideal (and superego) becomes the object of the aim-inhibited unconscious wishes derived from the psychosexual stage represented in the regression of the members' psychic systems. The particular ego defenses and mechanisms and the superego attitudes prevalent in the group, the characteristics of their behavior, will reflect this systemic regression. The quality of the group members' attachment to each other and the group's collective relationship to the leader will also be determined by the state of partial ego and superego regression.

Using this approach, an explanation can be provided for the oral phase of group formation. During group formation a circumscribed regression of the psychic systems to oral-stage derivatives as occurs in crowds would account for the shift toward narcissistic part-object identifications based upon superficial resemblances among the members, and for a shift in the aims and mode of drive discharge toward oral incorporation, with the wish to merge with the nurturing leader. The emergence of such affects as exaggerated feelings of helplessness coincide with the frustration of these dependent wishes by the leader, while a sense of exaggerated fulfillment and elation results from their fantasied gratifications. The mutual identification of the members around the wish to be fed by and to merge with the mother-leader, and to equate their own union in a group with union with the mother, reflects the partial oral regression produced in the psychic systems of all of the group members.

Whereas Freud's model of group organization conceived of the leader as the group's oedipal ego ideal, the newer structural model can account for the leader as the representative of the preoedipal ego ideal as well. The structural model is compatible with preoedipal organizations of group structure as well as the oedipal paradigm introduced by Freud. The structural model can therefore be used as a framework for the construction of a psychoanalytic theory of group development to explain the clinical development of groups through phases of organization derived from the various stages of infant development.

DISCUSSION

The paper by Whitman and Stock was chosen to begin this last part of the book because it serves as a bridge between the material in Section II and the remaining papers in Section III. Not unlike the theory of Bion and especially that of Ezriel, Whitman and Stock depict group process as the transposition of individual intrapsychic conflicts into group-level conflict states. Following the systematic analysis of patient productions developed by French (1952) for dyadic psychotherapy, they developed a similar approach for dealing with the expressed group member productions in therapy groups. More specifically, the shared expression of "the same intrapersonal problems"—a *disturbing impulse* and a *reactive motive* initially with different solutions for each individual member and subsequently with group solutions—is portrayed. They observed that while most members appeared to be experiencing the same general conflict, it took a somewhat different form for each individual, consonant with his unique life history. Within the context of the copresence of various conflictual themes in the group, each specific "group focal conflict" was chosen for analysis because it was closest to the surface and capable of explaining most of what was transpiring in a given session. There were repeated appearances of similar focal conflicts derived from the same, as yet unresolved, nuclear conflict. Furthermore, conflictual phases were found to be interspersed with periods of group interaction which were devoid of conflict. This last observation, together with the greater allowance for individual group member differences and varying degrees of repression, is more consonant with current notions of ego psychology than the concepts of Bion and Ezriel.

Erikson's argument regarding the curious gap in early Freudian theory, which maintained a dichotomy between the "individual-in-the mass" (Freud's group psychology) and the "individual-within-his family," with only vague references to "social factors," serves as a good beginning to illustrate how ego psychology has opened the way for a more meaningful conceptualization of the relationship between the individual and his group. The earlier psychoanalytic view of social (group) influences as being primarily restrictive in personality development and functioning is accordingly supplanted by significant observations, in tune with modern ego psychology, that these influences can also serve in a nonconflictual and growth-promoting manner. The complementary concepts of *ego identity* and *group identity* developed by Erikson lend support to the inseparability of individual and group behavior. Since the broader implications of his ideas for group psychoanalytic psychology will be elaborated on in the final chapter, it will suffice here to reiterate the specific meanings he attached to the twin concepts. He views ego identity as comprising three aspects: (1) a subjective experience, (2) a dynamic fact, and (3) a group psychological phenomenon. In the last-named connotation, ego identity refers to the individual's maintaining a sense of inner synthesis with his group's ideals and its basic ways of organizing experience. It is regrettable that Erikson has failed to date to elaborae on his rather general concept of group identity and to relate his ideas to those of other ego psychologists, especially of Hartmann.

My article on identification expands on Erikson's somewhat fragmentary concepts of an *individual* and *group iden-tity* by considering the relationship between an individual's self-involvement and his group identification. I view iden-tification with the group entity as an endopsychic process calling for a degree of ego involvement with a perceived object (group) or its symbolic representation. This kind of identification refers to the internalization of an aspect of the external world, as well as to a nonpathological, adaptive extension of the ego. A similar connotation of all identi-fications in personality functioning as a growth-promoting process has been depicted by G. Klein (1976). I proposed that the unconscious object representations of individuals which, together with self-representations are believed to constitute the self-concept, pertain to internalized past group experiences as well. In fact, these conscious and unconscious group perceptions are subject to reactivation in all subsequent group experiences, especially at moments of stress. My ideas regarding a variety of complex iden-tifications, object ties, and transferences in small groups are juxtaposed to Bion's more limited portrayal of "pro-jective" and "introjective" identifications exclusively as pathological mechanisms of defense. I also restate an ear-lier proposal of mine for viewing all group transactions on two major depth levels: contemporaneous-dynamic and genetic-regressive.

The universal problem inherent in people's simulta-neous need for and fear of group involvement is touched on in relation to the element of self-commitment involved in group identification. There is also reference to a pre-vious hypothesis (1955) that people's need to belong to groups may represent on the deepest levels a wish to re-store an earlier state of an unconflicted tie to a need-grat-ifying mother.

In my paper on regression in group psychotherapy, aimed at clarification of this concept in its application to group behavior, I suggest that a distinction be made between regression as a characteristic of personality pathology, as an aspect of all uncovering psychotherapy, and the kind of regression that has been an acknowledged aspect of group formation, beginning with Freud's monograph. I linked group psychological regression to ego psychology's "regression in the service of the ego" in the sense of a nonpathological and adaptive behavioral manifestation. In an attempt to elucidate the generally observed heightened levels of regression with accompanying anxiety manifestations in early phases of unstructured groups, I compared the initial stages in three models of group formations as described by Bion (chap. 3), Foulkes (chap. 5), and Kaplan and Roman (1963).

Saravay's article, the most recent included here, is, interestingly, largely focused on the earliest article depicted in this volume–Freud's group psychology. Saravay's ambitious aim is to revise and to update Freud's original formulations in the light of observed developments in therapy groups. He proposes using structural psychoanalytic concepts to explain the "oral" kind of regression noted in early phases of unstructured groups, as well as the gradual progression occurring in subsequent developmental phases. Saravay, not unlike Bion, speaks of Freud's formula for group formation as representing an "oedipal organization." One might guess that this relates in part to Freud's reference to the primal-horde "myth" which contains an oedipal theme. In fact, the primal-horde concept is not a necessary part of Freud's group psychology model. Redl who, as we noted, elaborated on that model does not even mention this aspect of Freud's contribution.

In his critique of Freud's group psychology, Saravay points to an inherent contradiction in the former's attempt to explain the nature of group cohesion. He questions how the primary-process kind of topographical regression in crowds can go hand in hand with Freud's proposed "maturation from secondary narcissism to object love." He suggests that subsequent psychoanalytic formulations regarding primitive object relations can be used more satisfactorily to explain both the group regression as well as the merging of the individual self with the crowd. Referring to my discussion of the marked regression in the early phases of group formation, Saravay explains this regression in terms of classical psychoanalytic drive-discharge theory. According to him, the inordinate pressure for drive discharge in the group, where there are no internalized object cathexes available to deal with the new and totally strange objects, evokes "... an equilibratory regression to the earliest form of object tie." The resulting shift in the internal distribution of drive energy from more stable, established identifications to more primitive object relations leads in turn to a "... regressive dedifferentiation of the ego and superego" of individual group members. Although the regressive shift in drive energy to effect group identification can occur without a leader, Saravay maintains that a simultaneous attachment to a leader facilitates this process. This is because the leader can become the object for the redirection of the regressively freed "instinctual wishes" as well as for the projection of the previously internalized object representations. Thus, Saravay's proposed structural model allows for *both*—an oral-regressive level around a shared wish to be sustained by a "mother-leader," as well as for a more advanced oedipal group level. In a way, Saravay parallels Bion's claim that Freud's group psychology is not "deep" enough insofar as it approximates only the "neurotic" family level. Unlike Bion, however, Saravay's suggested preoedipal group level comprises concepts drawn from American object relations theory exemplified by the writings of Jacobson (1964) rather than from those of Melanie Klein.

These issues will be subjected to closer scrutiny in the next, and final, chapter.

SECTION IV

OVERVIEW

11

CURRENT PSYCHOANALYTIC
GROUP THEORY

SAUL SCHEIDLINGER

For purposes of this discussion, psychoanalytic group theory will refer to any set of ideas which attempts to ascribe
some meaning, coherence, and regularity to observed behavior in groups, with particular attention to covert or
unconscious factors. In this sense, theories represent hypothetical constructs calling for further scientific validation via the use of independent observation and controlled
experiment.

A perusal of the articles in this volume readily suggests
that we have here a number of rich and creative, yet disappointingly disparate minimodels. Furthermore, some
are geared more to group therapy technique than to group
process theory. Since the authors represented here are
recognized authorities in this realm, it is apparent that a
satisfactory theoretical integration of the very complex
variables at work in groups has so far evaded the efforts
of even our best thinkers. Insofar as it is unrealistic to
expect an acceptable global group process theory in the
near future, it is my belief that we have to content ourselves
at present with "limited-domain" theorizing. This more
circumscribed approach involves concentrating in depth

on specific concepts as well as on minimodels and trying to evolve connecting paths, if not true bridges between them.

My purpose in this concluding chapter is, accordingly, to identify some such connecting paths among the different theoretical contributions offered in this volume, in the hope of achieving some degree of conceptual integration, together with questions for further inquiry.

In a most general sense, all of our contributors appear to accept the notion that in any group there is a continuous interplay between *individual personality* and *group process* manifestations on overt and covert levels. A variety of different explanations and emphases emerge, however, as soon as one poses more specific questions regarding the nature of these group interactions i.e. *what* interacts (self, ego, personalities, leader, members, shared emotions); *why* the interaction (motivation, direction); *how* the interaction (depth level, process, mechanisms); and, above all, which of the interacting elements are of primary and which of secondary importance.

INDIVIDUAL AND GROUP ELEMENTS

The early Freudian model of group psychology was relatively simple, based as it was on an as yet rudimentary psychoanalytic theory and little direct experience with groups. As the material in Section I revealed, Freud conceptualized group formation as evolving around the same model-object (father-leader person) and/or ideals, with individual members identifying with one another. Redl introduced the concept of a Central Person to allow for additional kinds of leader roles to those posited by Freud, with group formation involving the central person as either (a) an object of love or hate; (b) an object of identification (as in Freud's model) or; (c) an object for the reliving of similar conflicts. The constituent elements in group interaction thus were individual personalities whose egos (in the sense of self-preservative, reality, and control functions) were involved in special object relationships and identifications with the leader and with each other. The shared group emotionality was represented by the group members' common ties and perceptions of the leader (central person). Other group-level elements acknowledged by the early Freudians were group tasks, i.e., warfare, planning for an army, and religious services for a church—as well as various levels of cohesiveness and group organization.

Bion's system of group dynamics places major emphasis on group members' fantasied involvement with group-as-a-whole-phenomena, with the actual interaction of autonomous individual personalities within the group being acknowledged only indirectly. The two group "cultures" which he assumed to co-exist at any moment of a group's life, the Work-Group and a given Basic Assumption Group, each possesses its specific aims and relationship to a perceived leader.

Whereas the theories of Freud, Redl, and Bion were offered as being applicable to some extent to all groups, Ezriel presented his model as derived from and applicable to the group therapy setting exclusively. It involves the transposition of group member tension states caused by each individual's tripartite fantasied perceptions of the leader-therapist, i.e., required relationship; avoided relationship; and calamitous relationship—onto the group level, resulting in a "common group tension." Ezriel described this shared emotional theme as the common denominator of the dominant fantasies of the members. As was also true with Bion's scheme, Ezriel pays minimal attention to member-to-member relationships except insofar as they reflect the fantasied concerns regarding the leader.

Foulkes also cast his group process theories within the framework of a therapeutic method which he termed Therapeutic Group Analysis. He did, however, also readily comment on groups in general. He was emphatic in his belief that, while he had borrowed some of his group concepts from Freudian psychoanalysis, they were "equivalent to and not identical" with the meanings usually ascribed to them. In view of man's "basic social nature," Foulkes viewed the individual group member as enmeshed (modal point) in a group matrix, a network of relationships which became his focus for therapeutic attention. In this connection, he spoke of the group processes (originally the community) as primary elements not to be explained in terms of the interaction of individuals. While groups in general have agreed upon tasks (occupations), analytic groups are by plan devoid of a manifest purpose. All relationships and communications, be they individual or shared, that occur on at least four "depth" levels in the group are ultimately related to the earlier noted "transpersonal network." It is the latter that is the source as well as the effector of all communications. In order to underscore the nondirective role of the group therapist, Foulkes eschewed the term group leader, preferring instead that of conductor, thus emphasizing the latter's participant-observer and enabler role.

As already noted, Erikson, while acknowledging the great importance of group dynamics in personality and societal development, did not concern himself primarily with this issue. His major contribution was to demonstrate the fundamental cogwheeling interface and interaction between the developing personality and society, with particular stress on people's ever-present need for their group's guidance and support in the evolving sense of self, of self-esteem, as well as of their moral and ethnic value systems.

My own theoretical stance stresses the inseparability of individual and group psychological elements in their intrapsychic, interpersonal and group-as-a-whole contexts. I question the need for ascribing a theoretical primacy to any of these elements, which I perceive as a *Gestalt,* except where a group leader–change agent–guided by his philosophy of what would be most "curative" is moved by reality considerations to momentarily put stress on one or more of these elements in his planned interventions in behalf of individuals or of the group as an entity. Concerned lest the "group mind" fallacy of Le Bon (1920) become perpetuated, I suggested that every item of group behavior be viewed as the behavior of individual personalities in a special process of social and emotional interactions.

As was true of Ezriel's model, Whitman and Stock's theory is anchored in a conception of individual group patient's experiencing "focal conflicts" which need not necessarily be related to the group leader, thus possibly deriving their origin from peer interactions. These individual conflicts with their specific themes soon become transmuted into group level conflicts comprising the elements: Disturbing Motive, Reactive Motive, and Group Solution.

In his attempt to update Freudian group psychology, Saravay, it seems to me, too readily equated Freud's loose description of groups in general, including army and church, with various subsequent portrayals of therapy groups, especially by American authors. His major concern is with an adequate explanation for the regressive manifestations which Freud and more recent writers on group therapy noted in group formation and development.

MOTIVATIONAL SYSTEMS

When one turns to the crucial issue of motivation or

of need satisfaction ascribed to group behavior in the various group theories depicted in this volume, significant differences emerge, differences that seem to be related to each author's theoretical persuasion regarding psychoanalysis as a general psychology and as a therapeutic endeavor. In the early Freudian group psychology, (Section I), the contemporary theoretical concern with the issues of libidinal quantities, of tension reduction, with libidinal aims, and with a conscious ego struggling against powerful unconscious drives is all too evident. The speculations on the part of both Freud and Redl as to whether the aim-inhibited libidinal ties in groups are heterosexual or homosexual in nature as well as their minimal attention to aggression sound strangely out of date in the context of contemporary psychoanalytic theory. The same can be said regarding Freud's resort to phylogenetic regression (primal-horde theory) in explaining group psychology. This latter theme will be discussed further on in this chapter.

As already noted, it is difficult, if not impossible, to comprehend Bion's dramatic view of group psychology without some knowledge of Melanie Klein's psychoanalytic theories to which he adhered.

In the light of Melanie Klein's ideas, Bion's theoretical orientation and especially his view of group belonging in terms of individual defenses against "psychotic" anxieties, of depersonalization, and of intense internal conflicts involving fantasied primitive perceptions in the face of a relatively weak outer reality become more understandable.

Although Ezriel was a member of Bion's first group at London's Tavistock Clinic and was also exposed to Melanie Klein's theories as well as to the "object relations" theories of other British analysts, his group therapeutic scheme is, by comparison, elegant in its simplicity and parsimony. While his concept of a three-tiered set of relationships of each individual group member is embedded in a conflict model of personality, the latter is devoid of Kleinian primitive symbolism and mechanisms encompassing defenses against the all-powerful life and death instincts.

Foulkes appears to be a true eclectic, at least in his view of group psychology if not of personality theory in general. While openly expressing his "fundamental agreement" with Anna Freud's orientation in terms of individual personality theory, he dismissed Sigmund Freud's group psychological formulations as overly embedded in individual psychology. At the same time, without crediting Freud for a similar earlier observation, he viewed "man's social nature as basic to him" and the infant-mother and subsequent family relationships as the first social relationships.

Whitman and Stock's model embodies the translation of French's (1952) theory of psychotherapy to the group therapy situation. French's studies were conducted within the context of the so-called Chicago School of Psychoanalysis of which Franz Alexander was the prime mover (Alexander, French, et al., 1946). The overall theoretical orientation resided in a basic view of neurosis as a disturbance of four primary ego functions: (1) the internal perception of subjective needs, (2) reality testing, (3) integration of the data of internal and external perception, and (4) control. The ego's failure to mediate successfully between conflicting inner needs and environmental demands were seen as problems of integration. French studied the ego's integrative functions in detail, attempting to assess their qualitative and quantitative variations. Insofar as optimum ego in integration called for conscious ego awareness, this was to be achieved via a kind of emotional reconditioning, which Franz Alexander termed a corrective emotional experience: The therapist fosters a reliving of repressed traumatic childhood experiences with their parental responses, counteracting them with constructive and reality-geared verbal as well as nonverbal interventions. The Whitman and Stock and Whitaker and Lieberman (1964) approach represents a schematic way for viewing this process in the group setting where *individual* patient conflicts and solutions become *common, group-level* conflicts and and solutions.

Most of Erikson's (1959) monumental but disparate contributions to the psychosocial understanding of the life cycle, to psychohistory, and to ego psychology represent a series of efforts as yet not fully appreciated at a conceptual integration of the Freudian psychosexual theory and ego development, on the one hand, and societal (group) forces, on the other.

My own theoretical papers are presented within the broader framework of modern ego psychology with particular attention to the concepts of self- and object perceptions and representations as they apply to the dynamics of small groups.

Saravay's stance appears to be closely linked to Freudian drive-discharge theory, to the structural ego paradigm (ego, id, superego) and to the observations of such American writers on object relations theory as Jacobson (1964) and Kernberg (1966).

CONTENT AND PROCESS

The core of the early classical analytic group theory represented by Freud and Redl resides in the explanation of group cohesiveness in terms of attachments (identifications) among people which are the result of a shared emotionality centered around a father-leader or an ideology. Because the direct expression of sexual (and by implication also of aggressive) feelings runs counter to group cohesion, these impulsive derivatives were believed to be operative in aim-inhibited form. While references occur to commonly held ideals and to emotional states–among them group panic–as well as to themes such as dependency, sexuality, sibling rivalry, meals eaten in common, these are not presented in any organized way. Group processes with reference to suggestibility and organization are also discussed in brief, Freud juxtaposing labile crowds to more organized groups where individual autonomy and resistance to suggestion and regression are subject to reinforcement.

Both Freud and Redl were intrigued by the as yet incompletely understood phenomenon of emotional contagion in groups. Freud attempted to explain it in terms of a primitive kind of identification. Redl (1949) and Polansky et al. (1950) offered a more extensive set of explanatory constructs, in another context, relating it to the copresence of a number of group and individual factors.

In comparison to the loose and incomplete portrayal of content and process elements in Freudian group psychology, Bion's model is well rounded if not precise. In some ways, it attempts to build on, rather than to replace Freudian notions, as when Bion lists the Freudian examples of army and church as specialized Work-Groups, adding a third, however, the aristocracy.

The dominant content themes of the various group states are rendered explicit. For the Work-Group, the preoccupation with the group's manifest task; for the Basic-Assumption Groups, the themes of dependency, aggression, and sexuality, respectively. In terms of the individual group member, Bion ascribes special importance to the individual's relationship to the then operative dyad of the Work-Group and Basic-Assumption levels. While this is by no means spelled out, all the individuals appear to be simultaneously involved with either the reality-geared task-oriented issues of the Work-Group level or involuntarily pulled into the fantasy-laden, primary-process issues of the given Basic Assumption. The implication here is that some degree of individual autonomy is maintained by the group members when the Work-Group level is in ascendancy. Bion also makes repeated references to individual group member's primitive concerns with the group-as-a-whole as maternal part-objects (à la Melanie Klein) coupled with fears of being fused (loss of identity) with the group. It is not clear whether and how these concerns fit in with the Basic-Assumption fantasy themes which spell out the relationship in regard to the leader with greater precision. Not unlike Redl's observations, in Bion's scheme any individual (Work-Group leader or member) can be propelled into the role of leader in the context of a given Basic-Assumption state.

In trying to explain the processes wherein individual behavior, i.e., individual emotions and concerns become transformed into common, group-level concerns on the level of the Basic Assumption, Bion proposes the concept of valency, which is similar to Redl's notion of contagion.

Group content and process manifestations in Ezriel's theoretical scheme are rendered simple by the latter's portrayal of the three-phased individual conflict states (tensions) and their assumed transition to the common group tension level. The major process at work is that of transference to the therapist, which term is utilized by Ezriel in the broadest sense as involving the total set of attitudes and feelings toward the group-as-a-whole and toward the therapist-leader.

In his attempt to develop a generic set of concepts distinct from dyadic-psychotherapy and uniquely related to the group setting, Foulkes (1965) coined a number of terms pertaining to group processes. Among them are location, mirror reactions, occupation, preoccupation, translation, displacement, isolation, splitting, and communication. The latter term is especially noteworthy because it refers to all that transpires in the group; *what* is expressed, *how* it is expressed (verbally or nonverbally), and the extent to which it is within the realm of conscious awareness. Foulkes also used the structural psychoanalytic concepts of ego, id, and superego as they are reflected in group roles assumed by individuals or the group entity. The related concept of free group association is of interest, insofar as Foulkes saw it as operative also in nontherapy groups on the level of unconscious communications.

Erikson's twin concepts of ego and group identity, while extremely plausible and immediately applicable in clinical situations, are at the same time too global in character and hence in need of further refinement, especially with reference to the subtle processes wherein the group values, expectations, and communications become perceived and incorporated by the individual. Furthermore, these concepts of Erikson's are only tangentionally relevant to the psychology of small groups.

Whitman and Stock's theory is nonspecific regarding the themes of both the individual conflicts and the group focal conflicts. They cover, by implication, the whole range, from unconscious neurotic conflicts to contemporary problems of living. As is true with the parallel scheme of Ezriel's, they fail to spell out in detail how individual concerns evolve into group-level concerns.

Insofar as my contributions aim essentially at trying to clarify and integrate the relevant concepts already contained in the literature, I do not offer any new ideas regarding the content or processes in group behavior. My plea for distinguishing between coexisting reality-geared perceptions and interactions in the group process, on the one hand, and identifications as well as transferences, on the other, is worth noting at this juncture.

Saravay's stress with regard to group content and process is on the theme of orality and of primitive object relations expressed in the early phases of therapy groups which are subject to maturational progression in later phases of group development.

LEVELS OF INTERACTION

All of the group psychological models depicted in this volume postulate the operation of behavioral manifestations including motivational factors on the unconscious, preconscious and conscious levels. The differences lie in the way these various "depth" levels are conceptualized as well as the degree to which they are differentiated. Freud was the first to speak of certain groups assuming the "character of a regression." Neither he nor Redl, however, made any attempt to differentiate topographical (conscious /unconscious) regression from temporal ego regression in individual group members in the sense of loosening of ego controls as part of group involvement. Freud did note that various groups are characterized by various degress of regression ranging from "primary" groups (crowds) where regression and emotional lability are highest, through organized groups (army and church), to task-oriented groups which have " . . . acquired secondarily the characteristics of an individual" due to identifications based on work in common. Redl did not address himself to the issue of "depth" levels in group behavior, suggesting, by implication at least, that he was describing unconscious phenomena only.

Bion's group psychology, while allowing for a conscious Work-Group level, is unmistakably pre-empted by unconscious manifestations. In fact, his major criticism of Freud's group theories is that they do not go "deep" enough, that they deal with "neurotic" rather than with Bion's "psychotic" level of group manifestations. This becomes understandable in the broader context of Kleinian theory, which maintains that neurotic (oedipal) conflicts are mere defenses against underlying "psychotic" conflicts. Furthermore, not unlike other followers of Melanie Klein, Bion makes no attempt to distinguish between thoughts, fantasies, memory traces, impulses, and defenses other than by a loose employment of the terms projective and introjective identification. These latter differ from the generally accepted analogous classical psychoanalytic conceptions in that they entail an element of action, i.e., the object of projective identification as a kind of container is believed to actually feel the projected anger while the subject, in turn, experiences a sense of emotional depletion.

Ezriel conceived of the interactions in group therapy situations as unconscious transference relationships calling for therapist interpretations to be rendered conscious. He makes no explicit reference to a conscious level of group transactions. Foulkes by contrast delineated four levels of group communications ranging from the conscious social level to the deepest level of a collective unconscious.

The contributions in Section III give recognition to the idea that group behavioral manifestations operate on different levels of consciousness. Major attention is paid, however, to covert unconscious manifestations because these have been subject to neglect in most social-psychological writings on group behavior.

PHYLOGENETIC REGRESSION

Freud's idea that the primal-horde fratricide represents the beginning of group psychology and its memory resides in the archaic collective human unconscious, has also received some support from three of our other contributors. In addition to its explicit acceptance by Foulkes, Bion referred to it indirectly in his repeated emphasis on man's inborn groupishness, with Erikson acknowledging its utility in another context (1972). It is noteworthy that, while

Arlow and Brenner (1964) dismissed the concept of phylogenetic regression as being " . . . of limited use scientifically" in classical psychoanalysis, some contemporary writers on group process (Slater, 1966) as well as students of anthropology such as Neumann (1955) continue to give it serious consideration. As psychodynamic theory tends to lay increasingly greater stress on clinically demonstrable motivational factors, the future weight ascribed to phylogenesis remains an open question.

NEW DIRECTIONS FOR PSYCHOANALYTIC THEORY AND GROUP PSYCHOLOGY

Some basic facets of classical psychoanalytic theory have, over the last decade, been subjected to serious criticism from within its own camp. Foremost have been questions pertaining to the validity and usefulness of instinct theory and its related concept of psychic energy. As was underscored by George Klein (1976) and Schafer (1970), even modern ego psychology with its structural model has failed to correct the undue mechanistic flavor ascribed by psychoanalysis to human behavior and particularly to motivations. The need for a comprehensive theory of motivation which would also take into account the nonsexual propellants for behavior has also been argued with cogent forcefulness by the British proponents of the motivational primacy of object relations, among them Fairbairn (1952) and Guntrip (1971).

A related, very significant development pertains to a mushrooming interest in early object relations and internalized objects sparked by the clinical challenge posed by the "borderline" and narcissistic disorders. The writings of Kohut (1971, 1977) and of Kernberg (1975, 1976) with their emphasis on the psychology of the self in relation to external as well as internalized objects, have opened the way for a closer look at the relevant issues of individual identity with its "autonomous" and "relatedness" aspects (G. Klein, 1976).

The above-noted new directions in psychoanalytic theory as a general psychology with their stress on issues of intentionality and volition, on self-perceptions and self-involvements and, above all, on object relatedness are bound to forge a renewed emphasis on man's social behavior and, with it, on group dynamics. The much-needed further integration of psychoanalytic concepts with those of social psychology which I envisioned in 1952 (Scheidlinger) is thus facilitated and perhaps closer to fruition.

REFERENCES

Alexander, F., French, T.H., et al. (1946), *Psychoanalytic Therapy*. New York: Ronald Press.

Anthony, E.J. (1967), The generic elements in dyadic and in group psychotherapy. *Internat. J. Group Psychother.*, 17:57-70.

Appelbaum, S.A. (1963), The pleasure and reality principles in group process teaching. *Brit. J. Med. Psychol.*, 36:49-56.

Arlow, J. & Brenner, C. (1964), *Psychoanalytic Concepts and the Structural Theory*. New York: International Universities Press.

Arsenian, J., Semrad, E.V. & Shapiro, D. (1962), An analysis of integral functions in small groups. *Internat. J. Group Psychother.*, 12:421-434.

Augustine, Saint, *The City of God*. New York: Dutton, 1957.

Axelrad, S. & Maury, L.M. (1951), Identification as a mechanism of adaptation. In: *Psychoanalysis and Culture*, ed. G.W. Wilber & W. Muensterberger. New York: International Universities Press, pp. 168-184.

Bales, R.F. (1950), *Interaction Process Analysis*. Cambridge: Addison-Wesley.

Balint, A. (1943), Identification. *Internat. J. Psycho-Anal.*, 24:97-107.

Balint, M. (1960), Primary narcissism and primary love. *Psychoanal. Quart.*, 29:6-43.

Bellak, L. (1961), Free association: Conceptual and clinical aspects. *Internat. J. Psycho-Anal.*, 42:9-20.

Bennis, W.G. & Shepard, H.A. (1956), A theory of group development. *Human Relations*, 9:415-437.

Bion W.R. (1955), Group dynamics—A re-view. In: *New Directions in Psychoanalysis*, ed. M. Klein et al. New York: Basic Books.

——— (1959), *Experiences in Groups and Other Papers*. New York: Basic Books.

Bonner, H. (1959), *Group Dynamics*. New York: Ronald Press.

Bowlby, J. (1962), Separation anxiety: A critical review of the literature. *J. Child Psychol. & Psychiat.*, 1:251-269.

Brierley, M. (1951), *Trends in Psychoanalysis*. London: Hogarth Press.

Briskin, R. (1958), Identification in group therapy. *J. Abn. & Soc. Psychol.*, 56:195-198.

Buxbaum, E. (1945), Transference and group formation in children and adolescents. In: *The Psychoanalytic Study of the Child.* 1:351-366. New York: International Universities Press.

Cartwright, D. & Lippitt, R. (1957), Group dynamics and the individual. *Internat. J. Group Psychoth.*, 7:86-102.

Cattell, R.B. (1951), New concepts for measuring leadership in terms of group syntality. *Human Relations*, 4:161-184.

Croce, B. (1921), *The Essense of Aesthetic.* Darby, Pa.: Folcroft.

Day, M. (1967), The natural history of training groups. *Internat. J. Group Psychoth.*, 17:436-446.

Durkin, M. (1964), *The Group in Depth.* New York: International Universities Press.

English, H.B. & English, A.C. (1958), *A Comprehensive Dictionary of Psychological and Psychoanalytical Terms.* New York: David McKay.

Erikson, E.H. (1950), *Childhood and Society.* New York: Norton.

——— (1959), *Identity and the Life Cycle (Psychological Issues*, Monogr. 1). New York: International Universities Press.

——— (1972), Environment and virtues. In: *Arts and the Environment,* ed. G. Kepes. New York: Braziller.

Ezriel, H. (1960), Übertragung und psychoanalitische Deutung in der Einzelund Gruppen-Psychotherapie [Transference and psychoanalytic interpretation in individual and group psychotherapy]. *Psyche*, 14:496-523.

——— (1973), In: *Group Therapy*, eds. L.R. Wolberg & E.M. Schwartz. New York: Intercontinental Medical Book Corp, pp. 183-210.

Fairbairn, W.R.D. (1952), *Psychoanalytic Studies of the Personality.* London: Tavistock.

Fenichel, O. (1945), *The Psychoanalytic Theory of Neurosis.* New York: Norton.

Ferenczi, S. (1926), On the technique of psychoanalysis. In: *Further Contributions to the Theory and Technique of Psychoanalysis.* New York: Basic Books, 1952, pp. 177-188.

Festinger, L. et al. (1952), Some consequences of deindividuation in a group. *J. Abn. & Social Psychol.*, 47:382-389.

Fortes, M. (1970), An Ashanti case study. In: *Time, Social Structure, and Other Essays.* Atlantic Highlands, N.J.: Humanities Press.

Foulkes, S.H. (1951), Concerning leadership in group-analytic psychotherapy. *Internat. J. Group Psychoth.*, 1:319-329.

——— (1965), *Therapeutic Group Analysis.* New York: International Universities Press.

——— & Anthony, E.J. (1957), *Group Psychotherapy.* New York: Penguin.

Frank, J.D. (1957), Some determinants, manifestations, and effects of cohesiveness in therapy groups. *Internat. J. Group Psychoth.*, 7:53-63.

——— (1964), Training and therapy. In: *Group Theory and Laboratory*

Method, ed. L.P. Bradford et al. New York: John Wiley, pp. 442-451.

Frank, L.K. (1950), Introduction. In: *Projective Psychology.* New York: Knopf.

French, T.M. (1952), *The Integration of Behavior.* Chicago: University of Chicago Press.

Freud, A. (1936), *The Ego and the Mechanisms of Defense. Writings,* 2. New York: International Universities Press, 1966.

———— (1945), Indications for child analysis. *Writings,* 4:3-38. New York: International Universities Press, 1968.

———— & Dann, S. (1951), An experiment in group upbringing. *Writings,* 4:163-229. New York: International Universities Press, 1968.

Freud, S. (1908), "Civilized" sexual ethics and modern nervous sickness. *Standard Edition,* 9:179-204. London: Hogarth Press, 1959.

———— (1913), Totem and taboo. *Standard Edition,* 13:vii-162. London: Hogarth Press, 1955.

———— (1914), On narcissism. An introduction. *Standard Edition,* 14:69-102. London: Hogarth Press, 1957.

———— (1915), The unconscious. *Standard Edition,* 14:161-215. London: Hogarth Press, 1957.

———— (1920), Beyond the pleasure principle. *Standard Edition,* 18:3-64. London: Hogarth Press, 1955.

———— (1921), Group psychology and the analysis of the ego. *Standard Edition,* 18:67-143. London: Hogarth Press, 1955.

———— (1923), The ego and the id. *Standard Edition,* 19:3-66. London: Hogarth Press, 1961.

———— (1926), Inhibitions, symptoms and anxiety. *Standard Edition,* 20:77-174. London: Hogarth Press, 1959.

———— (1933), Why war. *Standard Edition,* 22:197-215. London: Hogarth Press, 1964.

———— (1940), An outline of psycho-analysis. *Standard Edition,* 23:141-207. London: Hogarth Press, 1964.

Fried, E. (1965), Some aspects of group dynamics and the analysis of transference and defenses. *Internat. J. Group Psychoth.,* 15:44-56.

Fried, M. (1963), Grieving for a lost home. In: *The Urban Condition,* ed. L.J. Duhl. New York: Basic Books, pp. 151-171.

Friedman, J. & Gassel, S. (1950), The chorus in Sophocles' *Oedipus Tyrannus. Psychoanal. Quart.,* 19:213-226.

———— ———— (1951), Orestes. *Psychoanal. Quart.,* 20:423-433.

Goldstein, K. (1939), *The Organism.* Boston: Beacon Press, 1963.

Greenacre, P. (1972), Crowds and crisis: Psychoanalytic considerations. In: *The Psychoanalytic Study of the Child,* 27:136-155. New York: Quadrangle Books.

Greenson, R.R. (1974), Transference: Freud or Klein. In: *Explorations in Psychoanalysis.* New York: International Universities Press, 1978, pp. 519-539.

Guntrip, H. (1961), *Personality Structure and Human Interaction.* New

York: International Universities Press.

———— (1971), *Psychoanalytic Theory, Therapy, and the Self.* New York: Basic Books.

Hartmann, H. (1939), *Ego Psychology and the Problem of Adaptation.* New York: International Universities Press, 1958.

———— (1950), Comments on the psychoanalytic theory of the ego. In: *Essays on Ego Psychology.* New York: International Universities Press, 1964, pp. 113-141.

Horwitz, L. (1964), Transference in training groups and therapy groups. *Internat. J. Group Psychoth.,* 14:202-213.

Jacobson, E. (1964), *The Self and the Object World.* New York: International Universities Press.

Janis, I.L. (1963), Group identification under conditions of external danger. *Brit. J. Med. Psychol.,* 36:227-238.

Jaques, E. (1955), Social systems as defense against persecutory and depressive anxiety. In: *New Directions in Psycho-Analysis,* ed. M. Klein et al. New York: Basic Books, pp. 478-498.

Kaplan, S.R. (1967), Therapy groups and training groups: Similarities and differences. *Internat. J. Group Psychoth.,* 17:473-504.

———— & Roman, M. (1963), Phases of development in an adult therapy group. *Internat. J. Group Psychoth.,* 13:10-26.

Kernberg, O. (1966), Structural derivatives of object relationships. *Internat. J. Psycho-Anal.,* 47:236-253.

———— (1975), *Borderline Conditions and Pathological Narcissism.* New York: Aronson.

———— (1976), *Object Relations Theory and Clinical Psychoanalysis.* New York: Aronson.

Klein, G.S. (1976), *Psychoanalytic Theory: An Exploration of Essentials.* New York: International Universities Press.

Klein, M. (1930), The importance of symbol formation in the development of the ego. In: *Contributions to Psycho-Analysis, 1921-1945.* London: Hogarth Press, 1948, pp. 236-250. New York: Norton.

———— (1932), *The Psycho-Analysis of Children.* New York: Norton.

———— (1946), Notes on some schizoid mechanisms. In: *Developments in Psycho-Analysis,* ed. J. Riviere. London: Hogarth Press, 1952, pp. 292-320.

———— (1948), *Contributions to Psychoanalysis: 1921-1945.* London: Hogarth Press.

———— Heimann, P., & Money-Kyrle, R., eds. (1955), *New Directions in Psychoanalysis.* New York: Basic Books.

Knox, R. (1951), *Enthusiasms.* Oxford: Oxford University Press.

Kohut, H. (1971), *The Analysis of the Self.* New York: International Universities Press.

———— (1977), *The Restoration of the Self.* New York: International Universities Press.

Kris, E. (1952), The psychology of caricature. In: *Psychoanalytic Explo-*

rations in Art. New York: International Universities Press, pp. 173-188.

Le Bon, L. (1920), *The Crowd: A Study of the Popular Mind.* London: Fisher Unwin.

Lewin, K. (1951), *Field Theory in Social Science.* New York: Harper, pp. 188-237.

McDougall, W. (1920), *The Group Mind.* New York: Putnam.

Mann, R.D. (1966), The development of the member-trainer relationship in self-analytic groups. *Human Relations,* 19:85-115.

Martin, E.A. & Hill, W.F. (1957), Toward a theory of group development. *Internat. J. Group Psychoth.,* 7:20-30.

Money-Kyrle, R. (1950), Varieties of group formation. *Psychoanalysis and the Social Sciences,* 2:313-329. New York: International Universities Press.

Muensterberger, W. (1955), On the psychobiological determinants of social life. In: *Psychoanalysis and the Social Sciences,* 4:7-25. New York: International Universities Press.

Murphy, G. (1947), *Personality.* New York: Harper.

Neumann, E. (1955), *The Great Mother.* New York: Pantheon.

Niebuhr, R. (1949), *The Nature and Destiny of Man.* New York: Scribner.

Nunberg, H. (1931), The synthetic function of the ego. In: *Practice and Theory of Psychoanalysis.* New York: International Universities Press, 1948, pp. 120-136.

——— (1951), Transference and reality. *Internat. J. Psycho-Anal.,* 32:1-9.

Peck H.B. (1963), Some relationships between group process and mental health phenomena in theory and practice. *Internat. J. Group Psychoth.,* 13:269-289.

Polansky, N., Lippitt, R. & Redl, F. (1950), An investigation of behavioral contagion in groups. *Human Relations,* 3:319-348.

——— et al. (1957), Determinants of the role-image of the patient in the psychiatric hospital. In: *The Patient and the Mental Hospital,* ed. M. Greenblatt. Glencoe, Ill.: The Free Press, pp. 380-401.

Powles, W.E. (1959), Psychosexual maturity in a therapy group of disturbed adolescents. *Internat. J. Group Psychoth.,* 9:429-441.

Rank, O. (1909), *The Myth of the Birth of the Hero.* New York: Nervous and Mental Disease Publishing Co., 1914.

Rapaport, D. (1959), *The Structure of Psychoanalytic Theory. A Systematizing Attempt (Psychological Issues,* Monogr. 6). New York: International Universities Press, 1960.

Rashkis, H.A. (1959), The development of group psychotherapy in a clinical research setting. *Internat. J. Group Psychoth.,* 9:504-509.

Redl, F. (1949), The phenomenon of contagion and "shock effect" in group therapy. In: *Searchlights on Delinquency,* ed., K.R. Eissler. New York: International Universities Press, pp. 315-328.

Rickman, J. (1951), Methodology and research in psychopathology. In:

Selected Contributions to Psycho-Analysis. New York: Basic Books, 1957, pp. 207-217.

Rochlin, G. (1959), The love complex. *J. Amer. Psychoanal. Assn.*, 7:299-316.

Sandler, J. (1960), On the concept of superego. In: *The Psychoanalytic Study of the Child*, 15:128-162. New York: International Universities Press.

Schafer, R. (1958), Regression in the service of the ego. In: *Assessment of Human Motives*, ed. G. Lindzey. New York: Rinehart, pp. 119-148.

———— (1970), The psychoanalytic vision of reality. *Internat. J. Psycho-Anal.*, 51:279-297.

Scheidlinger, S. (1952), *Psychoanalysis and Group Behavior.* New York: Norton.

———— (1955), The concept of identification in group psychotherapy. *Amer. J. Psychoth.*, 9:661-672.

———— (1960), Group process in group psychotherapy. *Amer. J. Psychoth.*, 14:104-120, 346-363.

———— (1966), The concept of empathy in group psychotherapy. *Internat. J. Group Psychoth.*, 16:413-424.

———— (1968a), Group psychotherapies in the sixties. *Amer. J. Psychoth.*, 22:170-184.

———— (1968b), Therapeutic group approaches in community mental health. *Social Work*, 13:87-95.

———— (1974), On the concept of the "mother-group." *Internat. J. Group Psychoth.*, 24:417-428.

———— & Pyrke, M. (1961), Group therapy of women with severe dependency problems. *Amer. J. Orthopsychiat.*, 31:766-785.

———— et al. (1955), Social group work in psychiatric residential settings. *Amer. J. Orthopsychiat.*, 26:709-750.

Schilder, P. (1935), *The Image and Appearance of the Human Body.* New York: International Universities Press, 1950.

———— (1936), The analysis of ideologies as a psychotherapeutic method, especially in group treatment. *Amer. J. Psychiat.*, 93:601-617.

———— (1940) Introductory remarks on groups. *J. Soc. Psychol.*, 12:83-100.

Schindler, W. (1951), Family patterns in group formation and therapy. *Internat. J. Group Psychoth.*, 1:100-105.

———— (1952), The "group personality" concept in group psychotherapy. *Internat. J. Group Psychoth.*, 2:311-315.

———— (1966), The role of the mother in group psychotherapy. *Internat. J. Group Psychoth.*, 16:198-200.

Schutz, W.C. (1958), *Firo: A Three-Dimensional Theory of Interpersonal Behavior.* New York: Rinehart.

Schwartz, E.K. & Wolf, A. (1963), Psychoanalysis in groups: Resistance to its use. *Amer. J. Psychoth.*, 17:457-464.

Searles, H.F. (1951), Data concerning certain manifestations of incorporation. *Psychiatry*, 14:397-413.

Segal, H. (1950), Some aspects of the analysis of a schizophrenic. *Internat. J. Psycho-Anal.*, 31:268–278.

Semrad, E.V. et al. (1963), The field of group psychotherapy. *Internat. J. Group Psychoth.*, 13:452-475.

Shepard, M.A. & Bennis, W.G. (1956), A theory of training by group methods. *Human Relations*, 9:403-414.

Slater, P.E. (1966), *Microcosm*. New York: John Wiley.

Spanjaard, J. (1959), Transference neurosis and psychoanalytic group psychotherapy. *Internat. J. Group Psychoth.*, 9:31-42.

Stock, D. and Lieberman, M.A. (1962), Methodological issues in the assessment of total-group phenomena in group psychotherapy. *Internat. J. Group Psychoth.*, 12:312-325.

———— & Whitman, R.M. (1957), Patients' and therapists' apperception of an episode in group therapy. *Human Relations*, 10:367-383.

Strachey, J. (1934), The nature of the therapeutic action of psychoanalysis. *Internat. J. Psycho-Anal.*, 15:127-159. Reprinted (1969) 50:275-292.

Sugar, M. (1971), Multitransferences and divariations in group therapy. *Internat. J. Group Psychoth.*, 21:444-445.

Sutherland, R.L. (1951), An application of the theory of psychosexual development to the learning process. *Bull. Menninger Clinic*, 15:91-99.

Tacitus, *Germania*. New York: Penquin, 1971.

Tarde, G. (1890), *Les Lois de l'Imitation*. Paris.

Trotter, W. (1916), *Instincts of the Herd in Peace and War*. London: Fisher Unwin.

Wender, L. (1936), Dynamics of group psychotherapy and its application. *J. Nerv. Ment. Dis.*, 84:54-57.

———— (1945), Group psychotherapy. In: *Group Psychotherapy: A Symposium*, ed. J.C. Moreno. Beacon, N.Y.: Beacon Press, pp. 108-110.

Wernicke, C. (1906), *Grundriss der Psychiatrie*. Leipzig: Barth.

Whitaker, D.S. & Lieberman, M.A. (1964), *Psychotherapy Through the Group Process*. New York: Atherton Press.

Winnicott, D.W. (1955), Metapsychological and clinical aspects of regression within the psychoanalytic set-up. In: *Collected Papers*. New York: Basic Books, 1958, pp. 278-294.

Yalom, I.D. (1970), *The Theory and Practice of Group Psychotherapy*. New York: Basic Books.

Yorke, C. (1971), Some suggestions for a critique of Kleinian psychology. *The Psychoanalytic Study of the Child*, 26:129-158. New York: Quadrangle Books.

Ziferstein, I. (1959), The role of identification in group psychotherapy. *Acta Psychotherapeutica* (Suppl.), 7:440-445.

INDEX